Street by Street

SOUTHEND BASILDON

BILLERICAY, CANVEY ISLAND, RAYLEIGH, SOUTH BENFLEET, STANFORD-LE-HOPE, WICKFORD

Ashingdon, Hadleigh, Hawkwell, Hockley, Laindon, Leigh-on-Sea, Pitsea, Rochford, Shoeburyness, Westcliff-on-Sea

Ist edition May 2001

Published by AA Publishing (a trading name of Automobile Association Developments Limited, whose registered office is Norfolk House, Priestley Road, Basingstoke, Hampshire, RG24 9NY. Registered number 1878835).

Mapping produced by the Cartographic Department of The Automobile Association.

A CIP Catalogue record for this book is available from the British Library.

Printed by GRAFIASA S.A., Porto, Portugal

The contents of this atlas are believed to be correct at the time of the latest revision. However, the publishers cannot be held responsible for loss occasioned to any person acting or refraining from action as a result of any material in this atlas, nor for any errors, omissions or changes in such material. The publishers would welcome information to correct any errors or omissions and to keep this atlas up to date. Please write to Publishing, The Automobile Association, Fanum House, Basing View, Basingstoke, Hampshire, RG21 4EA.

Ref: ML025

Key to map pages ii-iii

Key to map symbols iv-1

Enlarged scale pages 2-5

Street by Street 6-71

Index – towns & villages 72

Index – streets 73-86

Index – featured places 86-88

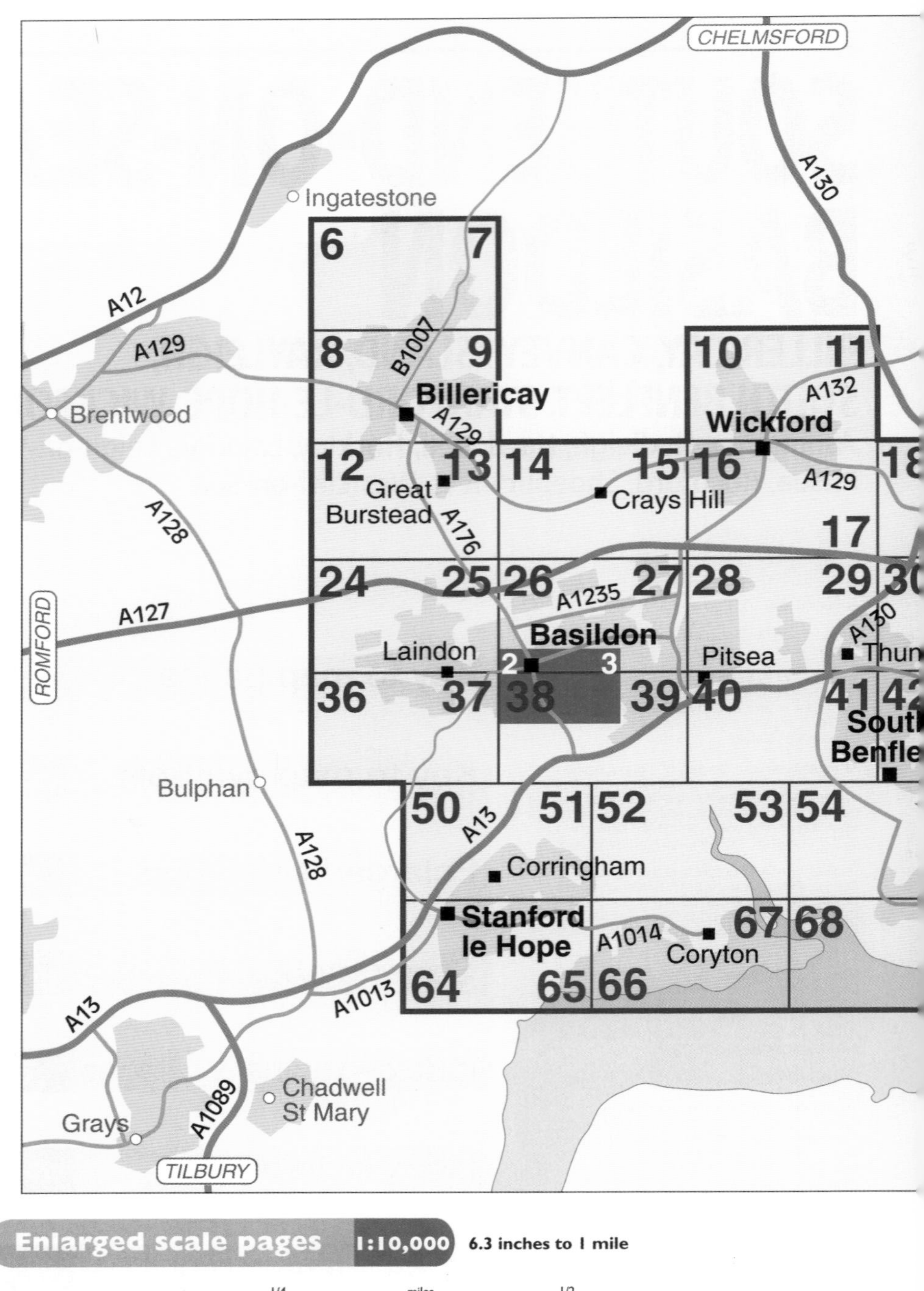

Enlarged scale pages 1:10,000

6.3 inches to 1 mile

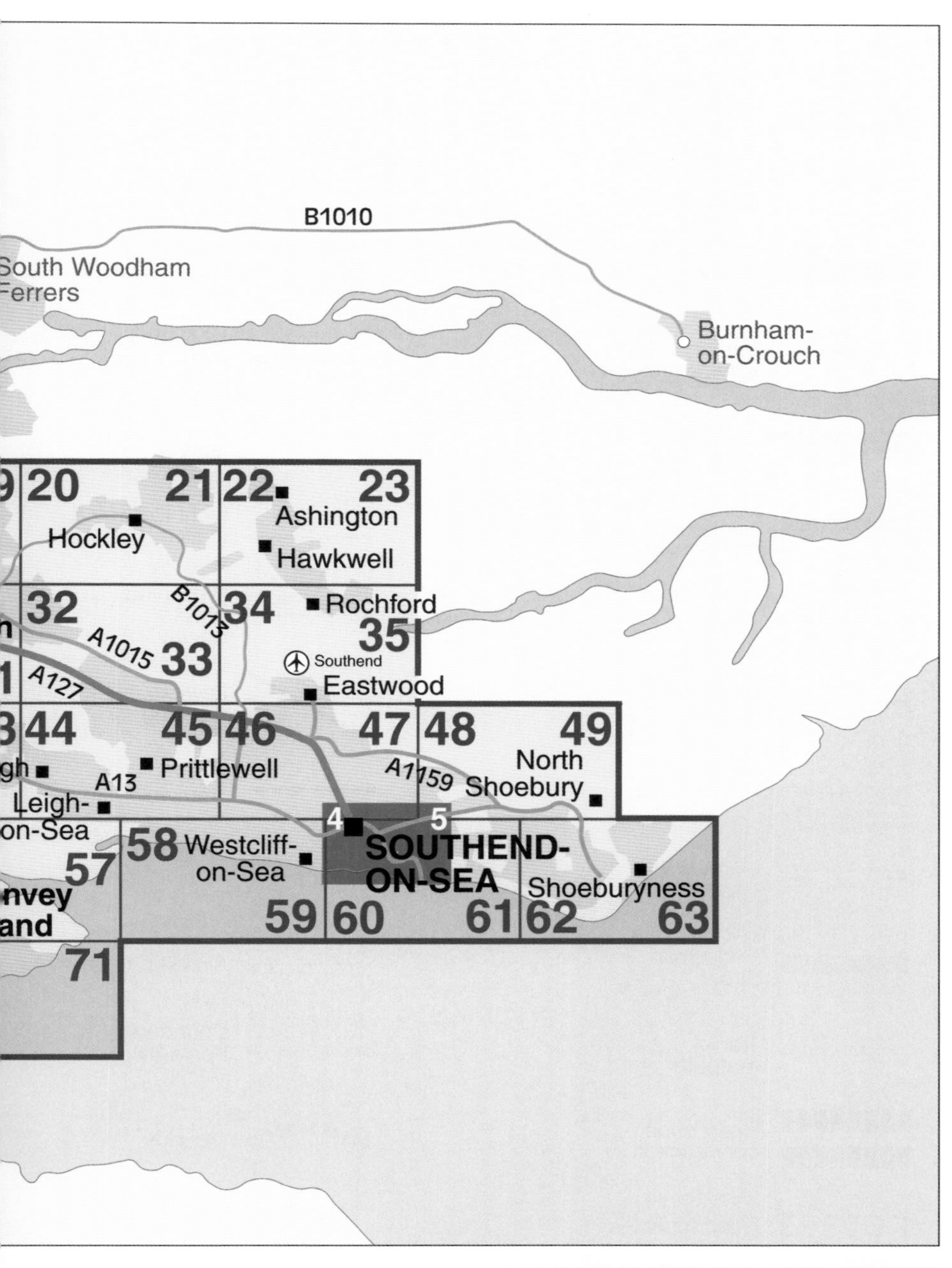

4.2 inches to 1 mile **Scale of main map pages 1:15,000**

0 1/4 miles 1/2 3/4 1

0 1/4 1/2 kilometres 3/4 1 1 1/4 1 1/2

Junction 9	Motorway & junction
Services	Motorway service area
	Primary road single/dual carriageway
Services	Primary road service area
	A road single/dual carriageway
	B road single/dual carriageway
	Other road single/dual carriageway
	Restricted road
	Private road
	One way street
	Pedestrian street
	Track/ footpath
	Road under construction
	Road tunnel
P	Parking
P+	Park & Ride
	Bus/Coach station
	Railway & main railway station
	Railway & minor railway station
	Underground station
	Light Railway & station
	Preserved private railway
LC	Level crossing
	Tramway
	Ferry route
	Airport runway
	Boundaries- borough/ district
	Mounds
93	Page continuation 1:15,000
7	Page continuation to enlarged scale 1:10,000

	River/canal, lake, pier
	Aqueduct, lock, weir
465 Winter Hill	Peak (with height in metres)
	Beach
	Coniferous woodland
	Broadleaved woodland
	Mixed woodland
	Park
	Cemetery
	Built-up area
	Featured building
	City wall
A&E	Accident & Emergency hospital
	Toilet
	Toilet with disabled facilities
	Petrol station
PH	Public house
PO	Post Office
	Public library
i	Tourist Information Centre
	Castle
	Historic house/ building
Wakehurst Place NT	National Trust property
M	Museum/ art gallery
	Church/chapel
	Country park
	Theatre/ performing arts
	Cinema

BASILDON
Lee Chapel
26
37
38
SS16
Ballards Walk Surgery
St Anne Line Junior & Infant School
Lee Chapel CP School
Crown & County Court
South West Essex Magistrates Court
Great Oaks Clinic
Basildon District Council
Eastgate Business Centre
Basildon Station
Woodlands Comprehensive School
Basildon College
Fobbing Farm Cl
BROADMAYNE
NETHER MAYNE
LAINDON LINK
B1007
A176
A1321
1 grid square represents 250 metres

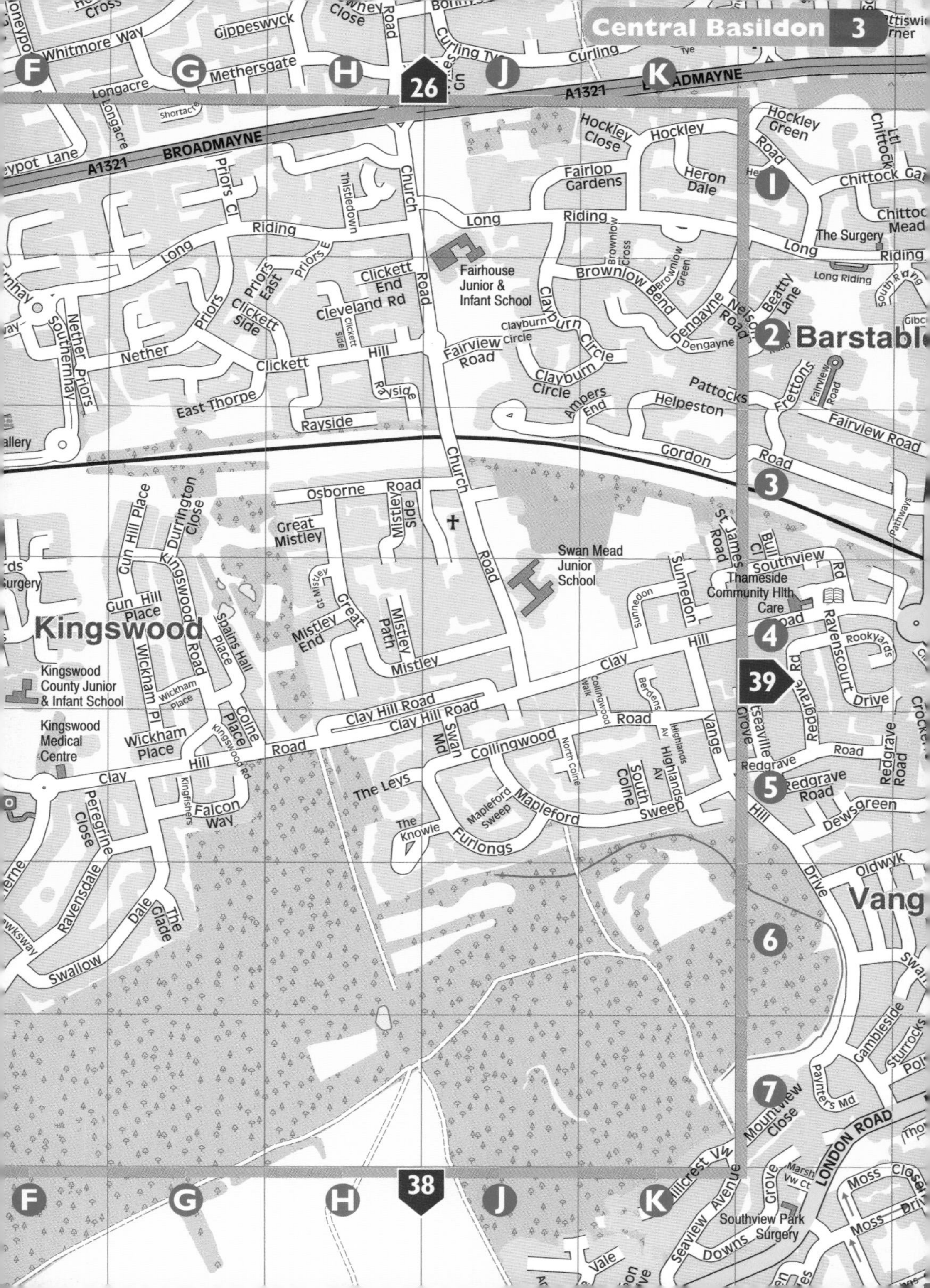
26
38
39
Whitmore Way
Gippeswyck
Methersgate
Longacre
Broadmayne
A1321
Hockley Close
Hockley
Hockley Green
Fairlop Gardens
Heron Dale
Chittock Gate
Long Riding
The Surgery
Priors Cl
Thistledown
Church Road
Fairhouse Junior & Infant School
Brownlow Cross
Brownlow Green
Brownlow Bend
Dengayne
Nelson Road
Beatty Lane
Barstable
Clickett End
Cleveland Rd
Clickett Hill
Clickett side
Priors East
Priors E
Nether Priors
Southernhay
Clayburn Circle
Fairview Road
Rayside
East Thorpe
Ambers End
Helpeston
Pattocks
Frettons
Gordon Road
Osborne Road
Great Mistley
Mistley Side
Mistley Path
Mistley End
Gun Hill Place
Durrington Close
Kingswood Road
Kingswood
Kingswood County Junior & Infant School
Kingswood Medical Centre
Swan Mead Junior School
St James Road
Sunnedon
Bull Cl
Southview Road
Thameside Community Hlth Care
Ravenscourt Drive
Rookyards
Redgrave Road
Clay Hill Road
Wickham Place
Spains Hall Place
Coline Place
Collingwood Road
Collingwood Walk
Berdens
Highlands Av
Vange Hill Drive
Seaville Grove
Dewsgreen
Swan Md
North Colne
South Colne
The Leys
The Knowle
Mapleford Sweep
Furlongs
Falcon Way
Kingfishers
Peregrine Close
Ravensdale
The Glade
Swallow Dale
Oldwyk
Vange
Gambleside
Sturrocks
Painters Md
Mountview Close
London Road
Hillcrest Vw
Seaview Avenue
Downs Grove
Marsh Vw Ct
Southview Park Surgery
Moss Close
Moss Drive
F
G
H
J
K
I
2
3
4
5
6
7

SOUTHEND-ON-SEA
Clifftown
QUEENSWAY A13
VICTORIA AVENUE
A127
A13
B1015
A1160
LONDON ROAD
West Road Mosque
Howards Chase
North Rd
Colchester Close
Avebury Road
Tudor Rd
Rochford Av
Rayleigh Av
Carnarvon Rd
Harcourt Avenue
South East Essex College
Police Station
Southend Borough Council
Crown Court
Magistrates Court
Great Eastern Avenue
Chelmsford Avenue
Boston Avenue
Baxter Avenue
Victoria Avenue
Sweyne Av
Albany Avenue
Hamlet Ct Mews
Balmoral Road
Salisbury Avenue
College
North Road
Milton Hall Junior School
Summercourt Road
Brighton Rd
Brighton Avenue
Mosque
Southend Victoria Station
Short Street
Milton St
Grainger Road
Greyhound Way
Stanfield Rd
Stadium Rd
Redstock Road
Bircham Road
Sycamore Grove
Maldon Road
St Ann's Road
Guildford Road
Prittlewell St
Coleman Street
SUTTON ROAD
Chartwell Gallery
Southchurch Rd
Chichester Road
Essex Street
Southchurch Rd
Doctors Surgery
Warrior Sq N
Warrior Sq East
Warrior Square
Tyrel Dr
Grange Gdns
Whitegate Road
Southend County Court
Quebec Avenue
Tylers Avenue
Baltic Av
Portland Avenue
York Road
Heygate Av
Chancellor Rd
Herbert Gv
Lucy Rd
Chinese Medical Centre
London Rd
Boston Av
Park Ter
Barons Court Infant School
Park Road
Park Street
Princes Street
Queens Road
Ashburnham Road
Gordon Road
College Wy
Napier Av
Elmer Avenue
Farringdon Service Rd
Elmer Ap
Luker Rd
High Street
Gordon Place
Park Crescent
Park La
Southend Central Station
Station Ap
Grover St
Pitmans Close
St Bernards High School
Milton Avenue
St Vincent's Road
Hamlet Road
Scratton Road
Milton Pl
Clifftown Road
Nelson St
Nelson Ms
Weston Rd
Clarence Road
Clarence St
Cambridge Road
Hotel
Wilson Road
Alexandra Road
Alexandra St
Runwell Ter
Cashiobury Ter
Capel Ter
Prittlewell Square
Devereux Rd
Clifton Mews
Royal Ms
Market Pl
The Royals Shopping Centre
Church Road
Tower Ct Mews Hotel
Beecroft Art Gallery
Westcliff Av
Trinity Av
Marine Av
Westcliff Parade
Clifftown Parade
Clifton Ter
Royal Terrace
Pier Hill
Esplanade
Western Esplanade
Westcliff Leisure Centre
Southend Pier
Southend Pier Railway
PO
A B C D E
1 2 3 4 5 6 7
47
59
60
4
1 grid square represents 250 metres

Southchurch
SS1
SOUTHCHURCH ROAD
A13
Southend East Station
Southend Adult Community College
Sacred Heart RC School
Porters Grange Junior & Infant School
Bournemouth Park Junior & Infants School
Central Avenue
South Avenue
Trinity Road
Stornoway Road
Branksome Road
Poynings Avenue
Vaughan Avenue
Pelham Road
Riviera Drive
Ambleside Drive
Woodgrange Drive
Windermere Road
York Rd
Northumberland Crescent
Northumberland Av
Shaftesbury Avenue
Beresford Road
Burnaby Rd
Manilla Rd
Prospect Close
Hawtree Cl
Outing Cl
Kursaal Way
Parade
EASTERN ESPLANADE
EASTERN ESP
B1016
A1160
SOUTHCHURCH AVENUE
Lifstan Way
Glebe Close
Butterys
Rectory Chase
Strand Gallery
The Surgery
Pavilion Cl
Droitwich Avenue
Glenmore Street
Stromness Pl
Bellevue Pl
Southchurch Hall Cl
Plas Newydd Hotel
47
60
61
F
G
H
J
K
1
2
3
4
5
6
7

D5
1 Berkeley Dr
2 Boleyn Cl
3 Brompton Cl
4 Dorchester Rd
5 Eccleston Gdns
6 Farriers Dr
7 Montpelier Cl
8 Pembroke Cl
9 Rutherford Cl
C5
Street names for this grid square are listed at the back of the index
Buttsbury
Ingatestone Road
Tyrrells
Tilehurst
Brocks Farm
Buttsbury
Elmbrook Farm
River Wid
Shoulder Hall
Padham's Green Road
Mountnessing Road
Little Blunts
Buckwyns Chase
Buckwyns Chase
Buckwyns Farm
Wardropers
Queen's Park
Church Road
Rosebay
Lawness
Betony Crs
Mallow Gdns
Devereux Way
Paget Dr
Milner Place
Arlington Way
Brandon Close
Connaught Way
Marlborough
Horses Close
Carlyle Gardens
Eaton Close
Goldington Crs
Vincent Way
Porchester Road
Ovington Gardens
Brightside County Junior & Infant School
Harebell Close
Wellington Mews
York Rd
Doctors Surgery
Mountnessing Road
Avenue
Upland Dr
Little Cowbridge Grange
The Links
Linda Gardens
Cherry Gardens
The Warren
Brightside
Coombes Cl
Upland Road
Fitzroy Close
Belgrave Road
Perry St
Bluebell Wood
Moat Edge
1 grid square represents 500 metres

E5
1 Blacksmith Cl
2 Westb'rne Gdns
F4
1 Princes Ct
2 Princes Ms
G5
1 Martingale Cl
2 Moore Cl
School Lane
Rectory Close
Thornton Place
The Lindens
Well Lane
Madles Lane
Marigold Lane
Peter
Lilystone Hall
Honeypot Lane
Ingatestone Road
STOCK ROAD
B1007
Smallgains Lane
Greenacre Lane
Small Gains Lane
Greenacre Farm
Great Blunts
The Vale
Oriental Galleries
Oakland Farm Industrial Estate
Queens Park Avenue
Princes Cl
Arundel Way
Lampern Crs
Potash Road
Sussex Way
Norsey View Drive
Cranmer Cl
Walsingham Way
Lisa Close
Central Av
The Priory
Perry Street
Robin Close
Brookside
Glanmire
Glencree
Bridleway
Dunfane
Longtail
Hollyford
Tylers Avenue
Burleigh Close
Marlowe Close
Graham Close
Orchard Avenue
Oakwood Drive
Doublet Mews
Broome Road
Derby Close
Martingale Road
Meade Road
Chepstow Close
Coach Ms
Mercer Road
Smythe Road
Goatsmoor Lane
Mill Hill Drive
Buttsbury Junior GM School
Trafalgar Way
Crawford Close
Bush Hall Road
Springfield Road
Infant School
Dukes Farm Close
Dukes Farm Road
PO
Mayflower Comprehensive School
Sadlers Close
Carson Road
Shire Close
Norsey Road
Jacqueline Gardens
The Grove
Juniper Close
Heath Road
Lodge Farm
The Knoll
Fern Close
Hillhouse Drive
Little Norsey Road
Dukes Rd
Lilford Road
Headley Road
Outwood
9

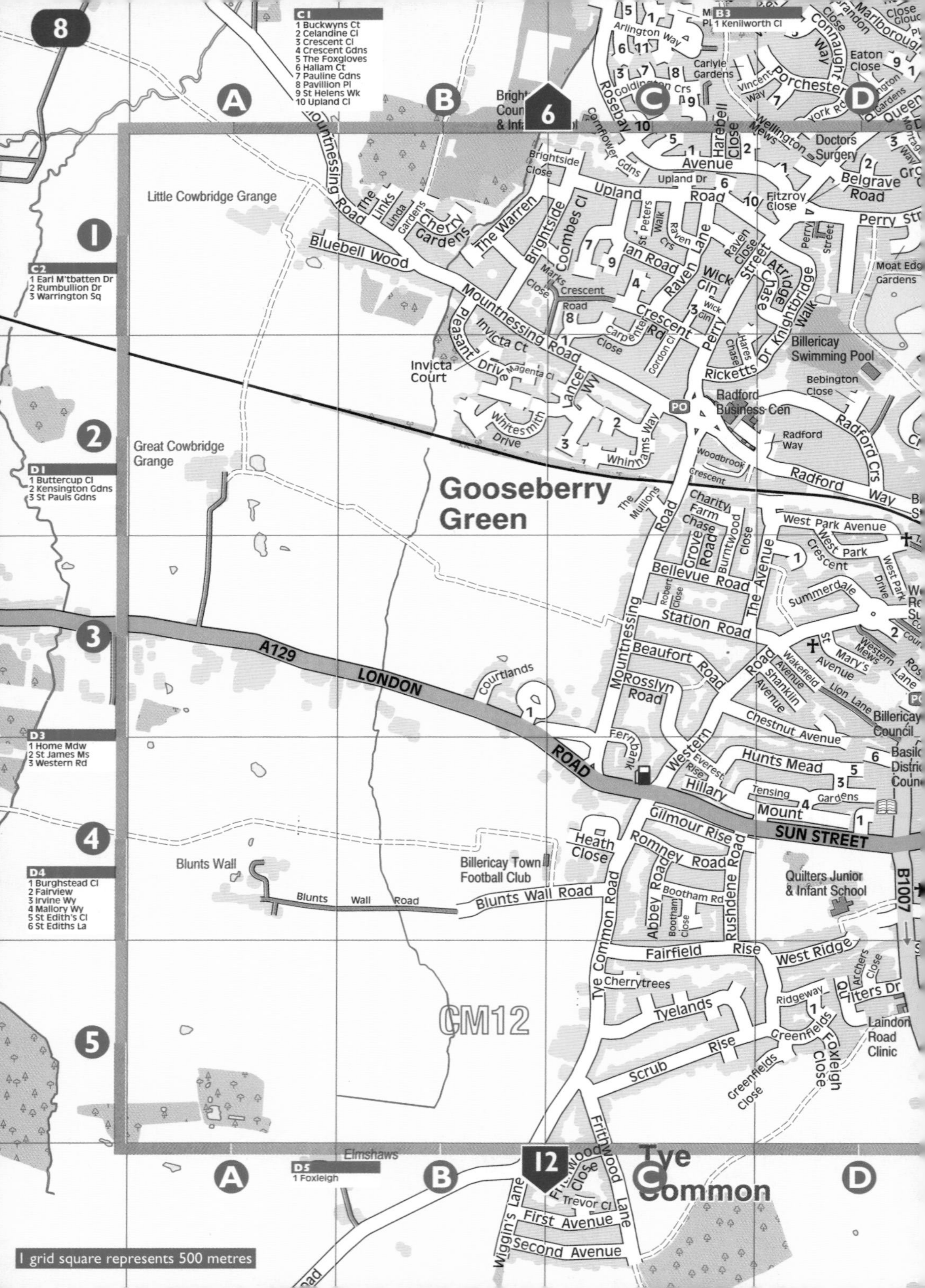

1 grid square represents 500 metres

E1
1 Newlands Cl
2 Sylvan Tryst
E2
1 Parklands
2 Radford Ct
E3
1 High Cloister
2 Hurlock Rd
3 Lower Cloister
4 Mayflower Rd
5 Pilgrims Cl
6 Saffron Wk
7 Weavers Cl
8 West Cloister
E4
1 Hillside Cl
2 West Cft
E5
1 School Rd
F3
1 Abbots Ride
2 The Chase
3 Copford Rd
4 David's Wk
5 Felsted Rd
6 Heather Bank
7 High Meadow
8 Jacksons Ms
9 Kelvedon Rd
10 Northfield Cl
11 Park Side
12 Shakespeare Av
F4
1 Wheatear Pl
2 Wren Cl
F5
1 Maple Mead
G3
1 Gascoigne Wy
2 Hatfield Dr
3 Henham Cl
4 Holbrook Cl
5 Shalford Rd
6 Stansted Cl
G4
1 Darell Wy
2 Warner Cl
G5
1 Highfield Ap
H3
1 Harrods Ct
H4
1 Stuart Wy
7
13
Marlowe Close
Buttsbury Junior GM School
Mill Hill Drive
Trafalgar
Street
Springfield Road
School
Jacqueline Gardens
Dukes Road
Farm Close
Crawford Close
STOCK ROAD
PO
Mayflower Comprehensive School
Oakwood
Coach Ms
Sadlers Close
Carson Rd
Shire Close
Norsey Road
Newlands Road
The Knoll
Hillhouse Close
Fern Close
Hillhouse Drive
The Grove
Little Dukes Rd
Lilford Road
Little Norsey Road
Juniper Close
Headley Road
Horace Rd
Norsey Road
Heath Road
Lodge Farm
Outwood Common Road
Norsey Wood (Nature Reserve)
The Spinney
St Johns School
Thameside Community Healthcare N H S Trust
St John's Road
Norsey Drive
Deerbank Road
The New Surgery
Norsey Close
Jacksons Cl
Kingswood
Ramsden Hall School
Break Egg Hill
Brackendale
Whiteways
The Mount
Mount View
Highland Grove
Crown Road
Feering Road
Lane
Dedham Road
Dedham Close
Rise
Hillway
Glenside
Outwood Common Road
Outwood Close
Outwood
Meadow
Daines Rd
Prince Edward Road
Sunnymede
Mons Avenue
Betoyne Close
Salesbury Drive
Outwood Farm Close
Outwood Farm
Chantry Way
Valley Road
Thynne Road
Chapel Court
Hillside Road
Prower Close
Martin Close
Langemore Way
South Ridge
Charfinch Crescent
Bunting Lane
Skylark Cl
Goldcrest Dr
Greens
Cavell Road
The Meadow Way
The Rising
Junior School
Greenway
Monoux Close
Morris Avenue
Balmoral Close
Farm Road
Beverley Rise
BILLERICAY
Farm
Lane
Outwood Farm Road
Road
Gatwick House
Bell Hill Close
A176
Jackdaw Close
Redwing Dr
Nuthatch Close
Common
Longrise
Linkdale
Lea Way
Crays View
Gatwick View
Stonechat Road
Fieldfare
The Swallows
The Rowans
Windmill Heights
Langham
A129
Beams
Highfield Road
Browns Farm
Kennel Lane
South Green
SOUTHEND ROAD
South Green Surgery
Canels Road
South Green County Infant

B5
1 Upper Market Rd
B3
1 Lapwing Rd
C3
1 Canewdon Cl
C5
1 Beccles Ct
2 Station Ap
3 Stilemans
4 Upper Market Rd
D4
1 Whitelands Cl
D5
1 Franklins Wy
Sudbury's Farm
Brock Hill
Brock Hill Dr
The Greenway
Waverley Crs
Lindon Road
Downham Road
Grange Road
Carlton Road
Delmar Gdns
Station Rd
Swallow Rd
Lapwing Rd
Haslemere Rd
Richmond Rd
Moreland Rd
Arundel Rd
Alderney Gardens
Church End
Runwell Gdns
Clare Av
David Av
Keith Av
Birs Cl
Runwell CP School
Canewdon Gdns
Regency Cl
Viking Wy
Tidworth Av
Church End Av
Church End Lane
Runwell Parish Council
Locarno Av
Egbert Gardens
Swan Lane
Windsor Gdns
Saxon Cl
Ethelred Gardens
Pearmain Cl
Carruthers Dr
Merlin Way
Harold Gardens
Rettendon Gdns
Ilgars Rd
RUNWELL ROAD
Athelstan Gardens
Guernsey Gardens
Clovelly Gdns
Doctors Surgery
The Hastings
Gdns
Herward Gdns
Alfred Gdns
Hengist Gdns
Edward Gdns
South Hanningfield Way
Meadow Lane
Vera Road
Cumm Road
Castledon Road
Castledon Farm
Station Avenue
Silver Wy
Jubilee Dr
Jersey Gardens
Elm Rd
Runwell Rd
Mount Road
Rowans Way
Cartlodge Av
Meadow Ct
Camomile Dr
Long Meadow Dr
Franklin Way Practice
SOUTHEND ROAD
A132
Crouch Dr
Lwr Southend Rd
The Broadway
River Crouch
Riverside Walk
Riverside Wk
Elizabeth Drive
Victoria Av
Charlotte Av
Reeds Way
Market Av
Wickford Swimming Pool
Wickford Health Cen
Wickford Stn
High Street
Kingley Cl
Kingley Dr
Louvaine Av
Victoria Crs
Eleanor Cha
Brookland
Wickford Junior School
Irvon Hl Rd
London Road Surgery
A129
St Peter's Ter
Basildon District Council
Wick Dr
West Beech Av
West Beech Cl
Wick Beech Av
Wick Lane
The Dell
1 grid square represents 500 metres

16

E5
1 Highcliffe Cl
2 St Catherines Cl
F5
1 Glencoe Dr
School
Runwell Hospital
Rettendon Place
A130
Woodham Road
High Ho
Lynfords Dr
Lynfords Av
The Chase
RUNWELL ROAD
A132
Lynfords Drive
Browns Av
Barnet Pk Road
Hawk Hill
Battlesbridge Station
Hawk La
River Crouch
Southlands Farm
SS11
Athelstan Gdns
Berens Cl
Springfield Rd
Whist Av
Rubicon Av
Beauchamps Drive
Royal Oak Dr
Mercury Cl
Belchamps Rd
Infant School
Redgate Cl
Ulting Wy
Warren Dr
Westfield Cl
Highcliffe Close
Avenue
Sharlands Cl
Beauchamps High School
Beauchamps
Alicia Walk
Highcliffe Wy
17
Spinney Cl
St Cleres Cres
Cherry Lane
Alicia Cl
A129
SOUTHEND ROAD
Rectory Gv
Jacks Cl
Lucerne Wk
Longfield Cl
Shot Fa
Enfield Rd
Rawreth Shot
Church

CM12
Tyelands
Laindon Road Clinic
Scrub Rise
Greenfields
Greenfields Close
Foxleigh Close
A
B
8
C
D
Elmshaws Farm
Frithwood Close
Frithwood Lane
Tye Common
Wiggin's Lane
Trevor Cl
First Avenue
Second Avenue
1
Tye Common Road
Farm Road
Salmon's Farm
Babshole Farm
2
Laindon Common
Road
Wiggins Lane
Common
River Crouch
Laindon
Tye Common Road
Hatches Farm Road
Hatches Farm
3
Clock House Road
Broomhills Chase
Botney Hill Road
Little Burstead
Botney Hill Road
Hill
4
Rectory Road
Chase Farm
Broor
Green Lane
5
New
A
B
24
C
D
Rectory Road
1 grid square represents 500 metres

South Green 13
F1
1 Carvers Wd
2 Foys Wk
3 Ganels Cl
4 Hammonds La
5 Hickstars La
6 Paddock Cl
7 Passingham Cl
8 Well Mead
F2
1 Froden Ct
2 Magnolias
G1
1 Briar Cl
2 Briar Vw
3 Patricia Gdns
4 Sebert Cl
5 The Willows
G2
1 Anthony Cl
2 Copperfield
3 Homefield Cl
4 Lorraine Cl
5 Stockwell Cl
Bell Close
Longrise
Crays View
Windmill Heights
Langham Crescent
Hunters Av
Kennel Lane
A176
A129
Jackdaw Close
Nuthatch Close
Stonechat Road
The Swallows
Beams Way
Common
The Rowans
Outwood
Highfield Road
South Green
Southend Road
South Green Surgery
South Green County Infant & Junior School
Selworthy Cl
Canels Road
Grange Road
Burstead Dr
Kevin Close
The Redinge
Kings Way
Froden Brook
Coopers Drive
Passingham Avenue
The Oaks
Haven Rise
Post Meadow
Tyrrells Road
Tyrone Rd
Tyrone Cl
Trinity Road
Trinity Close
Mill Road
Street
Church
Coxes Farm Road
St Peters RC Primary School
Browns Farm
Great Burstead
Cemetery
Church Street
Noak Hill Road
Noak Hill
The Hoe
Noak Hill Close
Margeth Road
St Agnes Road
Barleylands
Basildon District Council
Barleylands Road
Benson's Farm
Gate Lodge Way
Kimberly Drive
E
F
G
H
9
14
25

14
Browns Farm
A
B
C
D
Farm Road
1
2
3
4
5
Crays Hall Farm
Church Lane
Gurnard's Farm
Granites Chase
Granites Chase
River Crouch
SOUTHEND ROAD
A129
13
Barleylands
Basildon District Council
Stacey's Mt
HILL
Hope Road
PO
CRAYS
Crays
Oak Av
Queens Road
Jubilee Rd
Oak Av
Oak Road
Harding's Elms Rd
Barleylands Road
Oak Lane
Summerhill Farm
Wash Road
Pipps Hill Road North
26
Calvina Close
Kimberly Drive
Eastfield Road
Handleys Chase
A127
ARTERIAL ROAD
Pipps Hill
1 grid square represents 500 metres

Crays Hill
Woolshots Farm
A129 LONDON ROAD
Church Road
Branksome Avenue
Sugden Avenue
Southbourne Gv
Studland Avenue
Highcliff Dr
Parkstone
Woolshotts Rd
Newhouse Avenue
Ramsden View Road
Chase
Oak
Crays Hill County Primary School
Southlands Road
Corner Road
Approach Road
Gardiners Lane North
North Rd
Upper Rd
South Rd
Road
Pitsea Vw Rd
Borwick Lane
Doeshill Farm
Bury Farm Lane
Great Wasketts
Great Bromfords
Nevendon Rd
Nevendon Road
A127
Christopher Martin Road
Link
Honywood Road
Ilford Trading Est
Herons Gate Trading Est
Paycocke Road
Gardiners Way
Gardiners
Cricketers Retail Park
Cricketers Wy
Church Lane
Bishops Cl
Castledon Road
Elizabeth
Margarite Wy
Kingley Cl
Kingley Dr
Tudor Wy
Belmont Av
Belmont Close
Burne Av
The Chase
Alma Close
Trinder Wy
Leasway
Broomfords Drive
16
27
E F G H
1 2 3 4 5

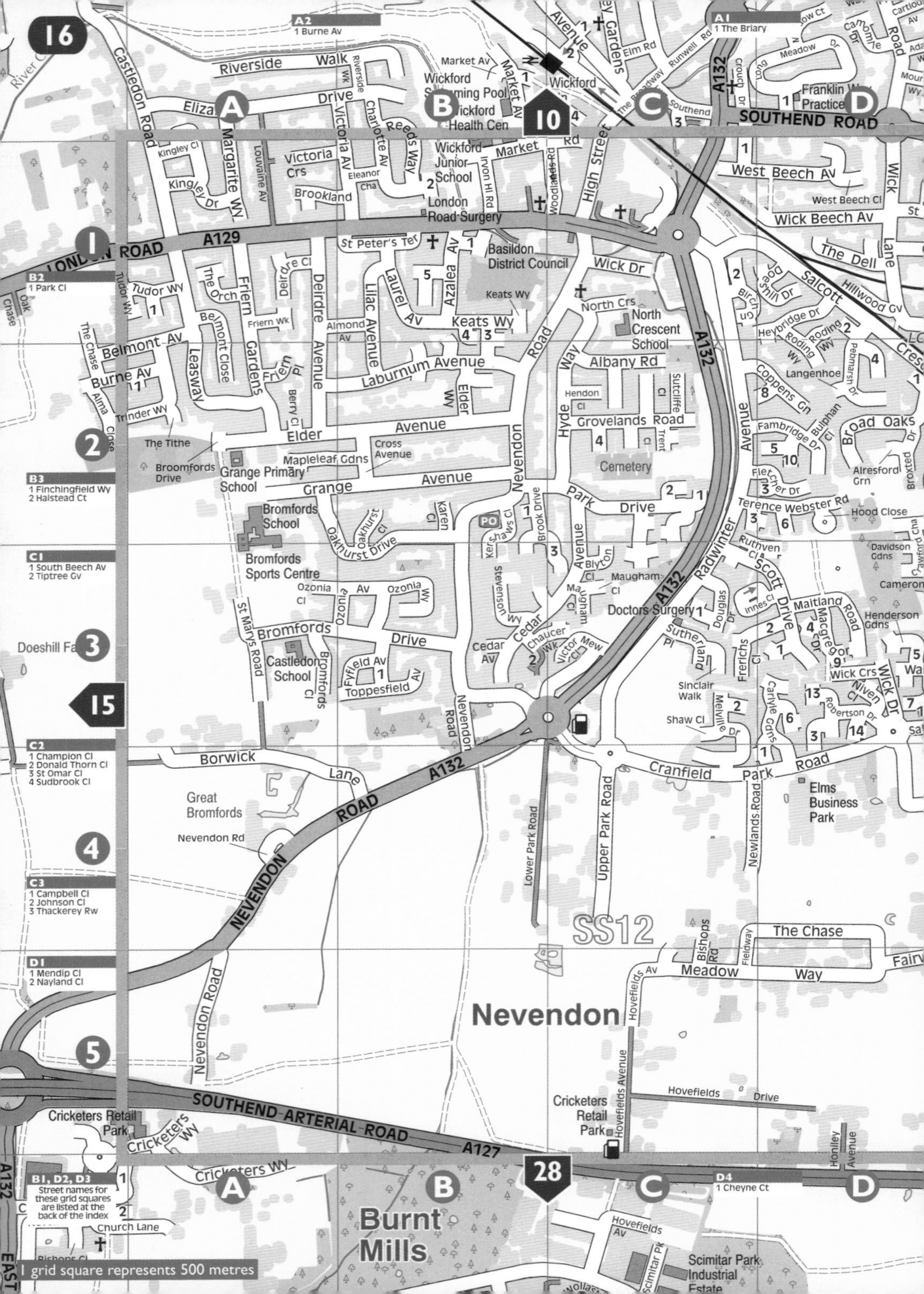

16
10
15
28
A2
1 Burne Av
A1
1 The Briary
B2
1 Park Cl
B3
1 Finchingfield Wy
2 Halstead Ct
C1
1 South Beech Av
2 Tiptree Gv
C2
1 Champion Cl
2 Donald Thorn Cl
3 St Omar Cl
4 Sudbrook Cl
C3
1 Campbell Cl
2 Johnson Cl
3 Thackerey Rw
D1
1 Mendip Cl
2 Nayland Cl
D4
1 Cheyne Ct
B1, D2, D3
Street names for these grid squares are listed at the back of the index
1 grid square represents 500 metres
Riverside Walk
Castledon Road
Drive
Victoria Av
Charlotte Av
Reeds Way
Wickford Swimming Pool
Wickford Health Cen
Market Av
Wickford
Southend Road
SOUTHEND ROAD
Elm Rd
Runwell Rd
The Broadway
A132
Franklin Wy Practice
Meadow Dr
Long Meadow Dr
Margarite Wy
Kingley Cl
Kingley Dr
Louvaine Av
Victoria Crs
Eleanor Cha
Brookland
Wickford Junior School
Market Rd
Ivyon Hl Rd
Woodlands Rd
High Street
London Road Surgery
West Beech Av
West Beech Cl
Wick Beech Av
Wick Lane
The Dell
LONDON ROAD
A129
St Peter's Ter
Basildon District Council
Wick Dr
Salcott
Hillwood Gv
Tudor Wy
The Orch
Friern Gardens
Deirdre Cl
Deirdre Avenue
Lilac Avenue
Laurel Av
Azalea Av
Keats Wy
North Crs
North Crescent School
Birch Gn
Doeshill Dr
Heybridge Dr
Roding Wy
Pebmarsh Dr
Oak Chase
The Chase
Belmont Av
Belmont Close
Friern Wk
Almond Av
Laburnum Avenue
Nevendon Road
Albany Rd
Hyde Way
Langenhoe
Coppens Gn
Burne Av
Alma Close
Trinder Wy
Leasway
Friern Pl
Berry Cl
Elder Wy
Hendon Cl
Sutcliffe Cl
Grovelands Road
Trent Cl
Avenue
Fambridge Dr
Bulphan Cl
Broad Oaks
Broxted Dr
Alresford Grn
The Tithe
Broomfords Drive
Grange Primary School
Mapleleaf Gdns
Cross Avenue
Elder Avenue
Grange Avenue
Cemetery
Fletcher Dr
Terence Webster Rd
Hood Close
Park Drive
Bromfords School
Oakhurst Drive
Oakhurst Cl
Karen Cl
PO
Kershaws Cl
Brook Drive
Bromfords Sports Centre
Stevenson Wy
Avenue
Blyton Cl
Maugham Cl
Radwinter Avenue
Ruthven Cl
Scott Drive
Davidson Gdns
Crawford Cha
Cameron
Ozonia Cl
Ozonia Av
Ozonia Wy
Cedar Av
Chaucer Wk
Victor Mew Cl
Doctors Surgery
Douglas Dr
Innes Cl
Maitland Road
Macgregor Dr
Henderson Gdns
St Marys Road
Bromfords Drive
Castledon School
Bromfords Cl
Fyfield Av
Toppesfield Av
Sutherland Pl
Sinclair Walk
Frerichs Cl
Carlyle Gdns
Wick Crs
Niven Cl
Wick Dr
Robertson Dr
Shaw Cl
Melville Dr
Doeshill Fa
Borwick Lane
ROAD
Cranfield Park Road
Newlands Road
Elms Business Park
Great Bromfords
Nevendon Rd
Lower Park Road
Upper Park Road
NEVENDON
SS12
The Chase
Bishops Rd
Fieldway
Meadow Way
Fairv
Hovefields Av
Nevendon
Nevendon Road
Hovefields Avenue
Hovefields Drive
Cricketers Retail Park
SOUTHEND ARTERIAL ROAD
A127
Cricketers Wy
Honiley Avenue
Church Lane
Bishops Cl
Burnt Mills
Hovefields Av
Scimitar Pk
Scimitar Park Industrial Estate
A132
EAST
River

Wickford 17
E1
1 Hawkins Cl
2 St David's Wy
E2
1 Arran Ct
2 Rochford Cl
E3
1 Boyd Ct
2 Brodie Wk
3 Duncan Cl
4 Irvine Pl
5 Knox Ct
6 Silva Island Wy
7 Stewart Pl
F1
1 Bakers Farm Cl
2 Sandown Cl
F2
1 Great Saling
2 Heathercroft Rd
3 Hornchurch Cl
4 Woodberry Rd
G1
1 Ambleside
2 Crouchview Cl
G3
1 Boreham Cl
2 Stapleford End
G2
1 Coltishall Cl
2 Honington Cl
3 North Weald Cl
4 Stanmore Rd
5 Tangmere Cl
11
18
29
Beauchamps High School
Rawreth Shot
Shot Farm
Shotgate
WICKFORD
A129 SOUTHEND ROAD
Enfield Rd
Oak Av
Cherry Lane
Alicia Avenue
Alicia Walk
Bridge Road
Lucerne Walk
Lucerne Wk
Lucerne Dr
Longfield Cl
Southend Rd
Bruce Grove
Gardens
Fifth Av
Fourth Avenue
Third Avenue
Second Avenue
First Avenue
Fanton Walk
Fanton Chase
Fanton Gdns
Heron Av
Brocks Business Park
Westfleet Trading Est
Beedell Av
Uxbridge Cl
Meadowland Rd
Wakescolne
Woodberry Rd
Blake Hall Drive
Hodgson Way
Hodgson Ct
Enterprise Wy
Mersea Crs
Crescent
Kendal Ct
Capitol Industrial Cen
Fulmar Wy
Hurricane Wy
Wethersfield Way
Boreham Cl
Sopwith Crescent
Hurricane Way
Hurricane Cl
Oban Ct
Orwell Ct
The Robert Frew Medical Centre
Tresco Way
Anglesey Gdns
Barra Gld
Tiree Cha
Salcott
Harris Cl
Dollymans Farm
Doublegate Lane
Old London
London Rd
Sappers Farm
Fanton Hall Farm
Fanton Av
Road
A127
SOUTHEND ARTERIAL ROAD
Morbec Farm
Harrow Road

C5
1 Ashfield
2 Boxford Cl
B1
1 Bedloes Av
D4
1 Leonard Dr
D5
1 Bromley Ms
2 Broomfield Av
3 Denham V
4 Goldhanger Cl
5 Gosfield Cl
6 Hanningfield Cl
7 Kelvedon Cl
8 Langham Dr
9 Latchingdon Cl
10 Navestock Cl
11 Newsum Gdns
12 Rettendon Cl
13 Sheering Ct
14 Wethersfield Cl
Burrells Farm
Church Road
Chelmsford Road
Bedloes Av
St Nicholas C of E Primary School
Rawreth
A130 CHELMSFORD RD
CHELMSFORD ROAD
Rawreth Lane
Rawreth Hall
Old London Road
Chelmsford Rd
A129 LONDON ROAD
London Road
Hotel
Doublegate Lane
Farm
Chelmsford Rd
A130
Lower Barn Farm
A129 LONDON
Beke Hall Chase North
Beke Hall Chase South
St Johns Drive
Beke Hall
Ltl Wheatley Cha
Louis Dr
London
Doctors Surg
Haddon Cl
Willingale Av
Bardfield
Aldham Gdns
Oakley Av
Langham Drive
Shelley Place
Polstead Cl
Morbec Farm
A127
1 grid square represents 500 metres

17
30

Rayleigh 19
E2
1 Laburnum Wy
2 Rowan Cl
3 Sycamore Cl
E3
1 Edinburgh Cl
E4
1 Belgrave Cl
2 Grosvenor Rd
E5
1 Clavering Ct
2 Elsenham Ct
3 Kingfisher Crs
4 Nightingale Cl
5 Peregrine Gdns
6 Swallow Cl
F3
1 Caversham Pk Av
F5
1 East Philbrick Crs
2 Harper Wy
G3
1 Dartmouth Cl
2 Paignton Cl
3 Torquay Cl
G4
1 Dene Cl
2 Lakeside
G5
1 Barringtons Cl
H3
1 Norman Crs
H4
1 Plowmans
2 Tyms Wy
Vanderbilt Avenue
Montefiore Avenue
Goldsmith Drive
Maple Drive
McCalmont Drive
Tryndehayes
Avenue
Drive
Hullbridge Road
Rutland Dr
Havana Drive
Trenders
Cheshunt Drive
Cheshunt Dr
Parkhurst
Hooley Drive
Lubard's Lodge
Park School
Laburnum Wy
Rawreth Lane
Doctors Surgery
Quest End Industrial Estate
Rawreth Industrial Estate
Manns Way
Lincoln Way
Norwich Crs
Truro Crs
Farm Vw
Exmouth Dr
Everest
Lubbards Cl
PO
Ferndale Rd
Saxon Cl
Kings Farm
Mortimer Road
Eastview Drive
Fairland Cl
Stirling Cl
Arundel Gdns
Victoria Av
Durham Way
Dawlish Crescent
Teignmouth Drive
Bristol Cl
Harberts Wy
Way
Brixham Close
Primary School
Deepdene Avenue
Pk
Canterbury Close
Brooklyn Drive
Hambro Avenue
Kembles
Hambro Hill
Hambro Close
Drakes Wy
Upr Lambricks
Lwr Lambricks
Ardley Way
Curtisway
Caustonway
Wellsfield
The Gattens
Wimarc Crs
Cheapside West
Sweyne Cl
Victoria Av
Vernon Av
Pearsons Av
Regent Cl
Downhall
Ely Cl
Willow Dr
Deepdene Avenue
Dene Gdns
Appledene Close
Rd
Preston Gdns
Hedgehope Avenue
Downhall Cl
The Sweyne Park School
Eastcheap
Hall
Gayleighs
Cheapside E
Cotswold Avenue
Uplands Pk Rd
Cem
The Chestnuts
HOCKLEY ROAD
Close
Sir Walter Raleigh Dr
London Rd
London Road Surg
LONDON ROAD
A129
Oakwood Rd
Marina Av
Cordelia Crs
Down
Sheriton Sq
Cherrydown
Malvern Close
Crescent
Chiltern Close
Mendip Close
Broadlands Avenue
Edward Francis Community Junior School
SS6
Hatfield Road
Waltham Road
Grange Gdns
Danbury Road
Langdon Rd
Kenilworth Gardens
Talbot Av
Infant School
Creswick Avenue
Philbrick Crescent West
Birch
Station
Link Rd
Upway
The Courts
Ruffles Close
Victoria Road
Byford Road
Nelson
Napier
Purleigh Rd
Falcon Cl
Glebe
Glebe Dr
Station Avenue
Rayleigh Station
STATION RD
London
Beech Av
Elm Drive
Elm Close
Fitzwimarc Secondary School
Road
Betjeman Close
Kestrel Grove
Lansdowne Drive
Approach
Mount Avenue
Hillview
Castle Dr
Hill
RAYLEIGH
B1013
Rectory Garth
Millfield Cl
Bracken Dell
Alexandra Rd
Princess Road
Albert Close
Heron Close
The
Dutch Cottage
31
Barfield Gallery
Crown Gdns
Leasway
Highmead
Love
Mount Cl
The Bailey
Francis Wk
CROWN HILL
A129
PO
Church View Surg
Bellingham La
BULL LA
WEBSTERS
Crown Hall
Essex Co Council
District Council Offices
Derwent Av
Rydal Cl
Kendal Cl
Kings Close
Louise Rd
Jubilee Rd
Bull Lane
Hilary Crescent
The Paddocks
Marshalls Close
Avondale Road

D2
1 Balmoral Gdns
2 Belvedere Av
3 Chevening Gdns
4 Laburnum Cl
5 Lambeth Ms
6 Marlborough Wk
7 St James's Wk
8 Sandringham Av
C2
1 Silvertree Cl
Mill Hill
SS5
Wadham Park Farm
Wadham Park Avenue
Church Rd
Murrels Lane
St Peters Road
Blounts Farm
Hockley Primary School
Folly Chase
Folly Lane
Sunnyfield Gdns
Hawthorne Gardens
Laburnum Grove
Fountain La
Manor Road
Osborne Avenue
Bull Lane
Home Farm
HIGH ROAD
ALDERMAN'S HILL B1013
Hillside Road
Woodside Road
Crown Road
Bullwood Approach
The Gattens
Hambro Close
Hill
Wellington Rd
Bullwood Hall Lane
Hockley Woods
Wellsfield
HOCKLEY ROAD
The Chestnuts
Nelson Gdns
Nelson Close
Nelson Road
Hamilton Mews
Wellington Road
Bullwood Hall
Victoria
Napier Road
Stevens Farm
Roach Valley Way
Ruffles Close
Byford Road
Betjeman Close
Blower Close
Alexandra Rd
Princess Road
Albert Close
Albert Road
Helena Road
Bracken Dell
Louise Rd
Bull Lane
Hilary Crescent
The Paddocks
Grove Close
Cecil Way
Milton Cl
Fisher's Farm
19
32
1 grid square represents 500 metres

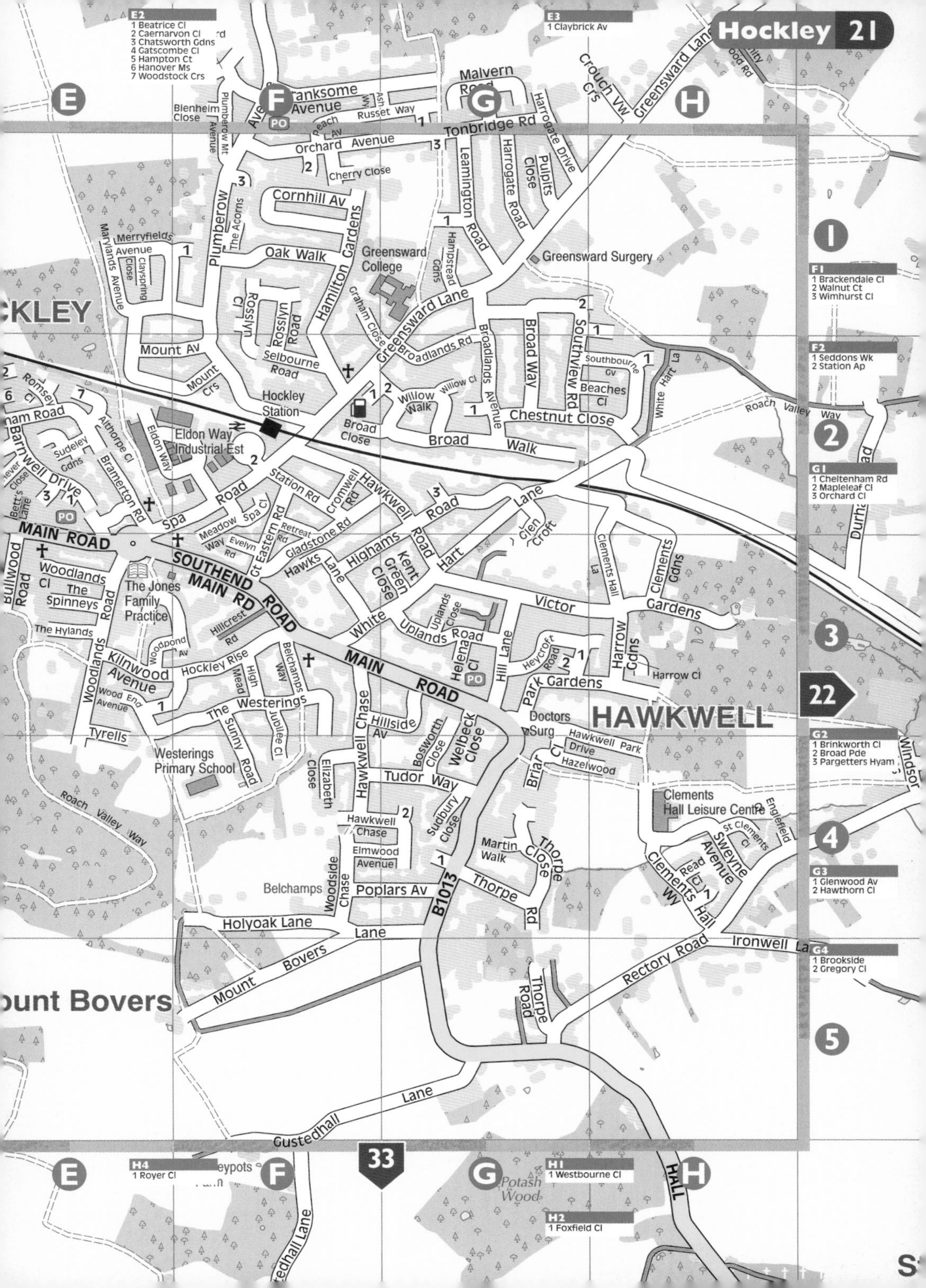
Hockley 21
E2
1 Beatrice Cl
2 Caernarvon Cl
3 Chatsworth Gdns
4 Gatscombe Cl
5 Hampton Ct
6 Hanover Ms
7 Woodstock Crs
E3
1 Claybrick Av
F1
1 Brackendale Cl
2 Walnut Ct
3 Wimhurst Cl
F2
1 Seddons Wk
2 Station Ap
G1
1 Cheltenham Rd
2 Mapleleaf Cl
3 Orchard Cl
G2
1 Brinkworth Cl
2 Broad Pde
3 Pargetters Hyam
G3
1 Glenwood Av
2 Hawthorn Cl
G4
1 Brookside
2 Gregory Cl
H1
1 Westbourne Cl
H2
1 Foxfield Cl
H4
1 Royer Cl
HAWKWELL
Mount Bovers
Hockley Station
Eldon Way Industrial Est
Greensward College
Greensward Surgery
The Jones Family Practice
Westerings Primary School
Clements Hall Leisure Centre
Doctors Surg
Belchamps
Potash Wood
MAIN ROAD
SOUTHEND ROAD
MAIN RD
B1013
Greensward Lane
Tonbridge Rd
Orchard Avenue
Plumberow Avenue
Hamilton Gardens
Leamington Road
Broadlands Avenue
Southview Rd
Chestnut Close
Broad Walk
Spa Road
Hawkwell Road
Hart Lane
White Hart La
Victor Gardens
Clements Hall La
Uplands Road
Hill Lane
Park Gardens
Hawkwell Chase
Tudor Way
Thorpe Road
Rectory Road
Ironwell La
Holyoak Lane
Mount Bovers Lane
Gustedhall Lane
Roach Valley Way
Woodlands Road
Kilnwood Avenue
The Westerings
22
33

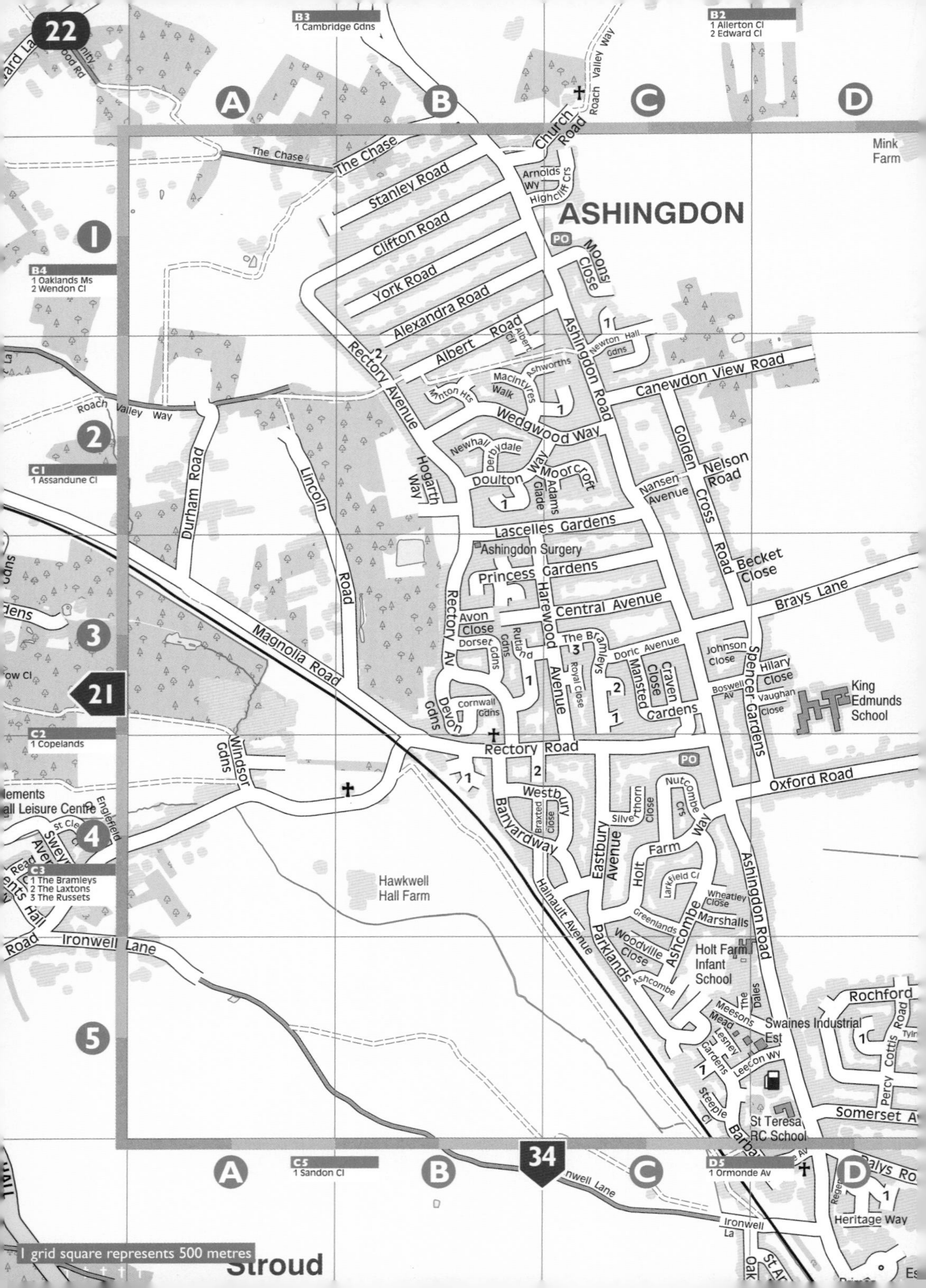
22
B3
1 Cambridge Gdns
B2
1 Allerton Cl
2 Edward Cl
A
B
C
D
Mink Farm
ASHINGDON
PO
The Chase
Church Road
Roach Valley Way
Arnolds Wy
Highcliff Crs
Stanley Road
Clifton Road
York Road
Alexandra Road
Albert Road
Albert Cl
Moons Close
Ashingdon Road
Newton Hall Gdns
Canewdon View Road
Rectory Avenue
Ashworths
Macintyres Walk
Wedgwood Way
Newhall
Derbydale
Doulton Way
Moorcroft
Adams Glade
Hogarth Way
Golden Cross Road
Nelson Road
Nansen Avenue
Lascelles Gardens
Ashingdon Surgery
Becket Close
Brays Lane
Princess Gardens
Central Avenue
Harewood Avenue
Avon Close
Rectory Av
Dorset Gdns
Rutland
The Bramleys
Royal Close
Doric Avenue
Mansted Gardens
Craven Close
Johnson Close
Spencer Gardens
Hilary Close
Boswell Av
Vaughan Close
King Edmunds School
Devon Gdns
Cornwall Gdns
Rectory Road
Oxford Road
Westbury
Banyardway
Braxted Close
Eastbury Avenue
Silverthorn Close
Nutcombe Crs
Holt Farm Way
Larkfield Cl
Wheatley Close
Marshalls
Greenlands
Ashcombe
Woodville Close
Parklands
Hainault Avenue
Holt Farm Infant School
The Dales
Meesons Mead
Swaines Industrial Est
Lesney Gardens
Leecon Wy
Steeple Cl
St Teresa RC School
Rochford
Cottis
Percy
Somerset
Lincoln Road
Durham Road
Magnolia Road
Roach Valley Way
Windsor Gdns
Hawkwell Hall Farm
Ironwell Lane
1
2
3
4
5
B4
1 Oaklands Ms
2 Wendon Cl
C1
1 Assandune Cl
21
C2
1 Copelands
Leisure Centre
Englefield
C3
1 The Bramleys
2 The Laxtons
3 The Russets
Road
34
C5
1 Sandon Cl
D5
1 Ormonde Av
Heritage Way
Ironwell La
1 grid square represents 500 metres
Stroud

E
F
G
H
1
2
3
4
5
Little Doggetts
Hyde Wood Lane
Apton Hall Farm
Scott's Hall
Apton Hall Road
Doggetts Chase
Little Stambridge Hall
Little Stambridge Hall Road
Ragstone Lodge
Brick Hous
Doggetts CP School
St Clare Mdw
Doggetts Cl
Lingfield Drive
Winters
Stambridge Road
Rochford Swimming Pool Services
Russell
Malting
Bobbing Cl
Middle Md
Oast Way
Prentice Close
Greenways
PO
Stambridge Road
Stambridge Primary School
ROCHFORD
Stew Elm F
Steward Farm La

35

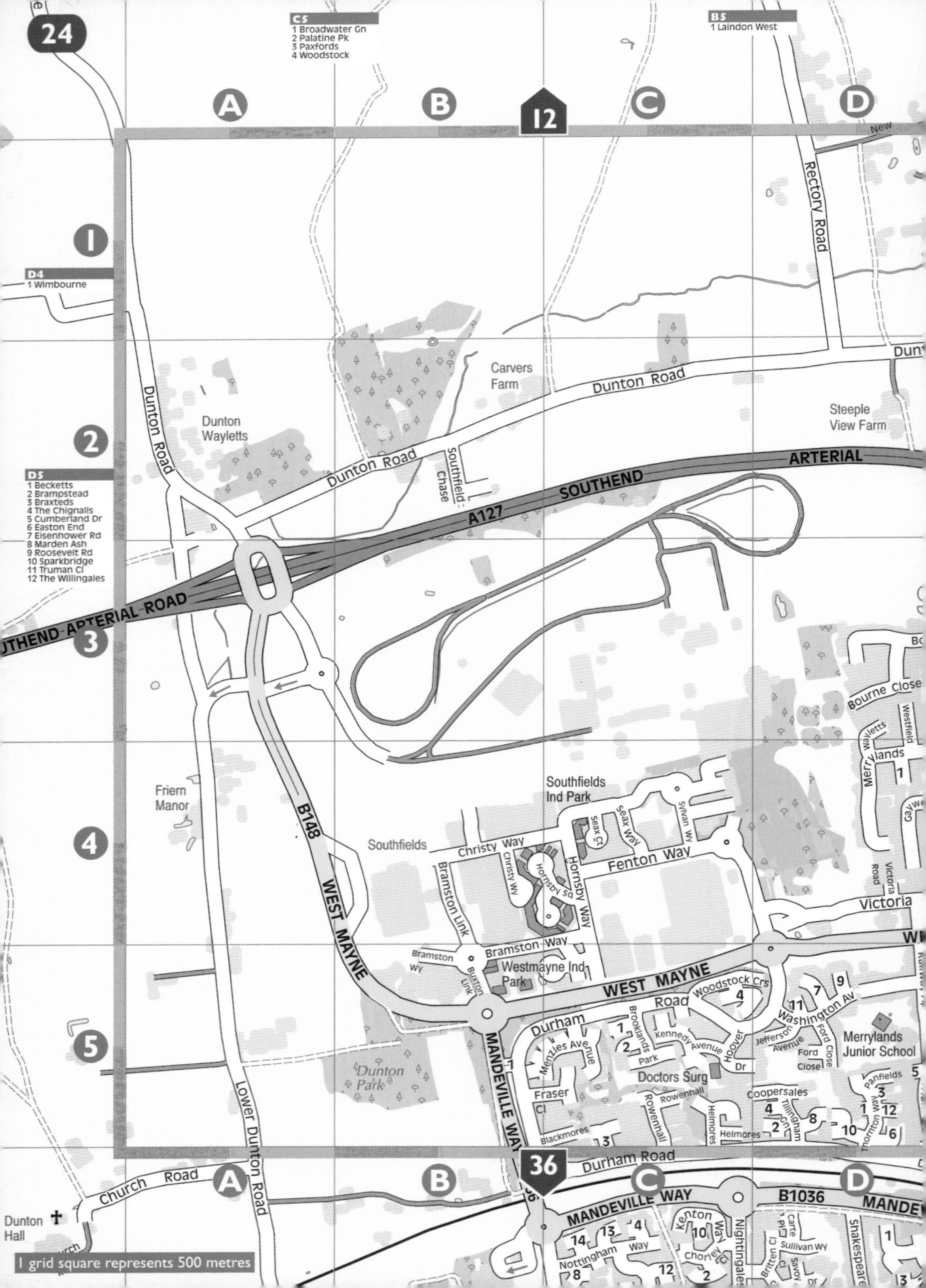
24
C5
1 Broadwater Gn
2 Palatine Pk
3 Paxfords
4 Woodstock
B5
1 Laindon West
A
B
12
C
D
D4
1 Wimbourne
D5
1 Becketts
2 Brampstead
3 Braxteds
4 The Chignalls
5 Cumberland Dr
6 Easton End
7 Eisenhower Rd
8 Marden Ash
9 Roosevelt Rd
10 Sparkbridge
11 Truman Cl
12 The Willingales
1
2
3
4
5
New
Rectory Road
Carvers Farm
Dunton Road
Steeple View Farm
Dunton Wayletts
Dunton Road
Southfield Chase
ARTERIAL
SOUTHEND
A127
SOUTHEND-ARTERIAL-ROAD
Bourne Close
Westfield
Wayletts
Merrylands
Southfields Ind Park
Seax Ct
Seax Way
Sylvan Wy
Friern Manor
B148
Southfields
Christy Way
Christy Wy
Hornsby Sq
Hornsby Way
Fenton Way
Bramston Link
Victoria Road
Victoria
WEST MAYNE
Bramston Way
Bramston Wy
Buxton Link
Westmayne Ind Park
WEST MAYNE
Woodstock Crs
Road
Durham
Brooklands Park
Kennedy Avenue
Hoover Dr
Jefferson Avenue
Washington Av
Ford Close
Ford Close
Merrylands Junior School
Menzies Avenue
MANDEVILLE WAY
Dunton Park
Doctors Surg
Fraser Cl
Rowenhall
Helmores
Coopersales
Tillingham Grn
Panfields
Thornton Way
Blackmores
Lower Dunton Road
Church Road
36
Durham Road
MANDEVILLE WAY
B1036
MANDE
Dunton Hall
Kenton Way
Nottingham Way
Chorley Cl
Nightingales
Britten Cl
Sullivan Wy
Savoy
Shakespeare
1 grid square represents 500 metres

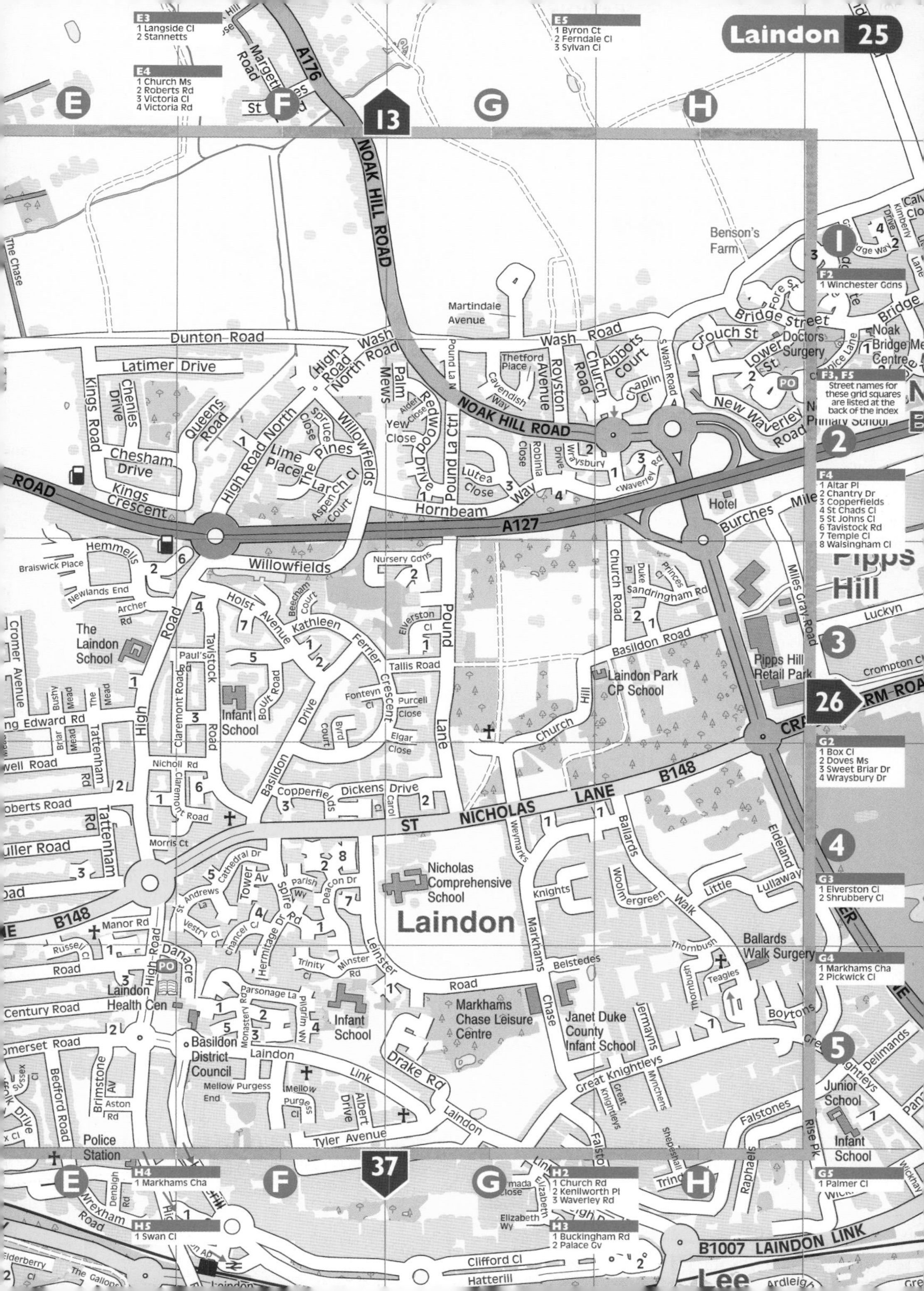
E3
1 Langside Cl
2 Stannetts
E4
1 Church Ms
2 Roberts Rd
3 Victoria Cl
4 Victoria Rd
E5
1 Byron Ct
2 Ferndale Cl
3 Sylvan Cl
F2
1 Winchester Gdns
F3, F5
Street names for these grid squares are listed at the back of the index
F4
1 Altar Pl
2 Chantry Dr
3 Copperfields
4 St Chads Cl
5 St Johns Cl
6 Tavistock Rd
7 Temple Cl
8 Walsingham Cl
G2
1 Box Cl
2 Doves Ms
3 Sweet Briar Dr
4 Wraysbury Dr
G3
1 Elverston Cl
2 Shrubbery Cl
G4
1 Markhams Cha
2 Pickwick Cl
G5
1 Palmer Cl
H2
1 Church Rd
2 Kenilworth Pl
3 Waverley Rd
H3
1 Buckingham Rd
2 Palace Gv
H4
1 Markhams Cha
H5
1 Swan Cl
E
F
G
H
I
2
3
4
5
13
26
37
A176
NOAK HILL ROAD
A127
B148
B1007 LAINDON LINK
ST NICHOLAS LANE
Dunton Road
Latimer Drive
Kings Road
Chenies Drive
Queens Road
Chesham Drive
Kings Crescent
High Road North
Lime Place
The Pines
Larch Cl
Spruce Close
Aspen Court
Willowfields
Palm Mews
Yew Close
Redwood Drive
Pound La Ctrl
Pound Lane
Hornbeam Way
Lutea Close
Martindale Avenue
Thetford Place
Cavendish Way
Royston Avenue
Church Road
Abbots Court
Chaplin Cl
Wash Road
Crouch St
Bridge Street
Lower St
New Waverley Road
Doctors Surgery
Benson's Farm
Hotel
Burches
Pipps Hill
Pipps Hill Retail Park
Miles Gray Road
Luckyn
Crompton Cl
Basildon Road
Sandringham Rd
Laindon Park CP School
Church Hill
Hemmells
Braiswick Place
Newlands End
Archer Rd
The Laindon School
Holst Avenue
Kathleen Ferrier Crescent
Beecham Court
Elverston Cl
Nursery Gdns
Tallis Road
Fonteyn Cl
Purcell Close
Elgar Close
Byrd Court
Basildon Drive
Copperfields
Dickens Drive
Tavistock Road
Claremont Road
Boult Road
Infant School
Cromer Avenue
Tattenham Rd
King Edward Rd
Nicholl Rd
Roberts Road
Fuller Road
Morris Ct
Weymarks
Ballards Walk
Eldeland
Lullaway
Little Lullaway
Woolmergreen
Knights
Markhams Chase
Nicholas Comprehensive School
Laindon
Cathedral Dr
Tower Av
Spire Rd
Parish Wy
Deacon Dr
St Andrews La
Vestry Cl
Chancel Cl
Hermitage Dr
Trinity Cl
Minster Rd
Leinster Road
Manor Rd
Russell Cl
Danacre
High Road
Laindon Health Cen
Century Road
Parsonage La
Monastery Rd
Pilgrim Wy
Infant School
Markhams Chase Leisure Centre
Belstedes
Janet Duke County Infant School
Jermayns
Thornbush
Teagles
Ballards Walk Surgery
Boytons
Great Knightleys
Mynchens
Somerset Road
Brimstone Av
Aston Rd
Bedford Road
Basildon District Council
Laindon Link
Mellow Purgess End
Mellow Purgess Cl
Albert Drive
Drake Rd
Tyler Avenue
Police Station
Junior School
Infant School
Falstones
Shepeshall
Raphaels
Rise Pk
Delimands
Wrexham Road
Denbigh Rd
Elizabeth Wy
Clifford Cl
Hatterill
Elderberry Cl
The Gallops
Ardleigh
Lee

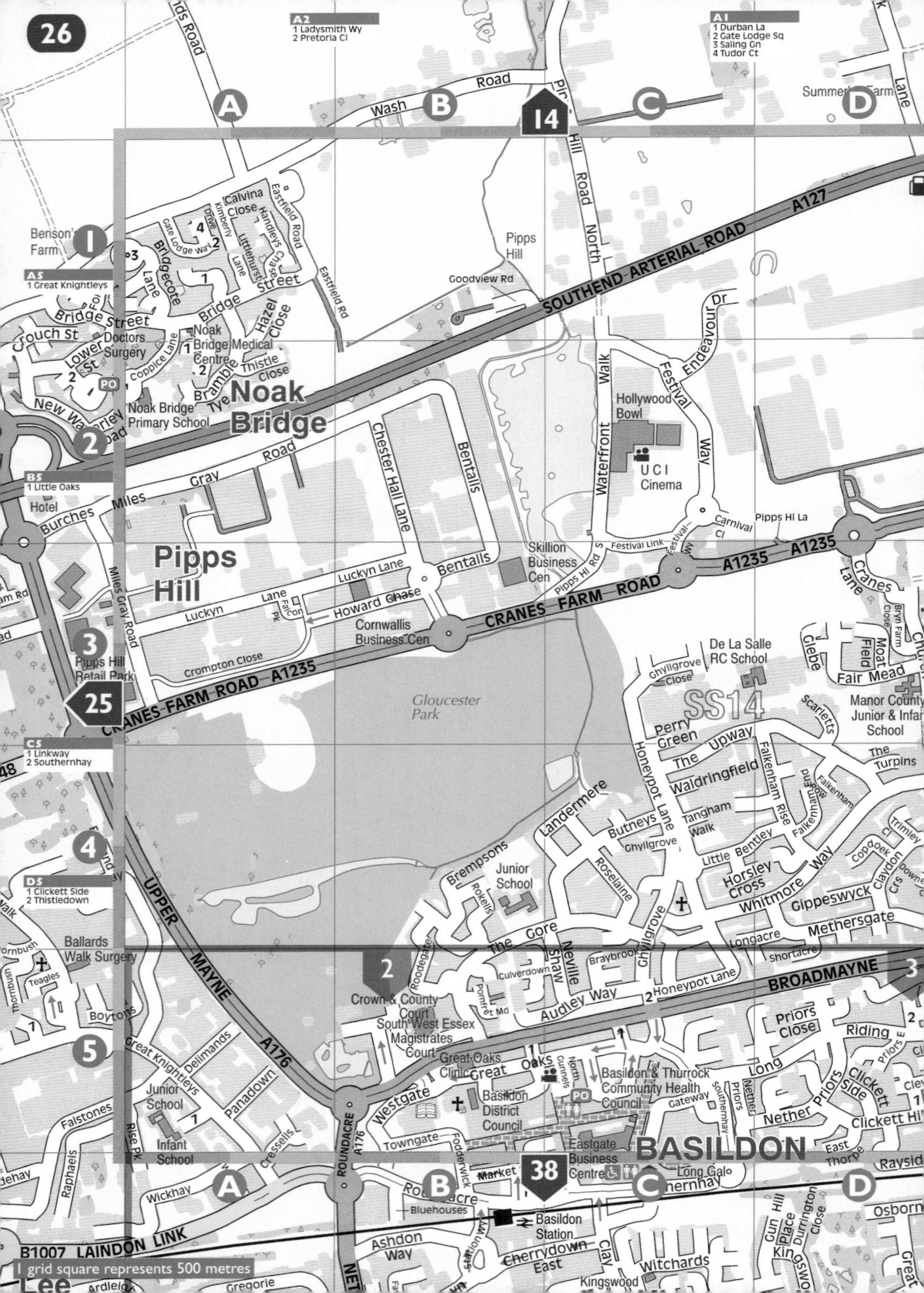
A2
1 Ladysmith Wy
2 Pretoria Cl
A1
1 Durban La
2 Gate Lodge Sq
3 Saling Gn
4 Tudor Ct
A5
1 Great Knightleys
B5
1 Little Oaks
C5
1 Linkway
2 Southernhay
D5
1 Clickett Side
2 Thistledown
Wash Road
14
Noak Bridge
Pipps Hill
SOUTHEND-ARTERIAL ROAD A127
CRANES FARM ROAD A1235
Gloucester Park
SS14
UPPER MAYNE A176
BROADMAYNE
BASILDON
Basildon Station
38
25
2
3
B1007 LAINDON LINK
1 grid square represents 500 metres

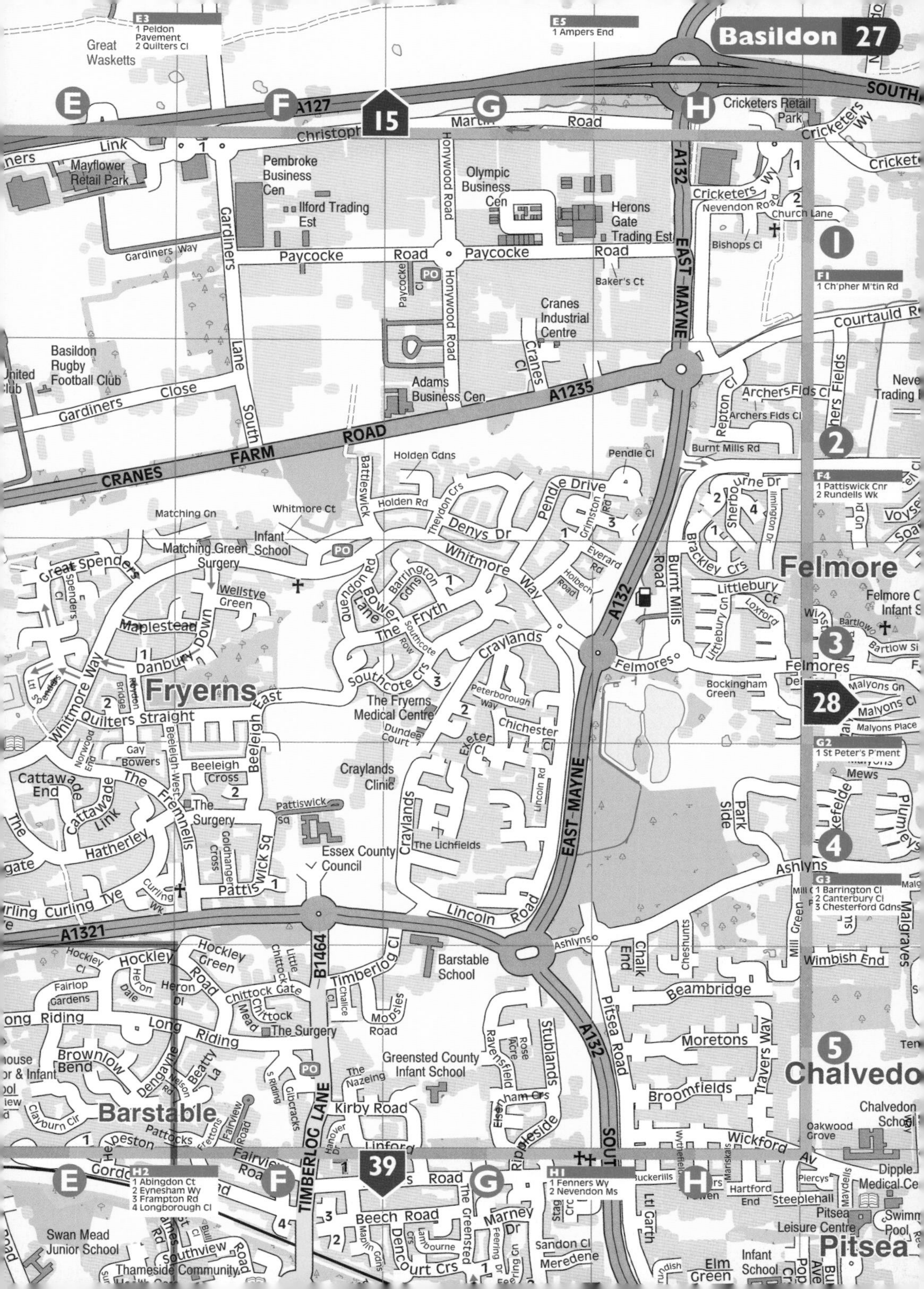
E3
1 Peldon Pavement
2 Quilters Cl
E5
1 Ampers End
F1
1 Ch'pher M'tin Rd
F4
1 Pattiswick Cnr
2 Rundells Wk
G2
1 St Peter's P'ment
G3
1 Barrington Cl
2 Canterbury Cl
3 Chesterford Gdns
H1
1 Fenners Wy
2 Nevendon Ms
H2
1 Abingdon Ct
2 Eynesham Wy
3 Frampton Rd
4 Longborough Cl
Great Wasketts
A127
Christopher Martin Road
Mayflower Retail Park
Pembroke Business Cen
Ilford Trading Est
Olympic Business Cen
Herons Gate Trading Est
Cricketers Retail Park
Cricketers Wy
Nevendon Road
Church Lane
Bishops Cl
Gardiners Way
Gardiners Lane
Paycocke Road
Honywood Road
Baker's Ct
Cranes Industrial Centre
Cranes Cl
Courtauld Rd
Basildon Rugby Football Club
Gardiners Close
South
Adams Business Cen
A1235
Cranes Farm Road
A132
East-Mayne
Repton Cl
Archers Flds Cl
Burnt Mills Rd
Holden Gdns
Holden Rd
Battleswick
Pendle Cl
Pendle Drive
Sherbourne Dr
Matching Gn
Whitmore Ct
Infant School
Matching Green Surgery
Great Spenders
Theydon Crs
Denys Dr
Grimston Rd
Everard Rd
Holbech Road
Burnt Mills Road
Brackley Crs
Littlebury Ct
Felmore
Felmore C Infant S
Wellstye Green
Maplestead
Quendon Rd
Bower Lane
Barrington Gdns
The Fryth
Whitmore Way
Southcote Row
Craylands
Felmores
Bockingham Green
Malyons Gn
Malyons Cl
Malyons Place
Danbury Down
Fryerns
Southcote Crs
The Fryerns Medical Centre
Peterborough Way
Chichester Cl
Quilters Straight
Beeleigh East
Beeleigh West
Dundee Court
Exeter Cl
Gay Bowers
Norwood End
Beeleigh Cross
Cattawade End
Cattawade Link
The Fremnells
The Surgery
Pattiswick Sq
Craylands Clinic
Lincoln Rd
Park Side
Mews
Hatherley
Goldhanger Cross
The Lichfields
Essex County Council
Ashlyns
Curling Tye
Curling Wk
A1321
Lincoln Road
Mill Green
Malgraves
B1464
Hockley Cl
Hockley Green
Hockley Road
Heron Dale
Heron Dl
Little Chittock
Chittock Gate
Chittock Mead
Timberlog Cl
Chalice Cl
Barstable School
Chalk End
Cheshunts
Wimbish End
Beambridge
Fairlop Gardens
Long Riding
The Surgery
Mopsies Road
Ravensfield
Rose Acre
Stublands
Pitsea Road
Moretons
Travers Way
Brownlow Bend
Dengayne
Nelson Rd
Beatty La
Greensted County Infant School
Chalvedon
Chalvedon School
Barstable
Clayburn Cir
Gilbracks
The Nazeing
Kirby Road
Eisenham Crs
Broomfields
Oakwood Grove
Fairview Road
Timberlog Lane
Hanover Dr
Linford
Rippleside
Wickford Av
Pattocks
Frettons
Helpeston
Gordon
Fairview Road
Wytheleld
Mariskals
Hartford End
Steeplehall
Piercys
Maydells
Dipple
Medical Ce
Swan Mead Junior School
Southview Road
Thameside Community
Beech Road
Dencourt Crs
The Greensted
Marney Dr
Feering Dr
Sandon Cl
Meredene
Ltl Garth
Elm Green
Infant School
Pitsea Leisure Centre
Swimm Pool
Pitsea

15
28
39

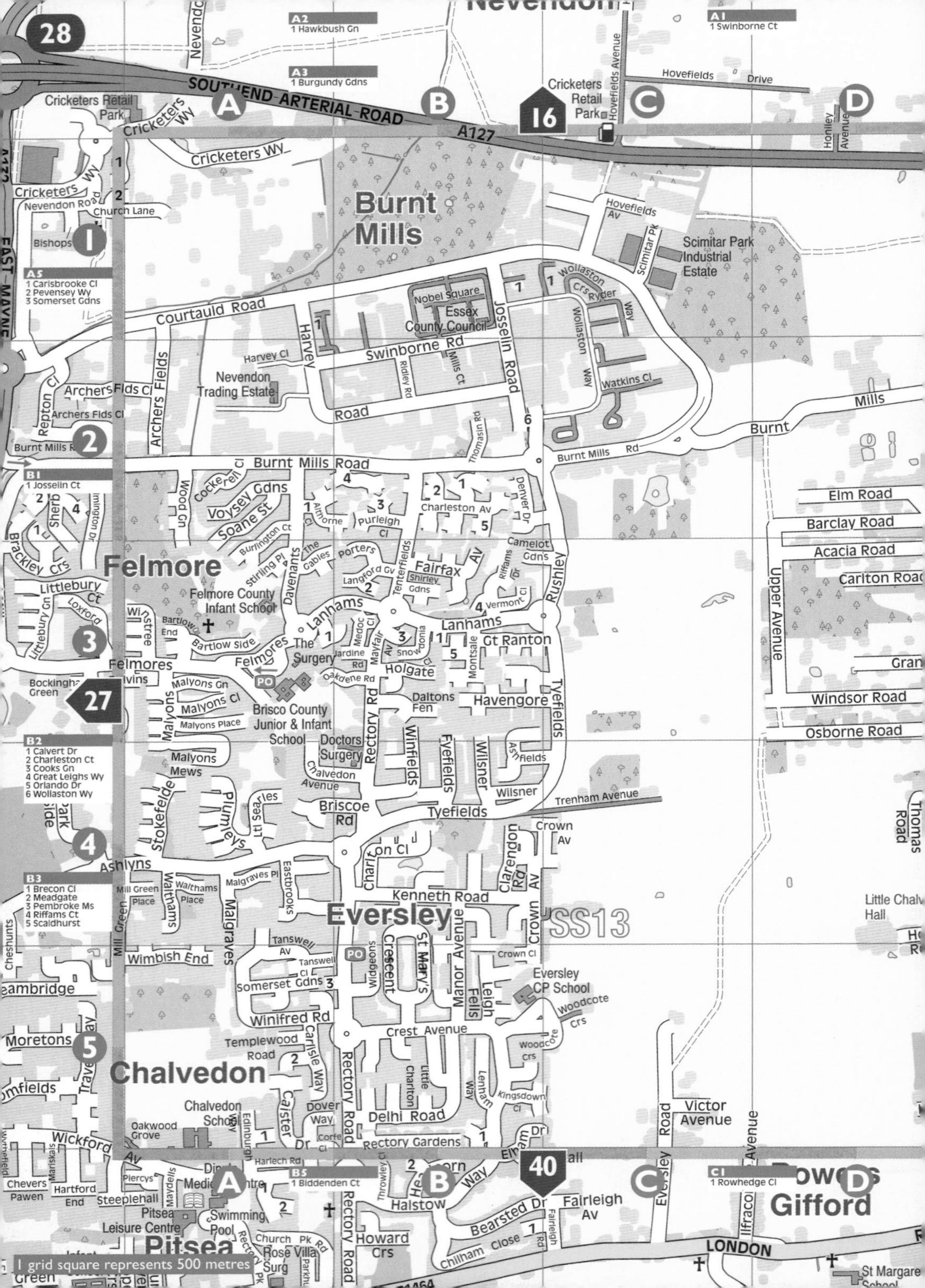
A2
1 Hawkbush Gn
A3
1 Burgundy Gdns
A1
1 Swinborne Ct
SOUTHEND ARTERIAL ROAD
A127
Cricketers Retail Park
Cricketers Wy
Hovefields Avenue
Hovefields Drive
16
Burnt Mills
Hovefields Av
Scimitar Pk
Scimitar Park Industrial Estate
Nobel Square
Essex County Council
Courtauld Road
Swinborne Rd
Josselin Road
Wollaston Crs
Ryder Way
Wollaston Way
Watkins Cl
Harvey Cl
Nevendon Trading Estate
Archers Fields
Archers Flds Cl
Repton Cl
Burnt Mills Road
Burnt Mills Rd
Thomasin Rd
A5
1 Carisbrooke Cl
2 Pevensey Wy
3 Somerset Gdns
B1
1 Josselin Ct
B2
1 Calvert Dr
2 Charleston Ct
3 Cooks Gn
4 Great Leighs Wy
5 Orlando Dr
6 Wollaston Wy
B3
1 Brecon Cl
2 Meadgate
3 Pembroke Ms
4 Riffams Ct
5 Scaldhurst
B5
1 Biddenden Ct
C1
1 Rowhedge Cl
Felmore
Felmore County Infant School
Voysey Gdns
Soane St
Cockerell Cl
Wood Gn
Burlington Ct
Stirling Pl
Davenants
The Gables
Porters
Langford Gv
Tenterfields
Fairfax Av
Shirley Gdns
Purleigh Cl
Charleston Av
Denver Dr
Camelot Gdns
Riffams Dr
Vermont Cl
Rushley
Lanhams
Gt Ranton
Montsale
Medoc Cl
Mayfair Av
Snowdonia Cl
Jardine Rd
The Surgery
Felmores
Bartlow End
Bartlow Side
Oakdene Rd
Holgate
Daltons Fen
Havengore
Tyefields
Malyons Gn
Malyons Cl
Malyons Place
Malyons Mews
Malyons
Brisco County Junior & Infant School
Doctors Surgery
Rectory Rd
Winfields
Fyefields
Wilsner
Ashfields
Chalvedon Avenue
Briscoe Rd
Trenham Avenue
Stokefelde
Plumleys
Ltl Searles
Ashlyns
Mill Green Place
Walthams Place
Malgraves Pl
Eastbrooks
Walthams
Malgraves
Charlton Cl
Crown Av
Clarendon Rd
Kenneth Road
Eversley
SS13
Tanswell Av
Tanswell Cl
Somerset Gdns
Widgeons
Crescent
St Mary's
Manor Avenue
Leigh Fells
Crown Cl
Eversley CP School
Woodcote Crs
Winifred Rd
Carlisle Way
Crest Avenue
Templewood Road
Chalvedon
Charlton
Little
Lenham Way
Kingsdown Cl
Chalvedon School
Oakwood Grove
Caister Dr
Dover Way
Corfe Cl
Delhi Road
Rectory Gardens
Edinburgh
Harlech Rd
Elyham Dr
Eversley Road
Victor Avenue
Upper Avenue
Ilfracombe Avenue
Elm Road
Barclay Road
Acacia Road
Carlton Road
Windsor Road
Osborne Road
Burnt Mills
Thomas Road
Little Chalvedon Hall
40
Fairleigh Av
Bearsted Dr
Chilham Close
Halstow Way
Throwley Cl
Rectory Road
Howard Crs
Church Pk Rd
Rose Villa Surg
Swimming Pool
Pitsea Leisure Centre
Pitsea
Medical Centre
Maydells
Piercys
Steeplehall
Hartford End
Chevers Pawen
Wickford Av
Pitsea
Gifford
LONDON
St Margaret's School
Nevendon Road
Church Lane
Bishops
Cricketers Wy
Burnt Mills Rd
Brackley Crs
Littlebury Ct
Littlebury Gn
Loxford
Felmores
Bockingham Green
27
Wimbish End
Moretons
Travers Way
EAST MAYNE
1 grid square represents 500 metres

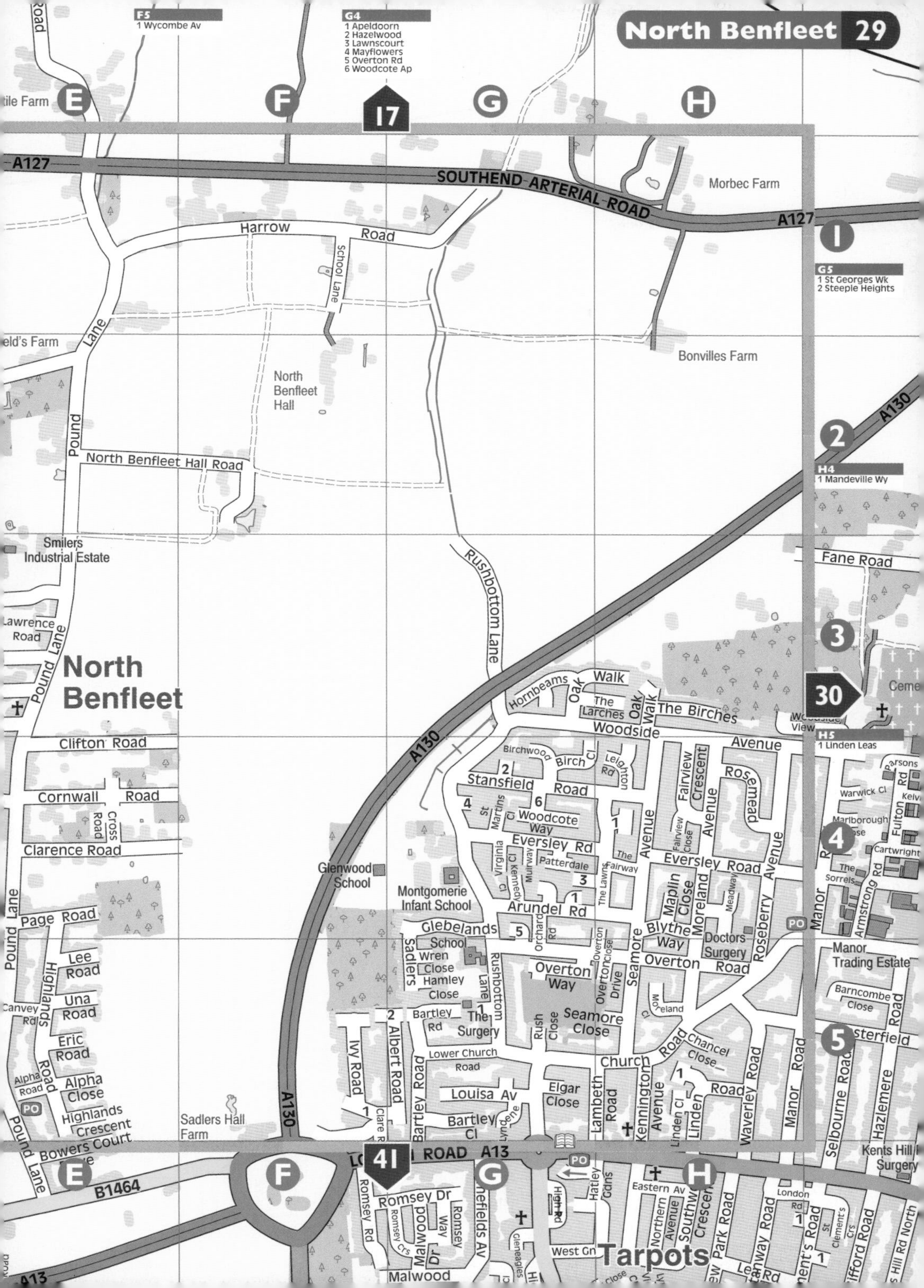
F5
1 Wycombe Av
G4
1 Apeldoorn
2 Hazelwood
3 Lawnscourt
4 Mayflowers
5 Overton Rd
6 Woodcote Ap
G5
1 St Georges Wk
2 Steeple Heights
H4
1 Mandeville Wy
H5
1 Linden Leas
17
30
41
A127
SOUTHEND ARTERIAL ROAD
Morbec Farm
Harrow Road
School Lane
Pound Lane
North Benfleet Hall
Bonvilles Farm
North Benfleet Hall Road
Smilers Industrial Estate
Rushbottom Lane
A130
Fane Road
Lawrence Road
North Benfleet
Clifton Road
Cornwall Road
Cross Road
Clarence Road
Page Road
Lee Road
Una Road
Eric Road
Canvey Rd
Highlands Road
Alpha Road
Alpha Close
Highlands Crescent
Bowers Court
Sadlers Hall Farm
Glenwood School
Montgomerie Infant School
Glebelands School
Sadlers
Wren Close
Hamley Close
Bartley Rd
The Surgery
Ivy Road
Albert Road
Clare Rd
Bartley Road
Lower Church Road
Louisa Av
Bartley Cl
Lyndene
Elgar Close
Hornbeams
Oak Walk
The Larches
The Birches
Woodside
Woodside View
Avenue
Birchwood
Birch Cl
Leighton Rd
Stansfield Road
St Martins Cl
Woodcote Way
Eversley Rd
Virginia Cl
Kennedy Cl
Muirway
Patterdale
The Lawns
The Fairway
Arundel Rd
Orchard Rd
Overton Way
Overton Close
Overton Drive
Seamore Close
Rush Close
Seamore
Fairview Crescent
Fairview Close
Rosemead
Avenue
Eversley Road
Maplin Close
Moreland
Meadway
Roseberry Avenue
Blythe Way
Doctors Surgery
Overton Road
Moreland Cl
Church Road
Chancel Close
Lambeth Road
Kennington Avenue
Linden Cl
Linden
Waverley Road
Manor Road
Parsons
Warwick Cl
Fulton Rd
Kelvin
Marlborough Close
Cartwright
The Sorrels
Armstrong Rd
Manor Trading Estate
Barncombe Close
Chesterfield
Selbourne Road
Hazlemere
Kents Hill Surgery
Cemetery
PO
London Road A13
B1464
A13
Romsey Dr
Romsey Rd
Romsey Crs
Malwood Dr
Romsey Way
Malwood
Gleneagles
High Rd
Hatley Gdns
West Gn
Tarpots
Eastern Av
Northern Avenue
Southwood Crescent
Park Road
Leinway Road
London Rd
St Clement's Crs
Clement's Road
Clifford Road
Kents Hill Rd North
Rd
E
F
G
H
I
2
3
4
5

C5
1 Chatsworth
2 Foxmeadows
A4
1 Shrewsbury Dr
Aldham Gdns
Bardfield
Oakley Av
Langham Drive
Polstead Cl
A
B
18
C
D
Morbec Farm
A127
1
D5
1 Grangeway
2 Swans Green Cl
Bonvilles Farm
A130
Lychgate
Industrial Est
Fane Road
Gt Whe
Farm
2
Burches Road
Fane Road
SOUTHE
3
29
Cemetery
Birches
Woodside
View
Avenue
Great Burches
Farm
Grange
Road
Coniston Road
Burches Road
Grange Road
Ullswater
Road
Goldfinch La
Crescent
Rosemead
Avenue
Parsons Rd
Warwick Cl
Kelvin Rd
Fulton Rd
Brunel Rd
Manor
Trading Estate
Marlborough
Close
Cartwright Rd
4
New
Thundersley
Windermere Road
Thirlmere Road
Borrowdale Road
Crossfell Rd
Allandale
Highview Road
The Common
Gt Burches Rd
Manor Road
The Sorrels
Armstrong Rd
Road
Moreland
Meadway
Roseberry Ave
Doctors
Surgery
PO
Primary
School
Keswick
Road
Bassenthwaite
Road
Thundersley
Silverdale
Langford Crs
Grandview
Drive
Prestwood
Close
Prestwood
Drive
Burches
Mead
Common Ap
Sayers
Cedar Pk Cl
Cedar Hall
Gdns
Manor
Trading Estate
Church Road
Road
Barncombe
Close
Road
5
Chancel
Close
Chesterfield
Avenue
Church
View
Road
Grasmere Road
Borrowdale
Rd
Borrowdale
Cl
Raymonds
Park Road
Road
Hart
Cl
2
1
Cedar Rd
Sunnymede Cl
Hart
Dark La
Church Road
The Rundels
Kingston
CP School
PO
Fox
Close
Stoneleighs
Deepdale
Princes
Av
Broadlands
Thundersley
Junior & Infant
School
Linden
Waverley Road
Road
Manor Road
Selbourne Road
Hazlemere
Kents Hill Road North
Spencer
Stanley
Road North
Kingston Way
Hydeway
Kents Hill Road
Thundersley Church Road
Road
Downer Road North
Rhoda Road North
B
42
Kenneth Road
C
Kings Park
D
Golden
Manor
Drive
Close
Chase
Wy
Villiers
Boyton
Cl
The Chase
Crescent
London
Rd
1
Road
St Clement's Crs
Road
North
Road
Drive
Lake Dr
Tudor Cl
Lodge Close
Chase
Dorothy
I grid square represents 500 metres

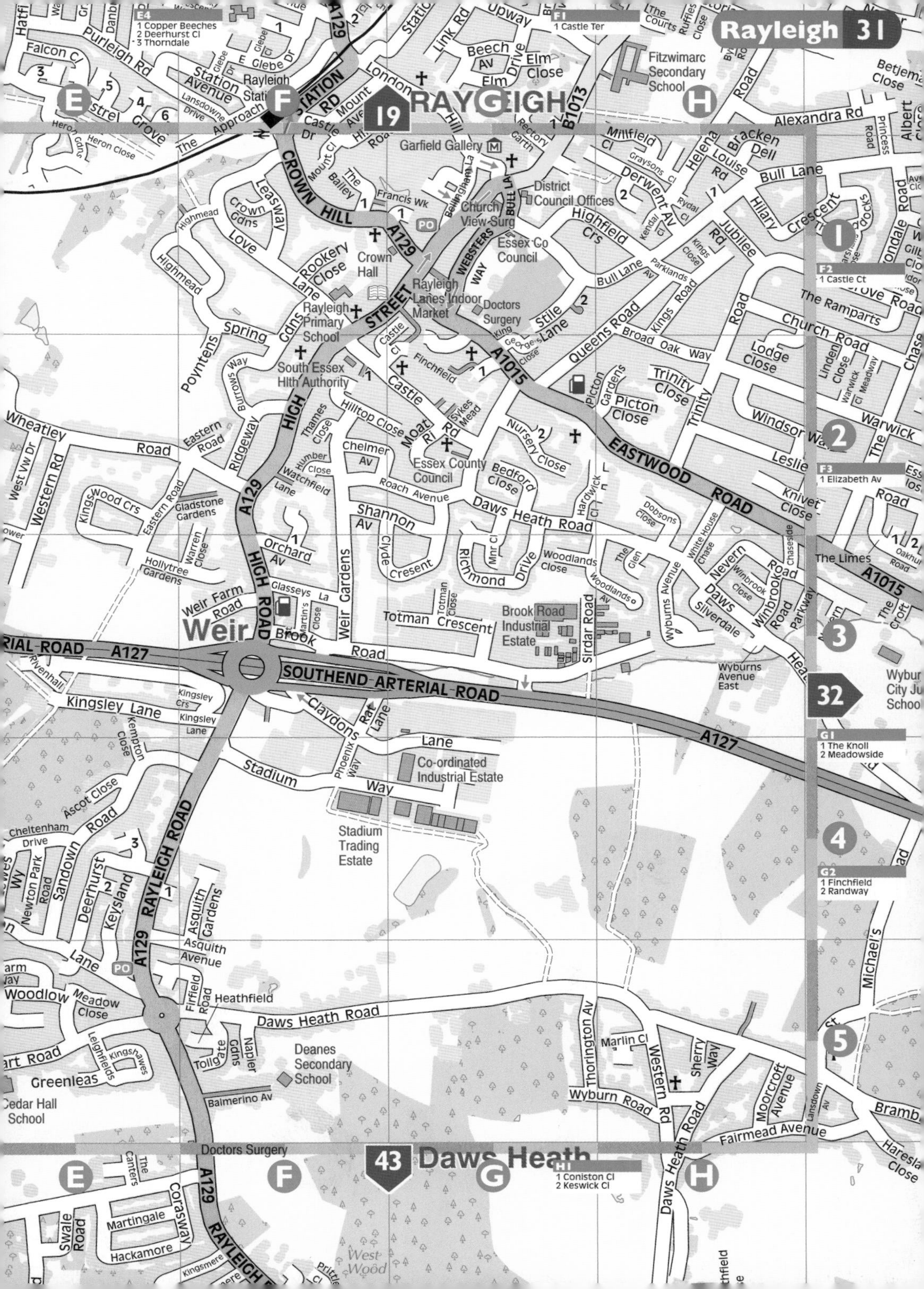
E4
1 Copper Beeches
2 Deerhurst Cl
3 Thorndale
F1
1 Castle Ter
F2
1 Castle Ct
F3
1 Elizabeth Av
G1
1 The Knoll
2 Meadowside
G2
1 Finchfield
2 Randway
H1
1 Coniston Cl
2 Keswick Cl
RAYLEIGH
19
32
43
Weir
Daws Heath
Rayleigh Station
Station Avenue
Purleigh Rd
Falcon Cl
Glebe Dr
Grove
Lansdowne Drive
The Approach
Heron Gdns
Heron Close
Station Rd
Crown Hill
Mount Cl
The Bailey
Castle Dr
Mount Av
London Hill
Link Rd
Upway
Beech Av
Elm Drive
Elm Close
Garfield Gallery
Bellingham La
Church View Surg
District Council Offices
Essex Co Council
Rectory Garth
B1013
Fitzwimarc Secondary School
Alexandra Rd
Millfield Cl
Graysons Cl
Derwent Av
Helena Rd
Bracken Dell
Louise Rd
Bull Lane
Hilary Crescent
Kendal Cl
Rydal Cl
Highfield Crs
Jubilee Rd
Kings Close
Parklands Av
Kings Road
Queens Road
Broad Oak Way
The Ramparts
Church Road
Lodge Close
Trinity Close
Trinity Road
Linden Close
Warwick Cl
Meadway
Windsor Way
Warwick
Leslie
Knivet Close
Betjeman Close
Princess Road
Albert Close
Chase
A129
A1015
A127
High Street
Webster's Way
Francis Wk
Crown Hall
Crown Gdns
Leasway
Love Lane
Highmead
Rookery Close
Rayleigh Lanes Indoor Market
Doctors Surgery
Rayleigh Primary School
Spring Gdns
Poyntens
Burrows Way
Castle Cl
Finchfield
King George's Close
Stile Lane
South Essex Hlth Authority
Castle Rd
Sykes Mead
Moat Rd
Hilltop Close
Thames Close
Picton Gardens
Picton Close
Nursery Close
Eastwood Road
Wheatley Road
Eastern Road
Ridgeway
High Road
Humber Close
Watchfield Lane
Chelmer Av
Essex County Council
Bedford Close
Roach Avenue
Daws Heath Road
Hardwick Cl
Dobsons Close
West Vw Dr
Western Rd
Kings Wood Crs
Eastern Road
Gladstone Gardens
Warren Close
Shannon Av
Clyde Cresent
Orchard Av
Richmond Drive
Mnr Cl
Woodlands Close
Woodlands Av
The Glen
Wyburns Avenue
White House Chase
Nevern Road
Winbrook Close
Chaseside
The Limes
Hollytree Gardens
Weir Farm Road
Glasseys La
Martin's Close
Weir Gardens
Totman Close
Totman Crescent
Brook Road Industrial Estate
Sirdar Road
Daws Silverdale
Winbrook Road
Parkway
Brook Road
Southend Arterial Road
Rivenhall
Kingsley Lane
Kingsley Crs
Kempton Close
Claydons Lane
Rat Lane
Phoenix Way
Co-ordinated Industrial Estate
Stadium Way
Wyburns Avenue East
Ascot Close
Cheltenham Drive
Sandown Road
Newton Park Road
Deerhurst
Keysland
Rayleigh Road
Asquith Gardens
Asquith Avenue
Stadium Trading Estate
Woodlow
Meadow Close
Firfield Road
Heathfield
Daws Heath Road
Leighfields
Kingshawes
Greenleas
Tollgate
Napier Gdns
Deanes Secondary School
Balmerino Av
Cedar Hall School
Thorington Av
Marlin Cl
Western Rd
Sherry Way
Wyburn Road
Daws Heath Road
Moorcroft Avenue
Lansdown Av
Fairmead Avenue
Michael's
Haresland Close
Doctors Surgery
The Canters
Corasway
Martingale
Swale Road
Hackamore
Kingsmere
West Wood
E
F
G
H
1
2
3
4
5

32
Napier Road
A2
1 Lodgelands Cl
Stevens Farm
A1
1 Bramfield Rd W
Roach Valley Way
Betjeman Close
Blower Close
Albert Road
Alexandra Rd
Princess Road
A
B
C
D
20
Bull Lane
Fisher's Farm
Bracken Dell
Louise Rd
Helena
Avondale Close
Grove Close
Cha End
Hilary
Crescent
The Paddocks
Avondale Road
Cecil Way
Gilbert Close
Tudor Close
Marshalls Close
Jubilee Rd
Kings Close
1
A3
1 Cedar Cl
2 Hawthorn Wy
Milton Cl
Sheridan Cl
Popes Wk
Shakespeare Avenue
Ashcombe Way
PO
Bramfield Rd East
Grove Road
The Ramparts
Church Road
Lodge Close
Linden Close
Warwick Cl
Meadway
The Chase
Copford Av
Brocksford Av
Grove Road
Albany Road
The Spinneys
Katherine Close
Grove Ct
Connaught Rd
Trinity
Windsor Way
2
Warwick Road
Warwick Gardens
Grove Junior & Infant School
Clarence Road
Warwick Green
Lancaster Road
Connaught Road
Leslie Road
B2
1 Dorothy Farm Rd
2 Holton Rd
3 Lillyville Wk
4 Thorington Rd
Essex Close
Worcester Drive
Leslie Gardens
York Rd
Kent Way
Disraeli Road
Ethel Road
Hillside Road
Nore Road
Rise
White House Chase
Chaseside
Nevern Road
Winbrook Close
Daws
Silverdale
Winbrook Road
The Limes
Oakhurst Road
Poplar Road
The Laurels
Lilian Place
York Road
York Close
York Rise
Kennedy Close
Gloucester Avenue
Connaught Road
The Drive
Warwick Road
Southwood Gardens
Avenue
Sandhill
Gravel Road
A1015
Parkway
Nevern Close
The Croft
South View Close
3
Heath Road
Wyburns Avenue East
31
Wyburns City Junior School
Lynwood Green
Bartletts
Rayleigh
Springwater Road
Boundary Road
Eastwood
B3
1 Lancaster Gdns
Springwater Gv
Springwater Close
Saffory Cl
Boley Cl
Tudor Road
Bosworth
RAYLE
Rayleigh Downs Road
Glenwood Avenue
Grovewood Avenue
Grovewood Cl
Langley Cl
Bramble Close
Bramble Road
Road
Pargat Drive
Bolney Drive
4
Michael's Road
Eastwood Old Road
Musket Gv
Ringwood Dr
Grove Hill
Belgrave Close
The Gables
Belgrave
Cornec Av
Eastwood Industrial Estate
Rd
Cabinet Way
Waylerts
Larchwood Close
A127
Bowman Av
Cornec Cha
Rutherford Cl
Progress
St
Pound Wood
5
Sherry Way
Moorcroft Avenue
Lansdown Av
Bramble
Fairmead Avenue
Haresland Close
Crescent
Woodside Close
Wroxham Close
Hickling Close
Mountain Ash Cl
Eastwood Old Road
Belgrave Road
Little Hays
Ashcombe Cl
Rothwell Cl
Bradford Bury
Stephenson Rd
Pine Cl
Ryde
44
Road
Bramble
The Ryde
Boyce Hill Cl
Belfairs Park Close
Belfairs Park Drive
Eastwood
Berkshire Close
Woodside
Orsett Av
Thorndon Park Close
The Fairway
Fairway Gdns
Park View Drive
Bramble Hall
Lane North
1 grid square represents 500 metres

Eastwood 33
E4
1 Chanton Cl
F4
1 Epping Cl
E
F
G
H
21
Gustedhall Lane
Honeypots Farm
Gustedhall Lane
Potash Wood
HALL ROAD
B1013
H5
1 Borman Cl
2 Lovell Ri
3 Mcdivitt Wk
Cemetery
The Lawn
Gusted Hall
Roach Valley Way
The Scrubs
Ark Lane
Flemings Farm
Blatches Farm
Roach Valley Way
34
Flemings Farm Road
Blatches Chase
Roach Valley
Green Lane
Riverdale
Anstey Close
Dering Crs
Dandies Drive
Dandies Chase
Dandies Close
Hartland Close
Nobles Green Road
Nobles Green Close
Kendal Way
Paddock Cl
The Spinneys
Symons Avenue
Eastwood Park Dr
Fairfield Road
Fairfield Gdns
Fairfield Crs
Alan Cl
Alan Grove
Benvenue Avenue
Heycroft Road
Winchester Close
Byfield
Scott Park Surgery
Repton Gv
Western Approaches
Fastnet
Rockall
Old Mead
Coniston
Collins Way
Lundy Close
Sunnybank Close
Meakins Cl
Fulford Dr
Neil Armstrong Way
White House Road
Macmurdo Road
Sairard Close
The Rodings
The Maze
PO
ROAD
A1015
Leighfields Av
Bellhouse Road
Rowan Walk
Steeplefield
Lambeth Road
Hudson Road
Hudson Crs
St Lawrence Gdns
Walters Cl
Willow Close
Applerow
Burfield Road
Orchard Grove
Orch Side
Whitehouse Mdw
Leslie Dr
Leslie Close
Chesterfield Cresent
The Cresent
Mansel Cl
Poppyfield Close
Park Av
Brooklands Av
Foursisters Way
Eastwood GM Junior School
Kingsdown School
Snakes Lane
Southend Borough Football Club
Mayflower
Comet Wy
Pinewood Avenue
Southernhay
Airborne Industrial Estate
Priory Wd
Hazelwood Grove
45
RAYLEIGH ROAD
Infant School
High School
Lympston Close
Bideford Cl
Kent Elms Close
ARTERIAL ROAD
Eastwood
PRINCE AVENUE
A127
Exford
Dunster Av
Abbotts Close
Shirley Rd
Bellhouse Crs
Brairwood Cl
5
4
3
2
1

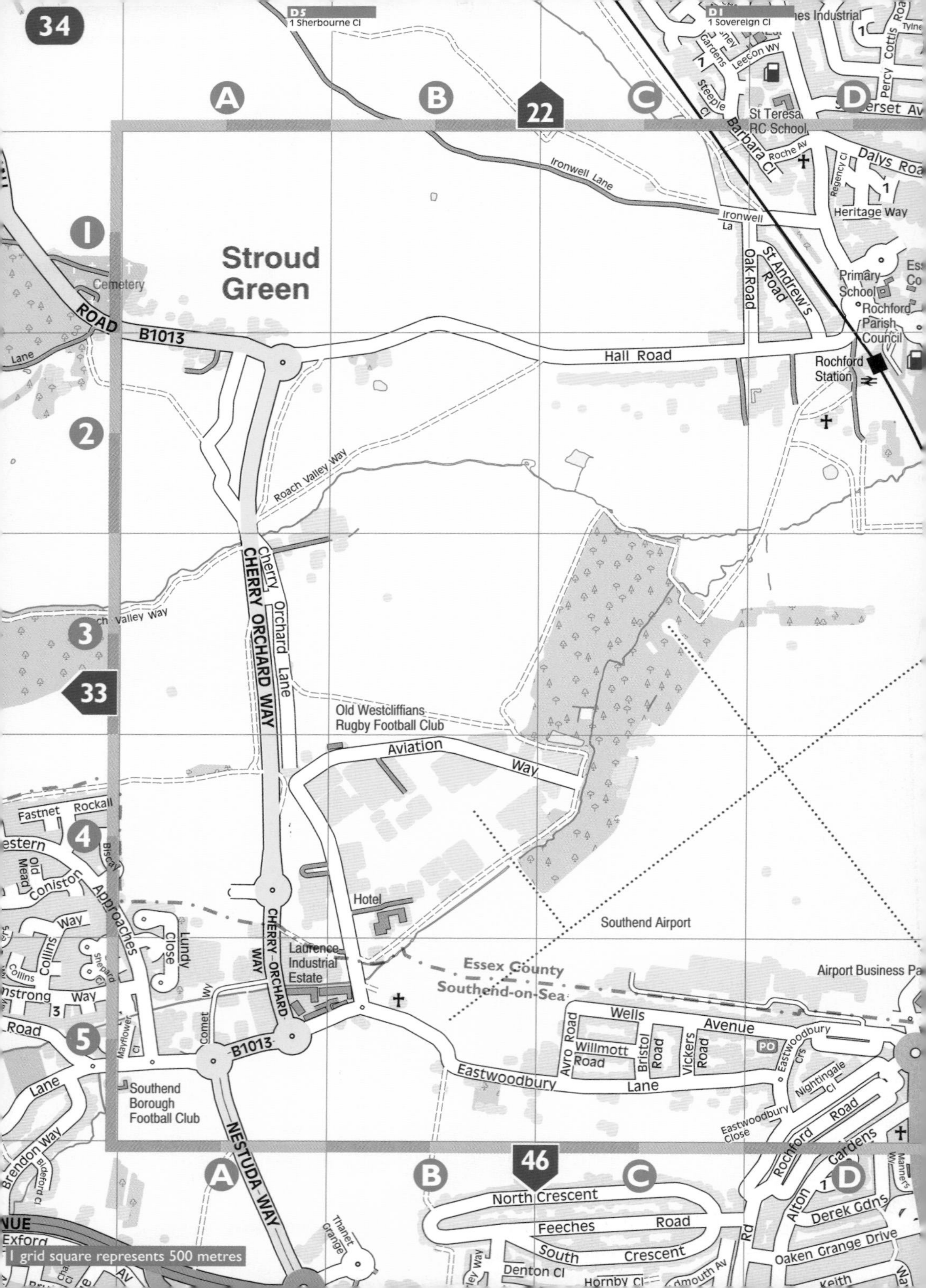

D5 1 Sherbourne Cl
D1 1 Sovereign Cl
A
B
22
C
D
Stroud Green
Cemetery
ROAD
B1013
Lane
Ironwell Lane
Ironwell La
Oak Road
St Andrew's Road
St Teresa's RC School
Barbara Cl
Roche Av
Dalys Road
Regency Cl
Heritage Way
Primary School
Rochford Parish Council
Rochford Station
Hall Road
Roach Valley Way
Cherry Orchard Lane
CHERRY ORCHARD WAY
Old Westcliffians Rugby Football Club
Aviation Way
Hotel
Laurence Industrial Estate
Southend Airport
Essex County
Southend-on-Sea
Airport Business Pa
Wells Avenue
Avro Road
Willmott Road
Bristol Road
Vickers Road
Eastwoodbury Lane
Eastwoodbury Crs
Eastwoodbury Close
Nightingale Cl
Rochford Road
PO
Fastnet
Rockall
Biscay
Old Mead
Coniston
Approaches
Way
Collins
Shepard Cl
Lundy Close
Comet Wy
Mayflower Cl
B1013
Road
Lane
Southend Borough Football Club
NESTUDA WAY
Brendon Way
Bideford Cl
North Crescent
Feeches Road
South Crescent
Thanet Grange
Denton Cl
Hornby Cl
Alton Gardens
Derek Gdns
Oaken Grange Drive
Keith
Rd
Exford
33
46
1
2
3
4
5
1 grid square represents 500 metres

E1
1 Middle Mead
2 Old Ship La
E2
1 Brayers Ms
2 Locks Hl
23
47
ROCHFORD
St Clare Mdw
Doggetts Cl
Lingfield Drive
Coombes Grove
Russell
Little Stambridge
Winters
Stambridge Road
Rochford Swimming Pool Services
Mornington Avenue
St Mark's Field
Bobbing Cl
Malting
Prentice Close
Middle Md
Oast Way
Greenways
Rd
PO
Weir Pond Rd
North St
East St
Rocheway
Townfield Road
Rochford Adult Community College
Rochford District Council
Lever La
Millview Meadows
The Trunnions
Spindle Beams
Police Stn
South St
Mill Lane
Stambridge Primary School
Broomhills
Riverside Industrial Estate
Riverside Industrial Est
Roach Valley Way
River
Tinker's Lane
Southend Road
Brickfields Way
Featherby Way
Purdeys Industrial Est
Millhead Way
Purdeys Way
Rochehall Way
Rose Way
Fleethall Road
Magnolia Way
Fleet Hall
Crowstone Preparatory School
Sutton Bridge Farm
Sutton Road
Shopland Road
Rochefort Drive
Leicester Avenue
Queen Elizabeth Chase
King Henry's Drive
Ann Boleyn Drive
Queensland Avenue
Ravenswood Chase
Sutton Court Drive
Warwick Drive
Brook Close
Prittle Brook
Sutton Hall
New Hall
Warners Bridge Chase
Southend Rugby Football Club
Sumpters Way
Temple Farm
Farriers Wy
Journeyman
The Vintners
Tailors Ct
Potters Wy
Tailors Way
The Candlemakers
The Cordwainers
The Wheelwrights
Fletchers Square
Craftsmans Square
Coopers Way
Chandlers Way
Essex County Council
Smither's Chase
Smither's Farm
Thorn
E
F
G
H
1
2
3
4
5

1 grid square represents 500 metres

E1
1 Courtney Park Rd
2 Elderberry Cl
3 Furze Gld
4 Mullberry Gdns
E2
1 Reed Pond Wk
E3
1 Lincefield
2 The Waterfalls
F1
1 Little Oxcroft
2 N'umberland Av
F2
1 Puckleside
2 Westmede
F3
1 Victoria Av
H2
1 Edgecotts
2 The Knares
H1
1 Ardleigh
2 Winter Folly
25
38
50
Lee Chapel
Westley Heights
Hills
Marks Hill (Nature Reserve)
One Tree Hill Country Park
Essex County
Thurrock
B1007 LAINDON LINK
B1036 MANDEVILLE WAY
STANEWAY
HIGH RD
B1007
Laindon Station
Police Station
Lee Chapel CP School
Junior School
Infant School
Dry Street
Lee Chapel Lane
The Chase
Kingston Hill
Homestead Drive
Southway
Stormonts Way
Green Lane
Leysings
Botelers
Gaynesford
Fletchers
The Knares
Paprills
Ardleigh
Ingaway
Wickhay
Trindehay
Falstones
Raphaels
Great Knightleys
Raleigh Dr
Elizabeth Wy
Armada Close
Hatterill
Clifford Cl
Tyler Av
Drake Rd
Laindon Link
Vowler Road
Emanuel Road
Samuel Rd
St David's Rd
Alexander Rd
Roseberry Av
Berry Lane
Wrexham Road
Denbigh Rd
High Road
Station Ap
The Gallops
Florence Way
Courtney Pk Rd
Stebbings
Mildmayes
Longwick
Fern Hill
Motehill
Irvine Way
Valence Way
Debden Gn
Breams Fld
Manning Gv
Albyns
The Hyde
Lippits Hill
Whitcroft
Delmores
The Firle
Shelsley Dr
Prescott
Wiscombe Hl
Corona Road
Ross Way
Grove Av
Firmans
Squirrels
Butlers Gv
High Oaks
Westley Rd
Stacey Drive
Beeleigh Av
Northlands Ap
Coombe Drive
Thames View
Grays Avenue
One Tree Hill
Somerset Road
Brimstone Av
Aston Rd
Bedford Road
Mellow Purgess End
Basildon

38
A2
1 Gernons
2 Kibcaps
3 Rantree Fold
4 Threshelford
South West Essex Magistrates Court
Great Oaks Clinic
Great Oaks
Basildon & Thurrock Community Health Council
A1
1 Wetherland
Riding
Long
Nether Priors
Clickett Side
Great Knightleys
Delimands
Junior School
Infant School
Falstones
Raphaels
Rise Pk
Cressells
Wickhay
A176
ROUNDACRE
Westgate
Towngate
Basildon District Council
Fodderwick
26
Eastgate Business Centre
BASILDON
Market Sq
Long Gallo
Southernhay
East Thorpe
Rayside
Roundacre
Bluehouses
Basildon Station
Osborne
B1007
LONDON LINK
Ashdon Way
Station Way
Cherrydown East
Clay Hill
Witchards
Gun Hill Place
Durrington Close
Kingswood Rd
B1
1 Lee Woottens La
Chapel
Great Gregorie
Ingaway
Cherrydown West
Faulners
Takely Ride
Takely End
Kingswood Surgery
Kingswood
Terling
Kingswood Junior & Infant School
Wickham Place
Spains Hall Pl
Mistley End
Coine Place
Paprills
Lee Chapel CP School
Gobions
Woodlands Comprehensive School
Waldegrave
Codenham Gn
Road
Kingswood Medical Centre
Clay Hill Road
Falcon Way
The Knares
Rantree Fold
Eastley
NETHER MAYNE
Codenham Straight
PO
The Knowe
Renacres
Sporhams
Morrells
Rantree
Fold
Whiteshott
Langleys
Wynters
Shaw
Latchetts
Herne
Hawksway
Ravensdale
Swallow Dale
The Glade
C2
1 Peregrine Cl
Furrowfelde
Lingcroft
Lee Woottens Lane
Sparrows
Curlew Crs
The Dell
Fletchers
Basildon College
Linnets
Toucan Way
2
3
Fobbing Farm Close
Basildon Hospital
A&E
37
C5
1 Highland Rd
Dry Street
Bells Hill
Hawkesbury Bush Lane
SS16
4
D2
1 Kingfishers
Dry Street
Leonard Road
Fort William Road
Hill Road
Vange Corner Drive
Vange Park Road
A13
5
STANFORD-LE-HOPE BY-PASS
B1420
LC
Moores Avenue
Brook Drive
High Road
Hovels Farm
One Tree Hill
Mirdle
51
SOUTHEND ROAD
A
B
C
D
1 grid square represents 500 metres

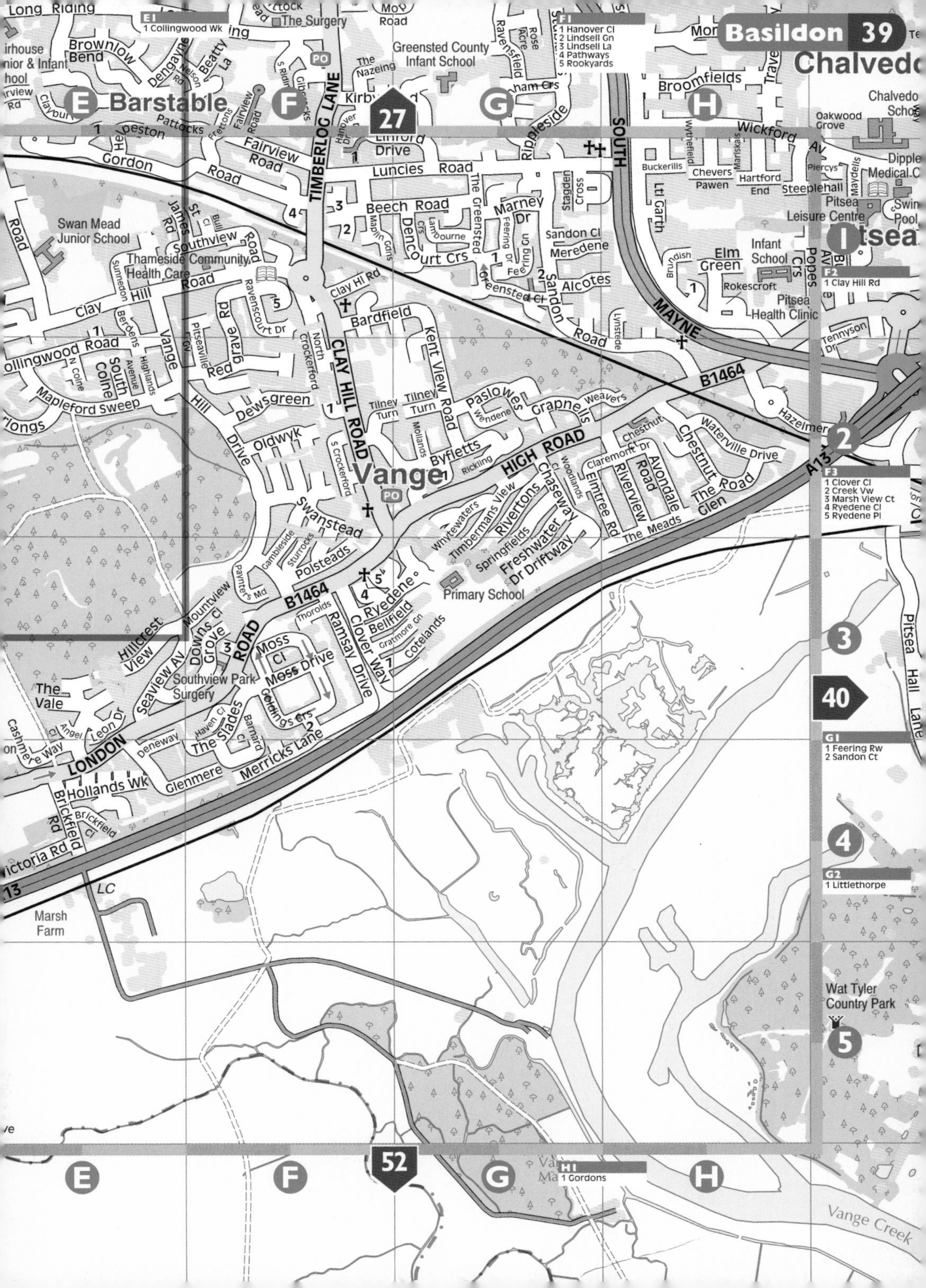
E1
1 Collingwood Wk
F1
1 Hanover Cl
2 Lindsell Gn
3 Lindsell La
4 Pathways
5 Rookyards
The Surgery
Greensted County
Infant School
Chalvedon
Chalvedon School
Oakwood Grove
Barstable
Brownlow Bend
Broomfields
Wickford Av
Gordon Road
Fairview Road
Luncies Road
Linford Drive
Beech Road
Marney Dr
TIMBERLOG LANE
SOUTH MAYNE
Dipple Medical Centre
Pitsea Leisure Centre
Swimming Pool
Pitsea
Steeplehall
Hartford End
Chevers Pawen
Buckerills
Swan Mead
Junior School
Thameside Community
Health Care
Clay Hill Road
Sandon Cl
Meredene
Alcotes
Sandon Road
Elm Green
Infant School
Rokescroft
Pitsea Health Clinic
F2
1 Clay Hill Rd
Tennyson Dr
Collingwood Road
South Colne
Mapleford Sweep
Red grave Rd
Bardfield
Kent View Road
CLAY HILL ROAD
Dewsgreen
Oldwyk
Tilney Turn
Paslowes
Grapnells
Weavers
B1464
Hazelmere
Waterville Drive
Chestnut Glen
The Road
HIGH ROAD
Vange
PO
Byfletts
Rickling
Chaseway
Riverview Road
Avondale Road
Elmtree Rd
The Meads
Rivertons
Freshwater Dr
Driftway
Springfields
Timbermans View
Whytewaters
Swanstead
Polsteads
Ryedene
Bellfield
Cotelands
Primary School
F3
1 Clover Cl
2 Creek Vw
3 Marsh View Ct
4 Ryedene Cl
5 Ryedene Pl
A13
Mountview
Hillcrest View
Downs Gr
Seaview Av
ROAD
Moss Cl
Moss Drive
Ramsay Drive
Clover Way
Southview Park Surgery
The Vale
Leon Dr
LONDON
Deneway
The Slades
Merricks Lane
Glenmere
Hollands Wk
Brickfield Rd
Victoria Rd
LC
Marsh Farm
G1
1 Feering Rw
2 Sandon Ct
G2
1 Littlethorpe
Pitsea Hall Lane
Wat Tyler
Country Park
H1
1 Gordons
Vange Creek
27
40
52
E
F
G
H
1
2
3
4
5

40
Chalvedon
Pitsea
Bowers Gifford
B1 1 Bradbourne Wy 2 Challock Lees
A1 1 Gifford Gn 2 St Gabriels Ct
28
39
53
Winifred Rd
Crest Avenue
Templewood Road
Rectory Road
Rectory Gardens
Caister
Dover Way
Delhi Rd
Corfe Cl
Charlton
Little
Lenham Way
Woodcote Crs
Kingsdown Cl
Victor Avenue
Eversley Road
Ilfracombe Avenue
Tunstall Cl
Headcorn Cl
Throwley Cl
Halstow Way
Bearsted Dr
Fairleigh Av
Fairleigh Rd
Chilham Close
Howard Crs
LONDON RD
St Margarets School
Church Road
Cemetery
B1464
A13
Wickford Av
Oakwood Grove
Edinburgh
Harlech Rd
Dipple Medical Centre
Piercys
Maydells
Steeplehall
Pitsea Leisure Centre
Swimming Pool
Church Pk Rd
Rectory Pk Dr
Rose Villa Surg
Parkhurst Rd
Chevers Pawen
Hartford End
Mariskals
Travers Way
Elm Green
Inf School
Rokescroft
Pitsea Health Clinic
Popes Crs
Burns Avenue
Tennyson Dr
Hazelmere
Waterville Drive
The Glen
St Michaels Av
Mountfields
Brackendale Avenue
Fieldway
Pitsea Station
Terminus Dr
Station Ap
LC
Junction Road
Pitsea Hall Lane
Pitsea Marsh
Wat Tyler Country Park
Pitseahall Fleet
Vange Creek
A
B
C
D
1
2
3
4
5
1 grid square represents 500 metres

G1
1 Gowan Brae
2 Oakwood Cl
G2
1 Dovesgate
H1
1 St Clement's Cl
2 Wellingbury
H2
1 Denesmere
2 Hawthorns
H4
1 Sanderlings
29
42
54
Tarpots
Hope's Green
LONDON ROAD A13
B1464
A13
A130
CANVEY WAY
HIGH ROAD
B1006
Sadlers Hall Farm
Jotmans Hall Farm
Jotmans Lane
Appleton School
Primary School
South Benfleet GM Primary School
Holy Family School
Kents Hill Surgery
The Surgery
Benfleet Station
Road
Eric Road
Alpha Road
Alpha Close
Pound Lane
Bowers Court Drive
Crescent
Bartley Rd
Bartley Road
Bartley Cl
Lower Church Road
Louisa Av
Lyndene
Rush Close
Seamore Close
Elgar Close
Church Road
Chancel Close
Lambeth Road
Kennington Avenue
Linden Cl
Waverley Road
Manor Road
Selbourne Road
Hazlemere
Romsey Rd
Romsey Dr
Romsey Crs
Romsey Way
Malwood Dr
Malwood Road
Homefields Av
Gleneagles
Bouldrewood Road
Gowan Cl
High Rd
Herongate
Saxonville
Elmhurst Avenue
Westwater
Chestnut Grove
Limetree Avenue
Wavertree Road
Uplands Cl
Uplands Road
High Beeches
Shorefield
Elm View Road
Hatley Gdns
Eastern Av
Northern Avenue
Southwold Crescent
New Park Road
Stanway Road
St Clement's Road
London Rd
West Gn
Croft Close
View Close
Lynn
Lea Rd
Croft Road
The Spinnakers
The Willows
Albion Rd
Elounda Ct
Martins Mews
Almere
Tamarisk
Bowers
Kents Hill
Villa Road
Sydney Rd
Merton Road
Holtynge
Oakleighs
Clifton
Clifton Way
Southcliff
Kimberley Road
Oakfield Cl
Oakfield Road
South View Rd
Cumberland Avenue
Wincoat Drive
Wincoat Cl
Melcombe Rd
Meggison Way
Cem
Perry Road
Watlington Road
Benfleet Park Road
Appleton Road
High Road
Richmond Avenue
Merrivale
Philmead Road
Tyrrell Road
Loten Rd
Boyce View Drive
Saxon Way
Danesfield
Greenways
Swallow Dr
Raven Drive
Woodham Park Dr
Peregrine
Curlew Drive
Woodham Road
Dove Dr
Linnet Dr
Woodham Drive
Kingfisher Drive
Brook Rd
Brook Road
Hope Road
Fleet Road
Hall Farm Road
Green
Fels
The
PO
E
F
G
H
I
1
2
3
4
5

42
30
41
55
SOUTH BENFLEET
Hope's Green
SS7
A
B
C
D
1
2
3
4
5
A5
1 St Marys Cl
A1
1 Glenridding
B2
1 Collingwood
2 Ridgemount
3 The Rowlands
4 Tippersfield
C1
1 Bradley Link
C2
1 Blackwater
2 Pear Trees
Chesterfield
Avenue
Church Road
Kingston CP Scho
Stoneleighs
Hart
Dark La
Sunnymede Cl
Thundersley Junior & Infant School
Kingston Way
Princes Av
Hydeway
Broadlands
Kenneth Road
Kings Park
Golden Manor Drive
Boyton Cl
The Chase
Lodge Close
Runnymede Chase
Dorothy Gdns
South East Essex Sixth Form College
Bradley Clos
Dubarry Close
Konnybrook
Castle Point Borough Co
Essex County Council
A13
KILN
Cherrymead
The Dale
Netherfield
Hermitage Av
Hermitage Close
Coombewood Drive
Lake Dr
Thundersley Gv
Glen Road
Mount Crs
Mount Road
Lime Road
Lime Rd
Southwell Road
Durley Close
Fernlea Road
Greenoaks
Underhill Road
Avenue Rd
Thundersley Park Road
Hill Road
Hill Cl
Granville Cl
The Chimes
Catherine
Clarence Road North
Clarence Road
Kale Rd
Avondale Road
Jarvis Road
Rhoda Road
Downer Road
Rhoda Road North
Downer Road North
Thundersley Church Road
Stanley
Spencer
Kents Hill Road North
Kents Hill Road Surgery
Hazlemere
Selbourne Road
Manor Road
Waverley Road
Linden Road
Crescent
Park Road
London Rd
St Clement's Road
St Clement's Crs
Gifford Road
Kents Hill Rd North
Bowers
Felstead
Holy Family School
Albion Rd
Elounda Ct
Martins Mews
Tamarisk
Almere
Kents Hill Junior School
Felstead Cl
Oakleighs
Avenue
Clifton Way
Southcliff
Earlswood
Clifton Close
Clarence Close
Road
Oakfield
Cumberland
Kents Avenue
Melcombe Rd
Constitution Hill
Con Way
Downsway
The Clinic
Golf Ride
Grove Road
Crescent Rd
HIGH ROAD
South Benfleet GM Primary School
Benfleet Business Centre
Boyce Gn
Queen's Road
King's Road
River View
Alexandra Road
Sweet Briar Avenue
Hillside Road
Hall Farm Road
Fleet Road
Hope Road
Brook Road
The Gallery
Green Rd
Hall Farm Cl
Adelaide Gardens
Church Cnr
Greenwood Av
Sidwell Cha
Sidwell Av
Sidwell Park
Sidwell La
St Mary's Drive
Norwood Drive
ESSEX
B1014 WAY
HIGH STREET
Doctors Surgery
School La
Karen Close
Grosvenor Rd
High Rd
Eastleigh Rd
Mill Hl
Station Road
High St
St Mary's Road
Benfleet Station
FERRY ROAD
Vicarage Hill
Hill Top Av
Round Hill Road
Kingfisher Drive
1 grid square represents 500 metres

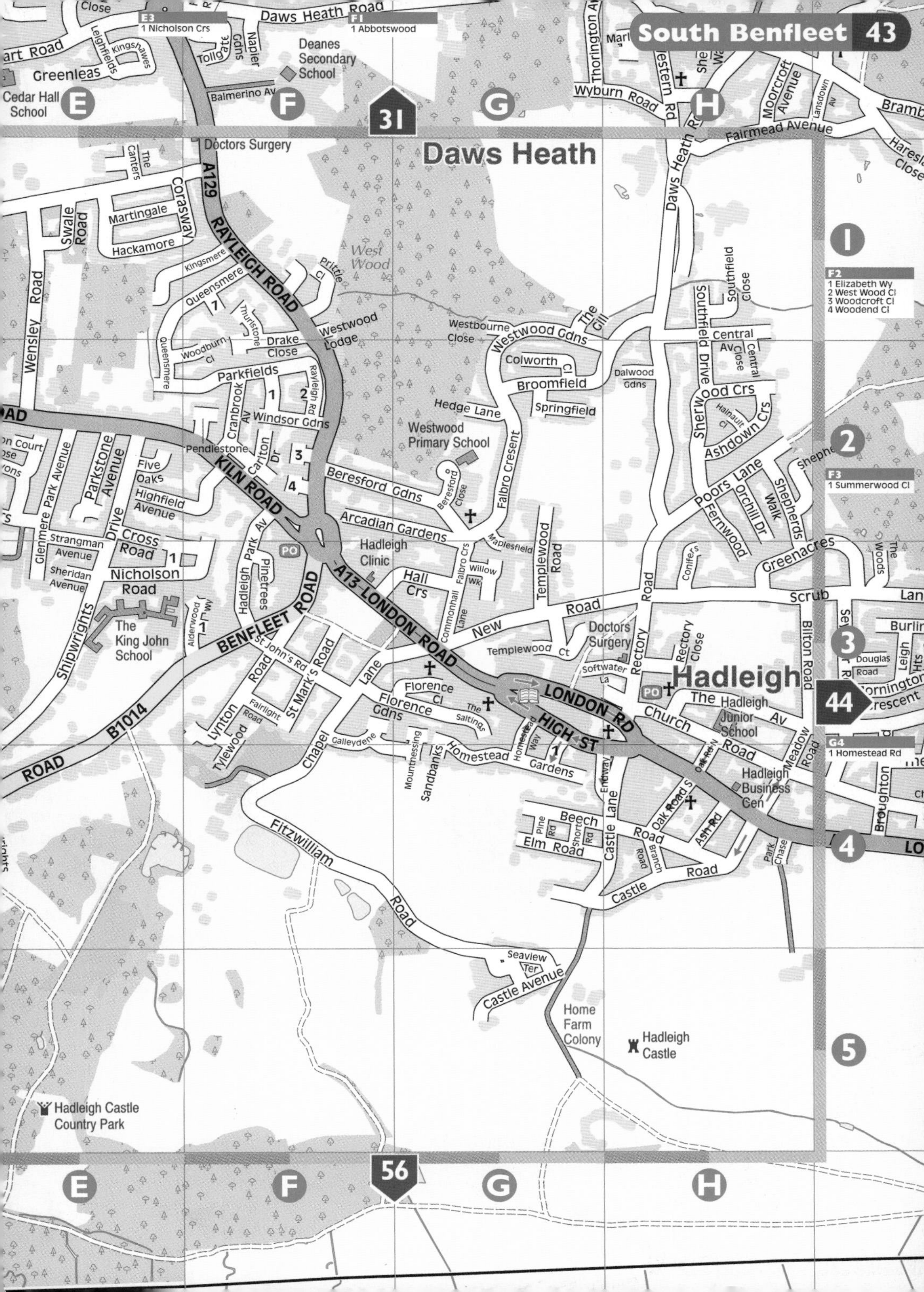

Daws Heath
Hadleigh
Daws Heath Road
E3 1 Nicholson Crs
F1 1 Abbotswood
F2 1 Elizabeth Wy 2 West Wood Cl 3 Woodcroft Cl 4 Woodend Cl
F3 1 Summerwood Cl
G4 1 Homestead Rd
Deanes Secondary School
Cedar Hall School
Greenleas
Kingshawes
Leighfields
Tollgate
Napier Gdns
Balmerino Av
Thorington Av
Wyburn Road
Moorcroft Avenue
Lansdown Av
Fairmead Avenue
Haresland Close
Doctors Surgery
A129 RAYLEIGH ROAD
The Canters
Coraway
Martingale
Hackamore
Swale Road
Wensley Road
Kingsmere
Queensmere
Thurlstone
Drake Close
Westwood Lodge
Woodburn Cl
Parkfields
Cranbrook Av
Rayleigh Rd
Windsor Gdns
Pendlestone
Carlton Dr
West Wood
Prittle Cl
Westbourne Close
Westwood Gdns
The Gill
Colworth Cl
Broomfield
Springfield
Dalwood Gdns
Hedge Lane
Westwood Primary School
Falbro Crescent
Southfield Drive
Southfield Close
Central Av
Central Close
Sherwood Crs
Hainault Cl
Ashdown Crs
Poors Lane
Fernwood
Orchill Dr
Shepherds Walk
Greenacres
The Woods
Scrub Lane
KILN ROAD
Five Oaks
Highfield Avenue
Parkstone Avenue
Glenmere Park Avenue
Drive
Cross Road
Strangman Avenue
Sheridan Avenue
Nicholson Road
Shipwrights
The King John School
Alderwood Wy
Hadleigh Park Av
Pinetrees
PO
Beresford Gdns
Beresford Close
Arcadian Gardens
Hadleigh Clinic
A13 LONDON ROAD
Hall Crs
Falbro Crs
Willow Wk
Maplesfield
Templewood Road
Commonhall Lane
New Road
Templewood Ct
Doctors Surgery
Rectory Road
Rectory Close
Softwater La
Bilton Road
Douglas Road
Burlington
Leigh Hts
Cornington Crescent
BENFLEET ROAD
B1014 ROAD
St John's Rd
St Mark's Road
Lynton Road
Fairlight Road
Tylewood
Chapel Lane
Florence Cl
Florence Gdns
The Saltings
Galleydene
Mounthessing
Sandbanks
Homestead Gardens
Homestead Way
LONDON RD
HIGH ST
The Hadleigh Junior School
Church Road
Meadow Road
Oak Rd N
Hadleigh Business Cen
Endway
Castle Lane
Beech Road
Pine Rd
Shorts Rd
Elm Road
Oak Road S
Ash Rd
Branch Road
Castle Road
Park Chase
Broughton
Fitzwilliam Road
Seaview Ter
Castle Avenue
Home Farm Colony
Hadleigh Castle
Hadleigh Castle Country Park
31
44
56
E F G H
1 2 3 4 5

44
B3
1 Ewan Cl
2 Woodfield Rd
A3
1 Pilgrims Wy
Pound Wood
Moorcroft Avenue
Lansdown Av
Fairmead Avenue
Haresland Close
Bramble Road
Bramble Crescent
32
Woodside Close
Wroxham Close
Mountain Ash Cl
Eastwood Old Road
Belgrave Road
Little Hays
Ashcombe Cl
Rothwell Cl
Bradford Bury
Stephenson Rd
Progress Way
Rutherford Cl
Pine Cl
Ryde Cl
The Ryde
Boyce Hill Cl
Belfairs Park Close
Belfairs Park Drive
Eastwood
Berkshire Close
Woodside
Orsett Av
Thorndon Park Close
The Fairway
Fairway Gdns
Park View Drive
Thorndon Park Drive
Thorndon Pk Crs
Moor Park Close
Woodberry Close
Linksway
Broadlawn
Bramble Hall
Poors Lane North
Grange Avenue
D1
1 Fairway Gdns Cl
2 Gleneagles Rd
Southfield Drive
Central Av
Central Close
Hainault Cl
Ashdown Crs
Shepherds Cl
Poors Lane
Orchill Dr
Shepherds Walk
Fernwood
Great Wood
Greenacres
The Woods
Sylvan Way
Warren Road
Woodland Cl
Sanctuary Road
Forest View Dr
Scrub Lane
Woodlands Park
Bilton Road
Seymour Road
Burlington Gardens
Buxton Close
Buxton Sq
Buxton Av
Cosgrove Avenue
Douglas Road
Leigh Hts
Temple Cl
Glebe Wy
Chandos Pde
Ewan Way
Marshall Close
Hadleigh
43
Hadleigh Junior School
Mornington Crescent
Links Way
Estate Rd
St Davids Dr
St Davids Ter
Vardon Drive
Prittle Brook
Adalia Crs
Adalia Way
Highlands Boulevard
Meadow Road
Broughton Road
The Crs
Hazel Close
Woodfield Road
Ormonde Avenue
Ormonde Gdns
Aberdeen Gdns
Braemar Crescent
Walker Drive
Agnes Avenue
Montague Av
Edinburgh Avenue
Forfar Cl
Cameron Close
Dundee Av
Dundee Close
Hadleigh Business Cen
Churchway
Heather Dr
Hamilton Close
Tennyson Close
Boulevard
Highlands Bvd
Belfairs Swimming Pool
Community College
A13 LONDON ROAD
Alma Close
Alma Road
Olive Avenue
Henry Dr
Stirling Av
Sutherland
Bailey Road
Barnard Road
Eaton Road
Fairview Gdns
Herschell Road
Gordon Rd
Sydney Rd
Doctors Surgery
PO
Highlands Surg
LONDON
The Eye Clinic
South Essex Clinical Trials Cen
Hazel Cl
Lapwater Close
St Michaels Preparatory School
Leigh Pk Cl
Tattersall Gardens
Quorn Gardens
Berkeley Gardens
Cottesmore Gdns
Thames Drive
Darenth Rd
Chapmans Walk
Chapmans Close
Medway Crs
Crescent Road
Park Rd
Canvey Road
Leigh Gdns
Western Road
Harley Street
Herschell Road
Vernon Road
Theobalds Rd
Marine Close
Thames Close
Gdns
Dynevor
Dale Rd
Hamboro Gardens
Ray Cl
Ray Wk
Marine Parade
57
Belton Way West
Castle Drive
Belton
High
Leigh-on-Sea Station
1 grid square represents 500 metres

A4 1 Kingsway Ms
A2 1 Badgers Cl
B1 1 Denton Ap
C2 1 Bell Wk
C4 1 Highfield Cl 2 Highfield Dr
D1 1 Audleys Cl 2 Caroline's Cl
D5 1 Avebury Rd 2 Balmoral Rd 3 Claremont Cl 4 Hamlet Court Ms
Southend Borough Football Club
PRINCE AVENUE
A127
NESTUDA WAY
SOUTHBOURNE GROVE
WESTBOURNE GROVE
A1158
Eastwoodbury Lane
North Crescent
Feeches Road
South Crescent
Prince Avenue Primary School
Earls Hall Infant School
Southend Hospital NHS Trust
Southend High School for Boys
Prittlewell Chase
Carlton Avenue
Carlingford Drive
Fairfax Drive
Westborough Road
VICTORIA AVE.
WEST ROAD
LONDON ROAD
A13
Chalkwell Hall Junior School
Lady of Lourdes RC School
College St Pierre
Alleyn Court Prep School
St Hildas School
Palace Theatre
Priory School
Southend Football Club
Primary School
West Road Mosque
Aaron House Clinic of Physiotherapy
Annandale Clinic
Southbourne Grove Surgery
Sooriakumaran Surgery
Doctors Surgery
Chinese Herbal Medical Centre
Preparatory School
Chalkwell
SS0
45
34
59
grid square represents 500 metres

E4
1 Penhurst Av
2 Wallis Av
F3
1 Stuart St
F4
1 Chestnut Gv
2 Grainger Cl
G4
1 Wordsworth Cl
H3
1 St Edmund's Cl
H4
1 Norwich Cl
2 Selbourne Rd
35
48
60
4
5
Southend Rugby Football Club
Temple Farm
Sumpters Way
Farriers Wy
Journeymans Wy
The Vintners
Tailors Ct
Potters Wy
Tailors Way
The Candlemakers
The Cordwainers
The Wheelwrights
Fletchers Square
Craftsmans Square
Chandlers Way
Coopers Way
Essex County Council
Smither's Chase
Smither's Farm
Sutton Road
Thornford Gardens
Talza Way
Cemetery
SS2
Stock Cl
Stock Industrial Park
Stock Road
Rosshill Industrial Park
Priory Park Industrial Est
Bentalls Close
Eastern Cl
Fossetts Way
Wellesley Hospital
Cecil Jones High School
PRIORY CRESCENT
EASTERN AVENUE
A1159
Eastern Avenue
Eastern Av
Waltham Crs
Weybourne Gardens
Weybourne Close
Cromwell Road
Wentworth Road
Prittlewell
Priory Crs
Ennismore Gardens
Station Av
Doctors Surg
Royston Avenue
Temple Sutton Primary & Infant School
Lewes Road
Lornes Cl
Avenue
Pantile Av
Peartree Cl
Regency Green
Priory Av
St Benet's Rd
Railway Ter
Station Ap
B1015
Prittlewell Stn
Edith Road
Hill Road
St Mary's Road
School
EAST STREET
Oakhurst Rd
Stuart Cl
Stuart Road
Dickens Close
Bournemouth Park Road
Lyndale Av
Walsingham Road
St Luke's Road
Norwich Avenue
Cluny Sq
Cumberland
Lonsdale Road
Rylands Road
Seaforth Avenue
Seaforth Gro
Crossfield Road
Durham Rd
Ruskin Avenue
Glenhurst Road
SUTTON ROAD
Kenway
Tickfield Av
Crowborough Rd
Tunbridge Road
Cedar Cl
Chestnut Gv
Maple Sq
Sycamore Grove
Tennyson Av
Lawn Av
Shelley Sq
Park
The Grove
Westbury
Browning Av
Vale Avenue
Gayton Road
Bircham Road
Byron Av
Ely Rd
Ferndale Rd
Selwyn Rd
Bournemouth Park Junior & Infants Sch
Redstock Rd
Stadium Road
Dryden Av
North Avenue
Central Avenue
South Avenue
A127
Colchester Road
Carnarvon Medical Centre
Carnarvon Rd
College
Harcourt Av
Gt Eastern Av
Police Sta
Southend Borough Council
Magistrates Court
Short Street
Greyhound Way
Grainger Road
Stanfield Road
Lyme Rd
Trinity Road
Branksome Road
Stornoway
Christchurch Road
Oban Road
Stromness Road
Bellevue Road
Ilfracombe Road
Lovelace Gdns
Surbiton Road
Richmond Street
Boston Avenue
Baxter Avenue
Maldon Road
Milton St
St Ann's Road
Swanage Road
Guildford Road
Wimborne Road
Southend Victoria Station
Prittlewell St
Coleman St
Boscombe Road
The Surgery
Stromness Place
A13
QUEENSWAY
Gallery
Essex St
Southchurch Rd
SOUTHCHURCH ROAD
London Road
Chinese Medical Cen
College Way
Chichester Road
Doctors Surg
Warrior Sq N
Warrior Sq
A1160
Tyrel Dr
Lancaster Gdns
Porters Grange Junior & Infant Sch
School
Windermere Rd
Chase Rd
Bellevue Place
Bellevue Av
Ilfracombe Avenue
Lovelace Avenue
Surbiton Avenue
Riviera
Southend East Stat
Queens Road
Gordon
Ambleside Drive
Park

48
B4 1 Eldbert Cl
A5 1 Droitwich Av
Stonebridge
Beauchamps
Shopland Hall Rd
Shopland Hall
Essex County
Southend-on-Sea
Clay Street Farm
B5 1 Pavilion Cl
C5 1 Coptfold Cl
D5 1 Broadclyst Cl
Barling Road
Rebels Lane
Cecil Jones High School
A1159
Eastern Av
Lornes Cl
Lloyd Wise Cl
Archer Av
Appletree Close
Archer Avenue
Archer Close
ROYAL ARTILLERY WAY
Lincoln Chase
Sherwood Way
Vallance Close
Welch Cl
Canterbury Av
Newington Avenue
Eastcote Gv
Hamstel Road
Cumberland Avenue
Lonsdale Road
Rylands Road
Crossfield Road
Durham Rd
Seaforth Grove
Westbury Road
Philpott Avenue
Whittingham Avenue
Chaingate Avenue
Wickmead Cl
Newington Close
Locksley Cl
Boyden Close
Claters Cl
Hamstel Primary School
St Nicholas School
Poynings Avenue
Central Avenue
South Avenue
Trinity Road
Ashurst Avenue
Petworth Gardens
Roedean Gdns
Roedean Close
Glynde Way
Castleton Road
Sackville Road
Thurston Avenue
Arlington Road
Steyning Avenue
Wick Chase
Vaughan Av
Pelham Road
The Surgery
Strand Gallery
Glenmore Street
Ilfracombe Road
Lovelace Gdns
Surbiton Road
Richmond Street
Moseley St
Beaufort Street
Stromness Road
Bellevue Road
Stromness Place
SOUTHCHURCH BOULEVARD
A13
Rectory Chase
Pilgrims Close
Wakering Road
SOUTHCHURCH BVD
Albert Rd
Armitage Road
Thorpe Hall Avenue
Fortescue Chase
Bovinger Way
Waterhale
Thorpe Bay School
Navestock Gdns
Wansfell Gardens
Willingale Way
Pleshey Close
The Willows
Burlescoombe
Southchurch
Lovelace Avenue
Oakleigh Avenue
Brighton Av
Fernbrook Av
Chinchilla Rd
Dalmatia Rd
Lifstan Way
Ilfracombe Avenue
Bellevue Avenue
Bellevue Place
Riviera Drive
Woodgrange Drive
47
61
5
1 grid square represents 500 metres

E5
1 Branscombe Wk
2 Burlesc'be Leas
G5
1 Withypool
Carpenters
Little Wakering
PO
E
F
G
H
I
H2
1 Townfield Wk
Barrow Hall Road
Barrow Hall Farm
Little Wakering Road
Havenside
The Crofts
Trotters
Old School Meadow
2
H4
1 Cookham Ct
2 Lambourni Cl
3 Woodley Wk
Oldbury Farm
B1017
SOUTHEND R
Essex County
Southend-on-Sea
Southend Road
Star Lane Industrial Estate
3
H5
Street names for this grid square are listed at the back of the index
STAR LANE B1017
4
POYNTERS LANE B1017
Bournes Green
Bournes Green Chase
Churchfields
Keighley Mews
Datchet Dr
Eton Wk
Kingston Av
Sunbury Ct
Caversham Av
Ravendale Way
Mountbatten Drive
Bray Ct
Sharnbrook
Sonning Way
Weybridge Walk
Wambrook
Parsons Lawn
Fitzwarren
Shillingstone
A13 NORTH SHOEBURY RD
BOURNES GREEN CHASE
Challacombe
Broadclyst Gardens
Cherrybrook
Plymtree
North
Appledore
Bishopsteignton
Chertsey Close
St Marys Cl
Maitland Place
Frobisher Way
Collingwood Way
Keyes Close
Colne Drive
North Shoebury Surgery
Woodcotes
Mallards
Puffin Pl
Peregrine Cl
Bow Cl
Way
5
Carmania Close
Cunningham Close
Fraser Close
Branscombe Sq
Chadacre Rd
Moat End
Burlescoombe Road
Chedington
Sedgemoor
Fallowfield
Swallowcliffe
Buckland
Road
Daines Close
Branscombe Gardens
Samuel Drive
Bournes Green Junior School
Ladram Way
Ladram Road
Ladram Close
Way
Cheldon Barton
Malmsmead
Hawkridge
Bickenhall
62
Weare Gifford
Doctors Surgery
Drewsteignton
Teignigrace
The Drakes
Linnet Close
Kingfisher Close
Jackdaw Close
Sandpiper Close
Herongate
St Georges
The Surgery
Barnstaple Road
Thorpe Bay Station
Maplin
Abbots Walk
Bishopsteignton
Yarnacott
Aylesbeare

D4
1 Aldria Rd
2 Foxfield Dr
Tree Hill
ntry Park
North
Coombe
Drive
Thames View
Grays
37
C5
1 Beckett Dr
2 Hobhouse Rd
Essex Coun
Thurrock
Goldsmiths
A
B
C
D
1
D5
1 Blythe Rd
2 Rachael Clarke Cl
HILL
Old
Hill
Avenue
Meadow Dr
South
Avenue
Sutton
Hall
Farm
SOUTH
2
3
STANFORD-LE-HOPE-BY-P
rens
rk Farm
4
Arden
Hall
5
Struan
Willowhill
Northlands
Cl
Hope Avenue
Branksome Avenue
Fourth Av
Alderman
Wk
Oxley Gdns
Avondale Gdns
Central
Foxfield Dr
Kelvinside
Avenue
Hall Cl
Pugh Pl
Tudor
Av
Anthony Drive
Regan
Cl
Havis Rd
Churchill
Crs
Third Avenue
Turold Road
Silverdale East
Branksome Avenue
Rose Valley
Crs
Pelham
Pl
Silverdale
Redlie
Cl
Andrew
Cl
Kathleen
Cl
Graham
Rodings Av
Way
Hollymead
STANFORD-LE-HOPE-BY-PASS
B1007
64
Russet Cl
Holst Cl
Bramleys
Link
Rd
Second Avenue
Gideons
Sandringham
Cl
Sheringham
St James
Av East
Balmoral
Av
Champion
Cl
Golding
Crs
Southend Road
Locke
Cl
Coxes
Cl
First Avenue
Bramleys
Martins
Cl
Nurse
St James
Av West
Parry
Cl
Dunstable
Weelkes Cl
Abbotts Hall
Infant School
1 grid square represents 500 metres

Corringham 51
E4
1 Ashdown Cl
2 Benton Gdns
3 Bracelet Cl
4 Hillview Gdns
5 Kenneth Gdns
6 Morley Link
7 W'dmanhurst Rd
E5
1 Bellmaine Av
2 Briceway
3 Nottage Cl
4 St Johns Ms
5 Tasman Cl
F5
1 Langland Cl
2 Limeslade Cl
G4
1 Fernside Cl
2 Glenfield Rd
Hovels Farm
STANFORD-LE-HOPE BY-PASS
A13
B1420
SOUTHEND ROAD
LAMPITS HILL
Farm Chase
Park Gate Rd
Woodlands Drive
Hertford Drive
Inglefield Road
Mill Lane
Whitehall Lane
Whitehall Farm
Patricia Drive
Greathouse Chase
Waterworks Lane
High Road
Southend Road
Milton Road
Howell Road
Buckley Cl
Gable Hall GM School
Williamsons Way
Colville Cl
Brampton Close
Lampits La
Lampits Lane
Edith Way
Wheatley Road
Weydale
Birchwood Road
Ashway
Thames Crescent
Langdon Way
Larkfield
Woodbrooke Way
Kersbrooke Way
Elmstead Cl
Finches Close
Digby
Sheldon Cl
Beechcombe
Recreation Av
PKWY
Road
Hill Terrace
Kenwood Road
Oakwood Road
Woolifers Av
Larkswood
Corringham Cemetery
Recreation Av
Ash Tree Surgery
Burr's Way
Road
Fobbing Road
The Hawthorns
Clarence Road
Herd Lane
Corringham County Primary School
The Avenue
Gardner Avenue
Burton Close
Qu Elizabeth Drive
Lyndhurst Road
Hawthorne Rd
Edinburgh Av
Crofton Av
Giffards Co Junior & Infant Sch
York Avenue
Windsor Avenue
Lampits Hl
Chamberlain Av
Crawley Cl
Gardner Avenue
Oxwich Close
Caswell Cl
Parkmill Cl
Ashley Cl
Balmoral Av
Giffords Cross Av
Arundel Drive
Carisbrooke Dr
Avenue
Pembroke Avenue
Bellmaine Av
Gardner Av
Norton Cl
Central
Montfort Av
Swimming Pool
Stanford-le-Hope Road
St John's Way
Springhouse Road
Corringham
The Surgery
CHURCH ROAD
Laburnum Drive
Harris Dr
Corringham Health Centre
Road
Colbourne Cl
Berwood Rd
Road
Andersons
Allistonway
Sorrells
Goldsmiths Av
Thames Close
Princes Avenue
Park Rd
Bibby Close
Giffords
Chase Rd
Thames Haven Road
Vincent Close
East Thurrock Football Club
ROOKERY HILL
Church Road
A1014
Lion Hill
Gildb
38
52
65

52
Hertford Drive
Woodlands Drive
A
B
39
C
D
Vange Marshes
1
Whitehall Lane
Whitehall Farm
2
Essex County
Thurrock
Patricia Drive
3
51
Marsh Lane
Fobbing Marshes
Lane
High Road
Wheelers Lane
4
The Avenue
Gildborne Close
PO
Fobbing
Hill Terrace
Lion Hill
Wharf Rd
Road
The Hawthorns
5
Corringham County Primary School
66
1 grid square represents 500 metres

Pitsea
Pitseahall Fleet
Vange Creek
Fobbing Horse
Oozedam
Holehaven
40
54
67
E
F
G
H
1
2
3
4
5

Bowers Marshes
A
B
41
C
D
1
2
3
53
4
5
A130
CANVEY WA
East Haven Creek
Northwick
Northwick Road
Roscommon Way
A
B
68
C
D
Charfleet Industrial Estate
Runwo Road
Kings Cl
W Point
1 grid square represents 500 metres

E5
1 St Andrews Cl
2 St James Cl
3 St Lukes Cl
4 St Peters Rd
F5
1 Central Av
G3
1 Lekoe Rd
G4
1 Braemore
2 Greendyke
3 Greenways
4 Helmsdale
H3
1 Ashleigh Cl
2 Ashworths
3 Chalk Rd
4 Hannah Cl
5 Leige Av
6 Woodberry Cl
H4
1 Brookside
2 Burnside
3 Norfolk Cl
4 Parklands
5 The Ridings
6 Sussex Wy
7 Terms Av
H5
1 Smartt Av
Benfleet Station
Ferry Road
Canvey Rd
B1014
Somnes Avenue
A130
Benfleet Creek
Waterside Farm
Winter Gardens Path
Waterside Farm Sports Centre
Island Golf
Winter Gardens
Dutch Village
Cornelius Vermuyden School
Northwick Park Junior& Infant School
Essex County Council
Briarswood Clinic
Junior School
St Katherine School
SS8
Brook Natural Health Centre
Hawkesbury Road Doctors Surg
Long Road Surgery
William Read CP School
Long Road
42
56
69

56
A5
1 Lede Rd
2 Roland La
A4
1 Climmen Rd
2 Cropenburg Wk
3 Hilversum Wy
4 Kent Av
5 Spanbeek Rd
6 Vadsoe Rd
7 Venlo Rd
8 Wessem Rd
Hadleigh Castle
Farm
43
B4
1 Camperdown Rd
2 Geesh Rd
3 Kellington Rd
4 Twyzel Rd
Hadleigh Marsh
B5
1 Aylett Cl
2 Herbert Rd
3 Keegan Pl
4 Mornington Crs
5 Rainbow Av
6 Sunningdale
Castle View Road
Beecroft Crs
Castle View School
55
C4
1 Abensburg Rd
2 Berg Av
3 Dovedale
4 Heeswyk Rd
5 Lakeside Crs
6 Newlands Rd
The Witterings
Hilton Rd
C5
1 Voorburg Rd
Sunken Marsh
Dovervelt Road
Wittem Road
Central Wall Road
CENTRAL WALL RD B1014
Buyi Av
Genk Cl
Jason Cl
Devon Wy
Gennep Rd
Helden Av
Kellington
Athos Road
Whernside Av
Miltsin Av
Kornberg Crs
Road
Strasbourg Rd
Newlands Rd
Corona Road
Heideburg Rd
Stanley Rd
Hindles Rd
Brandenburg Road
Tewkes Road
Helsburg Road
Landsburg Road
Munsterburg Rd
Eastfield Rd
Wilmslowe
Nordland Road
Creek Road
Dovervelt Road
Cassel Av
Hernen Rd
Meyel Av
Mornington Rd
Mornington Av
Dewyk Rd
Griffin Av
Namur Rd
Laars Av
Essex Rd
Amid Rd
Nevada Rd
Harrow Rd
Eton Cl
Harvest Road
Farm Rd
Antony Cl
Protea Wy
Short Rd
Thisselt Road
Waarden Road
Thielen Rd
Delft Rd
Kongres Road
Metz Avenue
Delfzul Rd
Letzen Road
Thelma Road
Paarl Road
Waarem Avenue
Vaagen Road
Linde Rd
Lilac Avenue
Larup Avenue
Waalwyk Dr
Foster Rd
Kamerwyk Av
Clarendon Rd
Grove Rd
Byron Cl
Goirle Av
Rainbow Road
Adelsburg Rd
Korndyk Av
The Carpet Gallery
Chamberlain Av
Cills Avenue
Barnards Av
Mitchells Av
Gains Cl
Gwendale Av
Smallgains Avenue
Geylen Rd
Limetree Rd
Wamburg Rd
Stevens Cl
Orange Rd
Gleten Rd
Westerland Av
Hassell Rd
Temptin Av
Norton Avenue
Bardenville Road
Hannett Road
Henson Avenue
HIGH STREET
KNIGHTSWICK ROAD
FURTHERWICK RD
FOKSVILLE RD
Venables Close
Bramble Road
May Avenue
Florence
Oxford
Normans Rd
Beach Road
Collindale Cl
Arcadia Road
Doctors
Woodville Rd
Wilrich Av
Baardwyk Av
Andyk Rd
Holbek Rd
Winterswyk Av
Beatrice Rd
St Josephs RC School
Stuart Cl
Roosevelt Av
Borrett Av
Pennial Rd
Fairlop Avenue
Avenue
rle Av
Dalen Av
Dollant Av
Brewster Cl
Lionel Road
Haron Cl
D4
1 Holmswood
Hawthorn Rd
Oak Road
Elm Road
Ash Road
70
A130
ROAD
Clifton
Caro Rd
Hilbery Rd
Juliers
Rosbach Rd
Ouida Rd
Delgada Rd
Rochford Road
Rosema
Marcos Road
Lappmark
St Annes
Gains
PO
Leigh
Windsor Close
1 grid square represents 500 metres

Tattersall
Western Road
Marine Close
Thames Gdns
Dynevor
Dale Rd
Chapmans Close
Road
Hamboro Gardens
Ray Cl
Ray Wk
Harley Street
Theobalds Rd
Grange Road
Marine Parade
Belton Way West
Castle Drive
Belton Way East
Belton Gardens
New
High Street
Leigh-on-Sea Station
Lynn Tait Gall
PH
E
F
G
H
I
44
2
3
4
5
58
Leigh
71
Two Tree Island
Hadleigh Ray
Southend-on-Sea
Essex County
Canvey Point
Castlepoint Museum
Prout Industrial Estate
Silverpoint Marine
Point Road
B1014
Approach Rd
Kollum
Maris Cl
Orrmo Rd

B1
1 Alexandra Rd
2 Sea Reach
A1
1 Broadway West
D1
1 Hillside Crs
2 Upland Rd
Glendale Gardens
Leigh Parish Council
The Tile Gallery
College St Pierre
The Surgery
Leigh Junior & Infant School
Chalkwell
Marine Parade
Rectory Grove
North Street
The Art Gal
Broadway W
Broadway
Belton Way East
Belton Gardens
New Road
High Street
John Cotgrove Gal
Leigh Hill
Cliff Parade
Grand Parade
Lynn Tait Gallery
Aly Dock
Leigh Creek
Chalkwell Station
The Ridge
Chalkwell Oaze
Leigh Sand
Ray Gut
Canvey Point
Chapman Sands
45
57
1 grid square represents 500 metres

Westcliff-on-Sea
Crow Stone
Marsh End Sand
Clifftow
SO
E1 1 Ridgeway Gdns
H1 1 Richmond Av 2 Summercourt Rd
H2 1 Lydford Rd 2 Shorefield Gdns 3 Wickford Rd
46
60
St Hildas School
Prep School
Doctors Surgery
Palace Theatre
The Surgery
Crown College
Milton Hall Junior School
Chinese Herbal Medical Centre
Mosque
Preparatory School
Hotel
Westcliff Station
St Bernards High School
Beecroft Art Gal
Westcliff Leisure Centre
Imperial Avenue
Crowstone Close
Rayleigh Av
Claremont Road
Albion Road
Albany Av
Cliff Av
Windsor Rd
Finchley Road
Genesta Road
Anerley Road
Burdett Avenue
St John's Road
St Helen's Road
Crosby Road
Galton Rd
The Ridgeway
Hall Park Av
The Leasway
Meadway
Chadwick Road
Seymour Road
Drake Road
Crowstone
Cotswold Road
Elderton Road
Cranley Road
Valkyrie Road
Argyll Road
Ceylon Rd
Britannia Gdns
Ailsa Rd
Satanita Rd
Meteor Road
Britannia Rd
Station Road
Ditton Court Rd
Hamlet
Canewdon
Preston Road
Cossington Rd
Hermitage Rd
Milton Rd
Avenue Ter
First Avenue
Second Av
Esplanade Gardens
Chalkwell
Chalkwell Esplanade
Leas Gdns
Crowstone Av
Whitefriars Crs
Grosvenor Rd
Grosvenor Mews
Admiral Ms
Cobham Rd
Pembury Rd
Palmerston Road
The Leas
Manor Rd
Clifton Dr
Seaforth Rd
Hamlet Ct Rd
Leonard Road
Station Rd
Retreat Rd
Hadleigh Road
Westcliff Av
Holland Rd
Palmeira Avenue
Shorefield Rd
Milton Av
San Remo Pde
Winton Av
Trinity Av
Marine Av
St Vincent's Road
Tower Ct
Hotel Mews
Western Esplanade
Westcliff Pde
Clifftown
Park Rd
Park La
Queens Road
Brighten Road
Salisbury Av
Balmoral Road
Osborne Road
Alexandra
Cambridge
LONDON ROAD
PO
1 2 3 4 5
E F G H I

60
SOUTHEND-ON-SEA
Clifftown
B1
1 Farringdon Service Rd
2 Grover St
3 Pitmans Cl
4 Station Ap
5 Warrior Sq East
A2
1 Cashiobury Ter
2 Milton Pl
3 Prittlewell Sq
B2
1 Capel Ter
2 Devereux Rd
C1
1 Grange Gdns
2 Quebec Cl
C2
1 Hartington Pl
2 Pleasant Ms
D1
1 Fairburn Cl
2 Fowler Cl
3 Langley Cl
4 Stanier Cl
QUEENSWAY
A13
A1160
SOUTHCHURCH ROAD
Southend Victoria Station
Southend Central Stn
Chartwell Gallery
Crown College
Milton Hall Junior School
St Bernards High School
Chinese Medical Cen
Infant School
Southend Co Court
The Royals Shopping Centre
Porters Grange Junior & Infant Sch
Doctors Surg
The Boscombe Surgery
Westcliff Leisure Centre
Southend Pier
Southend Pier Railway
Southend Flat
London Road
Queens Road
Hamlet Road
Scratton Road
Cambridge Rd
Alexandra Road
Clifftown Parade
Western Esplanade
Marine Parade
Royal Ter
Pier Hl
Lucy Road
Whitegate Rd
Tylers Av
York Road
Heygate Avenue
Warrior Sq
Essex St
Maldon Road
St Ann's Road
Guildford Road
Swanage Road
Wimborne Road
Boscombe Road
Stromness Place
Windermere Rd
Ambleside Drive
Kilworth Av
Southchurch Av
Kursaal Way
Beresford Rd
Burnaby Road
Woodgrange
Arnold Avenue
Hawtree Cl
Prospect Cl
Outing Cl
Seaway
Ash Wk
Pleasant Rd
Hartington Rd
Chancellor Rd
Herbert Gv
Church Rd
Alexandra St
Clarence St
Weston Road
Clifftown Road
Clifton Ms
Royal Ms
Nelson St
Runwell Ter
Wilson Rd
Hotel
Tower Ct
Mews
Westcliff Pde
St Vincent's Road
Park La
Park Street
Park Rd
Park Ter
Park Crs
Princes St
Ashburnham Road
Gordon Rd
Gordon Pl
Napier Av
Elmer Av
Elmer Ap
Luker Rd
College Way
Chichester Road
High St
Grover St
Baltic Av
Portland Av
Quebec Av
Hillcrest Road
Toledo Rd
Toledo Cl
Hastings Rd
Cromer Road
Albert Rd
Wesley Rd
St Leonard's Rd
Horace Rd
Stanley Rd
Old Southend Rd
Lancaster Gdns
Tyrel Dr
Honiton Rd
Cheltenham Road
Leamington Road
Park Lane
Southchurch Close
Christchurch Road
Oban Road
Stromness Road
Bellevue Road
Chase Rd
Bellevue Place
Southend Community
Salisbury Av
Balmoral Road
Albany Av
Cliff Av
Sweyne Av
Boston Avenue
Baxter Avenue
Brighten Road
Avenue Ter
Avenue Road
Westcliff Av
Trinity Av
Marine Av
Milton St
Milton Road
Southend Borough Magis Court
1 grid square represents 500 metres

F1
1 Woodgrange Cl
G1
1 Chelsworth Cl
H1
1 Burlescoombe Cl
2 Thorpe Hall Av
SOUTHCHURCH BOULEVARD
A13
Southchurch
SS1
Woodgrange Drive
Acacia Drive
Elm Grove
Fermoy Road
Thorpe Bay Surgery
Johnstone Road
Thorpe Bay
Greenways
Northumberland Crescent
Shaftesbury Avenue
Capadocia St
Colbert Avenue
Burges Road
EASTERN ESPLANADE
EASTERN ESP
B1016
THORPE ESPLANADE
Thorpe Bay
Hotel
48
62
E F G H
1 2 3 4 5

1 grid square represents 500 metres

F2
1 Southchurch Av
Carmania Close
Fraser Close
Raphael Drive
Picasso Way
Wakering Road
Centurion Cl
PO
Goya Rise
Rembrandt Close
Constable Way
Friars County Junior School
Rubens Cl
Whistler Rl
Vermeer Crs
Hogarth Drive
Ashanti Close
The Woodlands
Newell Avenue
Castle Cl
Peel Avenue
Elm Road
Vanguard Way
Seedbed Business Centre
The Goslings
Blackgate Road
LC
The Vanguards
Friars St
Wallace St
Shoebury Av
Terminal Close
Wakering Avenue
High Street
Gunners Road
Shoeburyness Station
Rosewood Lane
Primary School
Road
Hinguar St
Smith Street
George St
John St
Dane St
Rampart Street
Rampart Terrance
Chapel Road
Hospital Road
Shoeburyness
Dane's Av
Road
Beach
Sq Rd
Mess
Brodie Road
LC
Sandpit Road
Suttons Road
Walkey Way
Boyce Road
Rossiter Road
Pig's Bay
E
F
G
H
1
2
3
4
5

B1
1 Dowland Cl
A3
1 Old Jenkins Cl
2 Romsey Cl
B2
1 Gentry Cl
B3
1 Baryta Cl
2 The Hollies
3 Karen Cl
B4
1 Brockenhurst Dr
2 Wilson Cl
C1
1 Hudsons Cl
2 Laxtons
3 Worcester Cl
C3
1 The Green
2 Salisbury Av
3 Wharf Cl
D2
1 Cedars
2 Sanctuary Gdn
50
STANFORD-LE-HOPE BY-PASS
A13
B1007
A1013
STANFORD ROAD
A1014 THE MANORWAY
Hassengate Medical Cen
Abbotts Hall Infant School
Hassenbrook School
Primary School
Stanford Industrial Estate
Lingwood Clinic
The Surg
Regent Leisure Cen
Stanford-le-Hope Station
St Cleres Hall
St Cleres School
Cemetery
Mucking
Butts Lane
Mucking Wharf Road
Wharf Road
Bluehouse
London Road
Corringham Road
Billet Lane
Southend Road
Victoria Road
Scratton Road
Manor Road
Hassenbrook Road
Nursery Rd
Gideons Way
First Avenue
Second Avenue
Boyce Road
Dunstable Road
Prospect Avenue
Runnymede Road
Ruskin Road
Poley Road
Kingsman Rd
Caldwell Road
Park Road
Horndon Rd
1 grid square represents 500 metres

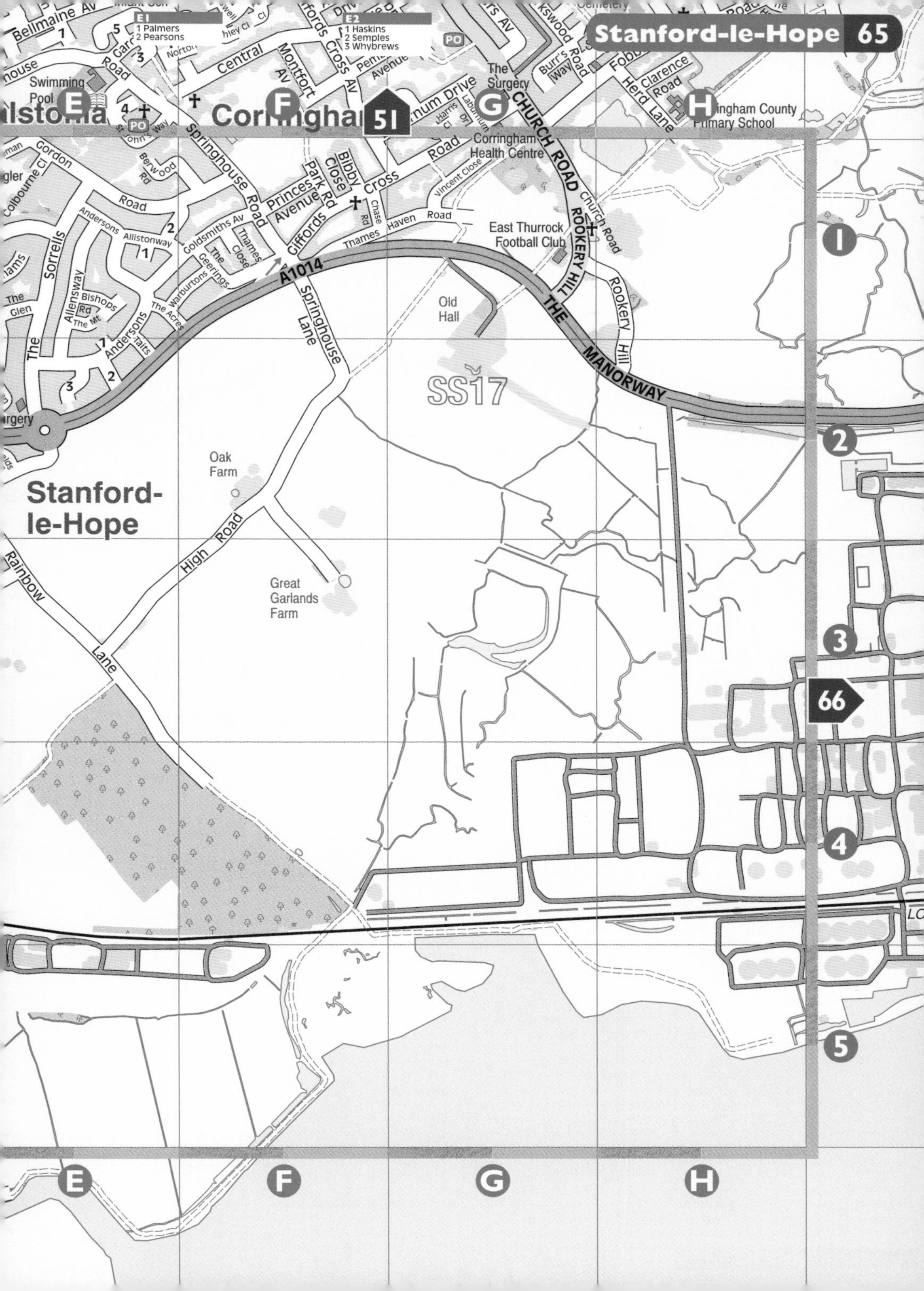
E1
1 Palmers
2 Pearsons
E2
1 Haskins
2 Semples
3 Whybrews
Bellmaine Av
Swimming Pool
Central
Montfort Av
Cross Av
Avenue
PO
The Surgery
Burr's Way
Road
Herd Lane
Clarence Road
Corringham County Primary School
Corringham
51
Springhouse Road
Gordon
Colbourne Cl
Road
Princes Avenue
Park Rd
Bibby Close
Cross
Road
Corringham Health Centre
Vincent Close
CHURCH ROAD
Church Road
Thames Haven Road
East Thurrock Football Club
Goldsmiths Av
Allistonway
Andersons
Sorrells
Thames Close
The Geerings
Giffords
Chase Rd
ROOKERY HILL
Rookery Hill
A1014
Springhouse Lane
Old Hall
THE MANORWAY
Allensway
Bishops Rd
The Mt
The Glen
The
Warburtons
The Acres
Andersons
Taits
SS17
Oak Farm
Stanford-le-Hope
High Road
Rainbow Lane
Great Garlands Farm
66
E
F
G
H
1
2
3
4
5

66
Hawthorns
Rd
Corringham County
Primary School
52
A
B
C
D
1
2
3
4
5
65
Oil Storage
Depot
LC
1 grid square represents 500 metres

E
F
53
G
H
Oozedam
Holehaven Creek
I
2
A1014
THE MANORWAY
Oil Refinery
Coryton
3
68
Shell Haven
Coryton Wharve
4
Thames Haven
5
Thurrock
Medway Towns
E
F
G
H

D1
1 Arjan Wy
2 Cambria Cl
54
A
B
C
D
1
2
3
4
5
67
Charfleet
Industrial
Estate
Runw
Road
Romainville
Way
W Point
Pl
Kings Cl
Kings
Road
Sandhurst
Koln
Cl
Lower
Horse
Shellhaven
Point
Hole
Haven
Coryton
Wharves
Sea
Reach
Thurrock
Medway Towns
1 grid square represents 500 metres

E1
1 Palmerstone Rd
2 Village Hall Cl
Essex
County
Council
Third Av
Link Rd
The Weald
Suffolk
Lincoln Way
Cedar Road
SS8
West Crescent
st Crescent
North Av
Paarl Road
Waarem Avenue
Vaagen Road
St Joseph RC School
Second Av
St Michaels Rd
St Pauls Rd
St Christophers Close
55
Aspen
Maple
Sycamore Close
Almond Walk
Linden Way
Little Gypps Close
Ltl Gypps Rd
Willow Cl
Church Cl
Princes Rd
Thameside Crs
Tilburg Road
Rembrandt Close
Daarle Av
Dalen Av
Dollant Av
Brewster Cl
Borrett Av
Pennial Rd
Fairlop Avenue
Beatrice Av
Lionel Road
Convent Road
St Johns Crs
St Agnes Dr
First Av
Birch Close
Pine Cl
Miramar Av
Long Rd
Village Dr
Green Avenue
New Road
Brook Natural Health Centre
Long Road Surgery
PO
Hawkesbury Road Doctors Surg
Canvey Village Surgery
Grasmere Road
Janette Av
Edith Rd
Edith Cl
Haven Cl
Laburnum Gv
Tudor Rd
Vikings Way
Shannon Way
Services Road
International Business Centre
Malvern Avenue
Vicarage Cl
Clinton Road
Coker Rd
Ormsby Road
Haven Road
Brooklands Square
Deepwater Rd
Montague Place
Ellesmere Rd
Woodhurst Road
Silverthorne
Infant School
Hawkesbury Road
Hawkesbury Close
Barbara Avenue
Antlers
Thames Road
A130
LONG ROAD
Cambridge Road
Hertford Rd
Hayes Lane
Green Lane
Matlock Road
Southwick Road
Southwick Gardens
William Read CP School
Stanford Road
Craven Av
Avon Road
Coniston Road
Downham Rd
Rose Road
Kitkatts Road
Beverley Avenue
Mayland Avenue
Ray Cl
Essex Cl
The Fielders
Lambourne
Thorney Bay Road
Berkeley Lane
Welbeck Road
Clifton Road
F1
1 Beechcroft Rd
2 The Redwoods
The Driveway
The Parkway
The Dry
Cottesmore
Bay Cl
Fernadale Crs
H1
1 Lylt Rd
Surgery
Cleveland
The Cherries
Western Esp
CANVEY ISLAND
Thorney Bay
Deadman's Point
70
H2
1 Chichester Cl
River Thames
Essex County
Medway Towns
E
F
G
H
I
1
2
3
4
5

70
56
69
A1
1 Bulow Av
2 Merlin Ct
A2
1 Blackmore Av
2 Howard Pl
3 Sylvan Cl
A3
1 The Cherries
B1
1 Nightingale Rd
B2
1 Ashingdale Cl
2 Atherstone Cl
3 Bruges Rd
C1
1 Maurice Rd
2 Teramo Rd
3 Torsi Rd
4 Vanderwalt Av
5 Yamburg Rd
C2
1 Brussum Rd
2 Compton Ct
3 Haarle Rd
4 Kolburg Rd
5 Zandi Rd
D1
1 Corsel Rd
2 Elderstep Av
3 Rosberg Rd
D2
1 Kenmore Cl
Goirle Av
Rainbow Road
Paarl Road
Waarem Avenue
Vaagen Road
Smallgains
Avenue
Borrett Av
Roosevelt Av
Pennial Rd
Fairlop Avenue
Dalen Av
Dollant Av
Brewster Cl
Lionel Road
Stuart Cl
Convent Road
Haron Cl
Beatrice Av
St Josephs RC School
FURTHERWICK RD
FOKSVILLE RD
The Carpet Gallery
Venables Close
Bramble Road
May Avenue
Hawthorn Road
Oak Road
Elm Road
Ash Road
A130
ROAD
Clifton Road
Runnymede Road
Westwood Road
Civic Halls
Windsor Close
Welbeck Road
The Driveway
Berkeley Lane
Avenue
The Parkway
The Dry
Cottesmore
Bay Cl
Jesmond Rd
The Av
Furtherwick Road
Blackthorne Road
Poplar Rd
Island Surgery
Labworth Road
Marine Ap
Grafton Road
Doctors Surg
Meynell Avenue
Thorp Leas
Atherstone Road
Ferndale Crs
Leigh Road
Meadway
The Surgery
Cleveland Road
Seaway
Beachway
Furtherwick Rd
Lovens Close
Lubbins Park Primary School
The Cherries
Western Esplanade
Thorney Bay
Deadman's Point
Gains Cl
Westerland Av
Hassell Rd
Geylen Rd
Limetree Rd
Wamburg Rd
Doctors Surg
Arcadia Road
Rosbach Rd
Ouida Rd
Delgada Rd
Rochford Road
Roserna Rd
Rayment Av
Hilbery Rd
Caro Rd
Julliers Rd
Odessa Rd
Julliers Cl
Delder Av
Marcos Road
San Remo Road
Taranto Road
Hope Road
Terni Rd
Telese Av
Lappmark Rd
St-Annes-Rd
STREET
Gainsborough Av
Gafzelle Dr
Winterswyk Av
Holbek
Temptin Av
Norton Avenue
Hallet Road
Bardenville Road
Hannett Road
PO
Leigh Beck
Sheldon Rd
Dovercliff Rd
Crescent Road
Marine Avenue
Station Road
Seaview Road
Westcliff Gdns
South Pde
Handel Road
Roggel Road
Maurice Road
Lottem Road
Hellendoorn Rd
Margraten Avenue
Shellbeach Road
Keer Avenue
Weel Road
Sprundel Av
Whiteways
Eastern Esplanade
A
B
C
D
1
2
3
4
5
1 grid square represents 500 metres

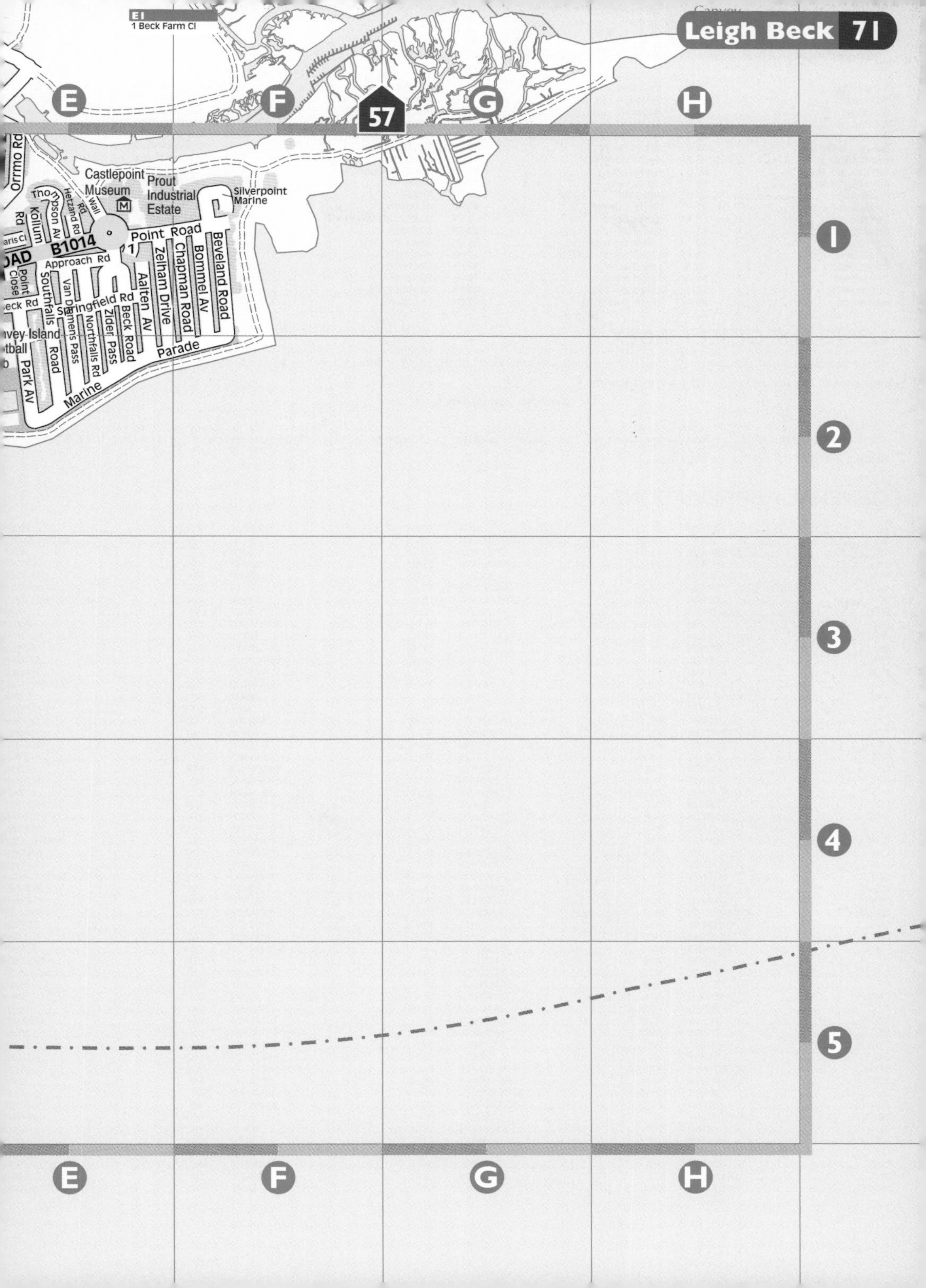
E1
1 Beck Farm Cl
E
F
57
G
H
Orrmo Rd
Castlepoint Museum
Prout Industrial Estate
Silverpoint Marine
Hetzand Rd
Wall
Kollum Rd
B1014
Point Road
Approach Rd
Point Close
Southfalls Road
Van Diemens Pass
Springfield Rd
Northfalls Rd
Zider Pass
Beck Road
Aalten Av
Zelham Drive
Chapman Road
Bommel Av
Beveland Road
Park Av
Marine Parade
1
2
3
4
5

Ashingdon 22 C1
Balstonia 51 E5
Basildon 2 C2
Billericay 9 E4
Bournes Green 49 E4
Bowers Gifford 40 D1
Burnt Mills 28 B1
Cambridge Town 62 B3
Canvey Island 69 F2
Chalkwell 58 D1
Chalvedon 27 H5
Clifftown 4 A6
Corringham 51 F5
Coryton 67 F3
Crays Hill 15 E3
Daws Heath 43 G1
Dry Street 38 A4
Dutch Village 55 E5
Eastwood 45 F1
Eversley 28 A4
Felmore 27 H3
Fobbing 52 A5
Fryerns 27 E3
Gooseberry Green 8 B2
Great Berry 36 D2
Great Burstead 13 F3
Hadleigh 43 H3
Hawkwell 21 H3
Hockley 20 D1
Hope's Green 41 H4
Kingswood 3 F4
Laindon 25 G4
Langdon Hills 36 D2
Lee Chapel 2 A4
Lee Chapel 37 H1
Leigh Beck 70 D1
Leigh-on-Sea 45 F4
Little Burstead 12 D4
Mill Hill 20 C1
Mount Bovers 21 E5
Mucking 64 C5
Nevendon 16 B5
New Thundersley 30 A4
Noak Bridge 26 A2
Noak Hill 13 F4
North Benfleet 29 E3
Pipps Hill 26 A3
Pitsea 40 A1
Prittlewell 46 D3
Queen's Park 6 D4
Rawreth 18 B1
Rawreth Shot 17 H1
Rayleigh 19 G6
Rochford 35 F1
Runwell 10 D4
Shoeburyness 63 F3
Shotgate 17 G2
South Benfleet .... 42 E
Southchurch .... 5 H
Southchurch .... 61 F
Southend-on-Sea .... 4 A
South Green .... 13 C
Stanford-le-Hope .... 65 E
Stroud Green .... 34 A
Sunken Marsh .... 56 E
Sunnymede .... 9 C
Tarpots .... 41 H
Thorpe Bay .... 62 A
Thundersley .... 30 E
Tye Common .... 12 C
Vange .... 39 F
Weir .... 31 F
Westcliff-on-Sea .... 59 F
Westley Heights .... 37 F
Wickford .... 17 E
Winter Gardens .... 55 F

USING THE STREET INDEX

Street names are listed alphabetically. Each street name is followed by its postal town or area locality, the Postcode District, the page number, and the reference to the square in which the name is found

Example: **Abbots Ride** BCAYE CM11........ **9** F3 1

Some entries are followed by a number in a blue box. This number indicates the location of the street within the referenced grid square. The full street name is listed at the side of the map page.

GENERAL ABBREVIATIONS

ACC	ACCESS
ALY	ALLEY
AP	APPROACH
AR	ARCADE
ASS	ASSOCIATION
AV	AVENUE
BCH	BEACH
BLDS	BUILDINGS
BND	BEND
BNK	BANK
BR	BRIDGE
BRK	BROOK
BTM	BOTTOM
BUS	BUSINESS
BVD	BOULEVARD
BY	BYPASS
CATH	CATHEDRAL
CEM	CEMETERY
CEN	CENTRE
CFT	CROFT
CH	CHURCH
CHA	CHASE
CHYD	CHURCHYARD
CIR	CIRCLE
CIRC	CIRCUS
CL	CLOSE
CLFS	CLIFFS
CMP	CAMP
CNR	CORNER
CO	COUNTY
COLL	COLLEGE
COM	COMMON
COMM	COMMISSION
CON	CONVENT
COT	COTTAGE
COTS	COTTAGES
CP	CAPE
CPS	COPSE
CR	CREEK
CREM	CREMATORIUM
CRS	CRESCENT
CSWY	CAUSEWAY
CT	COURT
CTRL	CENTRAL
CTS	COURTS
CTYD	COURTYARD
CUTT	CUTTINGS
CV	COVE
CYN	CANYON
DEPT	DEPARTMENT
DL	DALE
DM	DAM
DR	DRIVE
DRO	DROVE
DRY	DRIVEWAY
DWGS	DWELLINGS
E	EAST
EMB	EMBANKMENT
EMBY	EMBASSY
ESP	ESPLANADE
EST	ESTATE
EX	EXCHANGE
EXPY	EXPRESSWAY
EXT	EXTENSION
F/O	FLYOVER
FC	FOOTBALL CLUB
FK	FORK
FLD	FIELD
FLDS	FIELDS
FLS	FALLS
FLS	FLATS
FM	FARM
FT	FORT
FWY	FREEWAY
FY	FERRY
GA	GATE
GAL	GALLERY
GDN	GARDEN
GDNS	GARDENS
GLD	GLADE
GLN	GLEN
GN	GREEN
GND	GROUND
GRA	GRANGE
GRG	GARAGE
GT	GREAT
GTWY	GATEWAY
GV	GROVE
HGR	HIGHER
HL	HILL
HLS	HILLS
HO	HOUSE
HOL	HOLLOW
HOSP	HOSPITAL
HRB	HARBOUR
HTH	HEATH
HTS	HEIGHTS
HVN	HAVEN
HWY	HIGHWAY
IMP	IMPERIAL
IN	INLET
IND EST	INDUSTRIAL ESTATE
INF	INFIRMARY
INFO	INFORMATION
INT	INTERCHANGE
IS	ISLAND
JCT	JUNCTION
JTY	JETTY
KG	KING
KNL	KNOLL
L	LAKE
LA	LANE
LDG	LODGE
LGT	LIGHT
LK	LOCK
LKS	LAKES
LNDG	LANDING
LTL	LITTLE
LWR	LOWER
MAG	MAGISTRATE
MAN	MANSIONS
MD	MEAD
MDW	MEADOWS
MEM	MEMORIAL
MKT	MARKET
MKTS	MARKETS
ML	MALL
ML	MILL
MNR	MANOR
MS	MEWS
MSN	MISSION
MT	MOUNT
MTN	MOUNTAIN
MTS	MOUNTAINS
MUS	MUSEUM
MWY	MOTORWAY
N	NORTH
NE	NORTH EAST
NW	NORTH WEST
O/P	OVERPASS
OFF	OFFICE
ORCH	ORCHARD
OV	OVAL
PAL	PALACE
PAS	PASSAGE
PAV	PAVILION
PDE	PARADE
PH	PUBLIC HOUSE
PK	PARK
PKWY	PARKWAY
PL	PLACE
PLN	PLAIN
PLNS	PLAINS
PLZ	PLAZA
POL	POLICE STATION
PR	PRINCE
PREC	PRECINCT
PREP	PREPARATORY
PRIM	PRIMARY
PROM	PROMENADE
PRS	PRINCESS
PRT	PORT
PT	POINT
PTH	PATH
PZ	PIAZZA
QD	QUADRANT
QU	QUEEN
QY	QUAY
R	RIVER
RBT	ROUNDABOUT
RD	ROAD
RDG	RIDGE
REP	REPUBLIC
RES	RESERVOIR
RFC	RUGBY FOOTBALL CLUB
RI	RISE
RP	RAMP
RW	ROW
S	SOUTH
SCH	SCHOOL
SE	SOUTH EAST
SER	SERVICE AREA
SH	SHORE
SHOP	SHOPPING
SKWY	SKYWAY
SMT	SUMMIT
SOC	SOCIETY
SP	SPUR
SPR	SPRING
SQ	SQUARE
ST	STREET
STN	STATION
STR	STREAM
STRD	STRAND
SW	SOUTH WEST
TDG	TRADING
TER	TERRACE
THWY	THROUGHWAY
TNL	TUNNEL
TOLL	TOLLWAY
TPK	TURNPIKE
TR	TRACK
TRL	TRAIL
TWR	TOWER
U/P	UNDERPASS
UNI	UNIVERSITY
UPR	UPPER
V	VALE
VA	VALLEY
VIAD	VIADUCT
VIL	VILLA
VIS	VISTA
VLG	VILLAGE
VLS	VILLAS
VW	VIEW
W	WEST
WD	WOOD
WHF	WHARF
WK	WALK
WKS	WALKS
WLS	WELLS
WY	WAY
YD	YARD
YHA	YOUTH HOSTEL

POSTCODE TOWNS AND AREA ABBREVIATIONS

CAYE .... Billericay east	LAIN .... Laindon	RCHLM .... Rural Chelmsford	UPMR .... Upminster
CAYW .... Billericay west	LOS .... Leigh-on-Sea	SBF/HAD .... South Benfleet/Hadleigh	VGE .... Vange
SDN .... Basildon	PIT .... Pitsea	SBN/FI .... Shoeburyness/Foulness Island	WICKE .... Wickford east
VI .... Canvey Island	RAYL .... Rayleigh	SLH/COR .... Stanford-le-Hope/Corringham	WICKW .... Wickford west
OC/HUL .... Hockley/Hullbridge	RBRW/HUT .... Rural Brentwood/Hutton	SOS .... Southend-on-Sea	WOS/PRIT .... Westcliff-on-Sea/Prittlewell
IG .... Ingatestone	RCFD .... Rochford	SOSN .... Southend-on-Sea north	

Index - streets

A

alten Av CVI SS8 71 E1
bbey Rd BCAYW CM12 8 C4
bbots Ct LAIN SS15 25 H2
bbots Ride BCAYE CM11 9 F3 1
bbots Wk SBN/FI SS3 62 B1
bbotswood SBF/HAD SS7 43 F1 1
bbotts Cl LOS SS9 45 F1
bbotts Dr SLH/COR SS17 64 D2
bbotts Hall Cha SLH/COR SS17 64 D2
bensburg Rd CVI SS8 56 C4 1
berdeen Gdns LOS SS9 44 B4
bingdon Ct PIT SS13 27 H2 1
breys SBF/HAD SS7 30 D4
cacia Dr SOS SS1 61 H1
cacia Rd PIT SS13 28 D3
corn Pl VGE SS16 36 D1
he Acorns HOC/HUL SS5 21 F1
he Acres SLH/COR SS17 65 E1
dalia Crs LOS SS9 44 C4
dalia Wy LOS SS9 44 C4
dams Gld RCFD SS4 22 C2
dams Rd SLH/COR SS17 64 D3
dam Wy WICKE SS11 10 D5
delaide Gdns SBF/HAD SS7 42 A5
delsburg Rd CVI SS8 56 B5
dmirals Wk SBN/FI SS3 62 C4
dmiral Ms WOS/PRIT SS0 59 F2
gnes Av LOS SS9 44 C4
ilsa Rd WOS/PRIT SS0 59 F1
lan Cl LOS SS9 33 F5
lan Gv LOS SS9 33 F5
lbany Av WOS/PRIT SS0 46 D5
lbany Rd RAYL SS6 32 B2
WICKW SS12 16 C2
lbert Cl RAYL SS6 32 A1
RCFD SS4 22 B1
lbert Dr LAIN SS15 25 F5
lbert Rd RAYL SS6 32 A1
RCFD SS4 22 B2
SBF/HAD SS7 29 G5
SOS SS1 5 F5
SOS SS1 48 D5
lbion Rd SBF/HAD SS7 41 H2
WOS/PRIT SS0 46 D5
lbyns VGE SS16 37 F2
lcotes BSDN SS14 39 G1
lder Cl LAIN SS15 25 G2
lderleys SBF/HAD SS7 30 D5
lderman's Hl HOC/HUL SS5 20 C3
lderman Wk SLH/COR SS17 50 D4
lderney Gdns WICKE SS11 10 B3
lderwood Wy SBF/HAD SS7 43 F3
ldham Gdns RAYL SS6 18 C5
ldria Rd SLH/COR SS17 50 D4 1
ldrin Cl SLH/COR SS17 64 D2
ldrin Wy LOS SS9 33 H5
lexander Rd VGE SS16 37 E2
lexandra Rd LOS SS9 58 B1 1
RAYL SS6 19 H5
RCFD SS4 22 B2
SBF/HAD SS7 42 A4
SOS SS1 4 A5
lexandra St SOS SS1 4 D5
lexandria Dr RAYL SS6 18 D4
lfred Gdns WICKE SS11 10 C4
licia Av WICKE SS11 17 F1
licia Cl WICKE SS11 17 F1
licia Wk WICKE SS11 17 F1
licia Wy WICKE SS11 17 F1
llandale SBF/HAD SS7 30 D4
llensway SLH/COR SS17 65 E1
llerton Cl RCFD SS4 22 B2 1
lley Dock LOS SS9 58 A1
lleyn Pl WOS/PRIT SS0 46 B5
llistonway SLH/COR SS17 65 E1
lma Cl SBF/HAD SS7 44 A4
WICKW SS12 15 H2
lma Rd SBF/HAD SS7 44 B4
lmere SBF/HAD SS7 42 A2
lmond Av WICKW SS12 16 A1
Almond Wk CVI SS8 55 G5
Alnwick Cl VGE SS16 36 C1 1
Alpha Cl PIT SS13 29 E5
Alpha Rd PIT SS13 29 E5
Alresford Gn WICKW SS12 16 D2
Altar Pl LAIN SS15 25 F4 1
Althorne Cl PIT SS13 28 A2
Althorpe Cl HOC/HUL SS5 21 E2
Alton Gdns SOSN SS2 46 D1
Ambleside WICKE SS11 17 G1 1
Ambleside Dr SOS SS1 5 G4
Ambleside Wk CVI SS8 55 G5
Ameland Rd CVI SS8 55 H3
Amersham Av VGE SS16 36 C1 2
Amid Rd CVI SS8 56 B4
Ampers End BSDN SS14 3 J3
Anders Fall LOS SS9 33 H5
Andersons SLH/COR SS17 65 E1
Andrew Cl SLH/COR SS17 50 C5
Andyk Rd CVI SS8 70 D1
Anerley Rd WOS/PRIT SS0 59 G1
Angel Cl VGE SS16 39 E3
Anglesey Gdns WICKW SS12 17 E3
Ann Boleyn Dr RCFD SS4 35 E4
Anson Cha SBN/FI SS3 62 D1
Anstey Cl LOS SS9 33 E4
Anthony Cl BCAYE CM11 13 G2 1
Anthony Dr SLH/COR SS17 50 D5
Antlers CVI SS8 69 G2
Antony Cl CVI SS8 56 A4
Antrim Rd SBN/FI SS3 62 C2
Anvil Wy BCAYW CM12 7 E5
Apeldoorn SBF/HAD SS7 29 G4 1
Appleby Dr VGE SS16 36 C1
Appledene Cl RAYL SS6 19 G4
Appledore SBN/FI SS3 49 F5
Applerow LOS SS9 33 G5
Appleton Rd SBF/HAD SS7 41 G3
Appletree Cl SOSN SS2 48 B3
Apple Tree Wy WICKE SS11 11 E5
Approach Rd BCAYE CM11 15 E3
CVI SS8 71 E1
The Approach RAYL SS6 31 F1
Apton Hall Rd RCFD SS4 23 F2
Aragon Cl SOSN SS2 46 D2
Arcadian Gdns SBF/HAD SS7 43 F2
Arcadia Rd CVI SS8 70 C1
Archer Av SOSN SS2 48 A3
Archer Cl SOSN SS2 48 B3
Archer Rd LAIN SS15 25 E3
Archers Cl BCAYW CM12 8 D5
Archers Flds PIT SS13 28 A2
Archers Fields Cl PIT SS13 27 H2
Ardleigh VGE SS16 37 H1 1
Ardley Wy RAYL SS6 19 G4
Argyll Rd WOS/PRIT SS0 59 G1
Arjan Wy CVI SS8 68 D1 1
Ark La RCFD SS4 33 H2
Arlington Rd SOSN SS2 48 B5
Arlington Wy BCAYW CM12 6 C5
Armada Cl LAIN SS15 37 G1
Armadale CVI SS8 55 G5
Armagh Rd SBN/FI SS3 62 C2
Armath La VGE SS16 36 C2
Armitage Rd SOS SS1 48 D5
Armstrong Cl SLH/COR SS17 64 D2
Armstrong Rd SBF/HAD SS7 30 A4
Arne Cl SLH/COR SS17 64 C1
Arne Ct LAIN SS15 25 F3 1
Arne Ms LAIN SS15 25 F3 2
Arnold Av SOS SS1 5 H5
Arnolds Wy RCFD SS4 22 B1
Arran Ct WICKW SS12 17 E2 1
Arundel Dr SLH/COR SS17 51 F5
Arundel Gdns RAYL SS6 19 E3
WOS/PRIT SS0 45 H3
Arundel Rd SBF/HAD SS7 29 G4
WICKE SS11 10 B3
Arundel Wy BCAYW CM12 7 F4
Ascot Cl SBF/HAD SS7 31 E4
Ashanti Cl SBN/FI SS3 63 E1
Ashburnham Rd SOS SS1 4 B3
Ashcombe RCFD SS4 22 C5
Ashcombe Cl LOS SS9 32 C5
Ashcombe Wy RAYL SS6 32 A1
Ashdon Wy VGE SS16 2 C3
Ashdown Cl SLH/COR SS17 51 E4 1
Ashdown Crs SBF/HAD SS7 43 H2
Ashfield RAYL SS6 18 C5 1
Ashfields PIT SS13 28 B4
Ashingdale Cl CVI SS8 70 B2 1
Ashleigh Cl CVI SS8 55 H3 1
Ashleigh Dr LOS SS9 58 C1
Ashley Cl SLH/COR SS17 51 F5
Ashlyns PIT SS13 27 G5
Ash Rd CVI SS8 70 B1
SBF/HAD SS7 43 H4
Ashurst Av SOSN SS2 48 C4
Ash Wk SOS SS1 5 F5
Ashway SLH/COR SS17 51 G4
Ashworths CVI SS8 55 H3 2
RCFD SS4 22 B2
Aspen Cl CVI SS8 55 F5
Aspen Ct LAIN SS15 25 F2
Asquith Av SBF/HAD SS7 31 F5
Asquith Gdns SBF/HAD SS7 31 F4
Assandune Cl RCFD SS4 22 C1 1
Aston Rd LAIN SS15 25 E5
Athelstan Gdns WICKE SS11 10 C4
Atherstone Cl CVI SS8 70 B2 2
Atherstone Rd CVI SS8 70 B2
Athos Rd CVI SS8 56 B4
Atridge Cha BCAYW CM12 8 D1
Audleys Cl SOSN SS2 46 D1 1
Audley Wy BSDN SS14 2 D1
Avebury Rd WOS/PRIT SS0 46 D5 1
Avenue Rd LOS SS9 58 B1
SBF/HAD SS7 42 B3
WOS/PRIT SS0 59 H1
Avenue Ter WOS/PRIT SS0 59 H1
The Avenue BCAYW CM12 8 D3
CVI SS8 70 A1
SBF/HAD SS7 43 H3
SLH/COR SS17 52 A4
Aviation Wy SOSN SS2 34 B4
Avon Cl RCFD SS4 22 B3
Avondale Cl RAYL SS6 32 A1
Avondale Dr LOS SS9 45 G2
Avondale Gdns SLH/COR SS17 50 D4
Avondale Rd RAYL SS6 32 A1
SBF/HAD SS7 42 A3
VGE SS16 39 H2
Avon Rd CVI SS8 69 H1
Avon Wy SBN/FI SS3 62 C3
Avro Rd SOSN SS2 34 C5
Aylesbeare SBN/FI SS3 62 C1
Aylesbury Dr VGE SS16 36 C1
Aylett Cl CVI SS8 56 B5 1
Azalea Av WICKW SS12 16 B1

B

Baardwyk Av CVI SS8 70 D1
Back La RCFD SS4 34 D2
Badger Hall Av SBF/HAD SS7 42 D2
Badgers Cl WOS/PRIT SS0 46 A2 1
Badgers Mt HOC/HUL SS5 20 D3
The Badgers VGE SS16 36 D2
Badgers Wy SBF/HAD SS7 42 D2
Bailey Rd LOS SS9 44 C4
The Bailey RAYL SS6 31 F1
Baker's Ct BSDN SS14 27 H1
Bakers Farm Cl WICKE SS11 17 F1 1
Balfour Cl WICKW SS12 16 D3 1
Ballards Wk LAIN SS15 25 H4
Balmerino Av SBF/HAD SS7 31 F5
Balmoral Av SLH/COR SS17 51 F5
Balmoral Cl BCAYE CM11 9 H4
Balmoral Gdns HOC/HUL SS5 20 D2 1
Balmoral Rd WOS/PRIT SS0 46 D5 2
Balstonia Dr SLH/COR SS17 50 D4
Baltic Av SOS SS1 4 D4
Bannister Gn WICKW SS12 16 D2 1
Banyardway RCFD SS4 22 B4
Barbara Av CVI SS8 69 G1
Barbara Cl RCFD SS4 22 C5
Barclay Rd PIT SS13 28 D2
Bardenville Rd CVI SS8 70 D1
Bardfield VGE SS16 39 F1
Bardfield Wy RAYL SS6 18 D5
Barge Pier Rd SBN/FI SS3 62 D4
Barley Cl VGE SS16 36 D3
Barleylands Rd LAIN SS15 14 A5
Barling Rd SBN/FI SS3 48 D2
Barnard Cl VGE SS16 39 F3
Barnard Rd LOS SS9 44 C4
Barnards Av CVI SS8 56 C5
Barncombe Cl SBF/HAD SS7 30 A5
Barnet Park Rd WICKE SS11 11 E3
Barnstable Cl SOS SS1 61 H1
Barnstaple Rd SOS SS1 62 A1
Barnwell Dr HOC/HUL SS5 21 E2
The Barnyard VGE SS16 36 D2
Barons Wy VGE SS16 37 E2
Barra Gld WICKW SS12 17 E3
Barrington Cl BSDN SS14 27 G3 1
SBN/FI SS3 49 H5 1
Barrington Gdns BSDN SS14 27 G3
Barringtons Cl RAYL SS6 19 G5 1
Barrow Hall Rd SBN/FI SS3 49 F1
Barrowsand SOS SS1 62 A3
Barstable Rd SLH/COR SS17 64 C2
Bartletts RAYL SS6 32 B3
Bartley Cl SBF/HAD SS7 29 G5
Bartley Rd SBF/HAD SS7 29 G5
Bartlow End PIT SS13 28 A3
Bartlow Side PIT SS13 28 A3
Baryta Cl SLH/COR SS17 64 B3 1
Basildon Dr LAIN SS15 25 F4
Basildon Rd LAIN SS15 25 H3
Bassenthwaite Rd SBF/HAD SS7 30 B5
Batavia Rd CVI SS8 55 E5
Battleswick BSDN SS14 27 F2
Baxter Av SOSN SS2 4 A1
Bay Cl CVI SS8 70 A2
Beach Av LOS SS9 58 D1
Beaches Cl HOC/HUL SS5 21 G2
Beach House Gdns CVI SS8 70 D2
Beach Rd CVI SS8 56 C5
SBN/FI SS3 63 E4
SOS SS1 5 G6
Beachway CVI SS8 70 A2
Beambridge PIT SS13 27 H5
Beams Wy BCAYE CM11 9 F5
Bearsted Dr PIT SS13 40 B1
Beatrice Av CVI SS8 56 A5
Beatrice Cl HOC/HUL SS5 21 E2 1
Beatty La BSDN SS14 27 F5
Beauchamps Dr WICKE SS11 17 F1
Beaufort Rd BCAYW CM12 8 C3
Beaufort St SOSN SS2 5 K1
Beazley End WICKW SS12 16 D2 2
Bebington Cl BCAYW CM12 8 D2
Beccles Ct WICKE SS11 10 C5 1
Becket Cl RCFD SS4 22 C3
Beckett Dr SLH/COR SS17 50 C5 1
Becketts LAIN SS15 24 D5 1
Beck Farm Cl CVI SS8 71 E1 1
Beck Rd CVI SS8 71 E1
Bedford Cl RAYL SS6 31 G2
Bedford Rd LAIN SS15 25 E5
Bedloes Av WICKE SS11 18 B1 1
Beecham Ct LAIN SS15 25 F3
Beech Av RAYL SS6 19 G5
Beechcombe SLH/COR SS17 51 G4
Beechcroft Rd CVI SS8 69 F1 1
Beechmont Gdns SOSN SS2 46 D2
Beech Rd BSDN SS14 39 F1
SBF/HAD SS7 43 G4
Beecroft Crs CVI SS8 55 H3
Beedell Av WICKE SS11 17 E2
WOS/PRIT SS0 46 C4
Beeleigh Av VGE SS16 37 F3
Beeleigh Cl SOSN SS2 46 D3
Beeleigh Cross BSDN SS14 27 F4
Beeleigh East BSDN SS14 27 F4
Beeleigh West BSDN SS14 27 E3
Beke Hall Cha North RAYL SS6 18 B4
Beke Hall Cha South RAYL SS6 18 B5
Belchamps Rd WICKE SS11 11 E5

Belchamps Wy HOC/HUL SS5 .... 21 F3
Belfairs Cl LOS SS9 .... 45 E4
Belfairs Dr LOS SS9 .... 45 E4
Belfairs Park Cl LOS SS9 .... 44 D1
Belfairs Park Dr LOS SS9 .... 44 C1
Belgrave Cl LOS SS9 .... 32 C4
RAYL SS6 .... 19 E4 1
Belgrave Rd BCAYW CM12 .... 8 D1
LOS SS9 .... 32 C5
Bellevue Av SOS SS1 .... 5 H3
Bellevue Pl SOS SS1 .... 5 H3
Bellevue Rd BCAYW CM12 .... 8 C3
SOSN SS2 .... 5 H2
Bellfield VGE SS16 .... 39 F3
Bell Hill Cl BCAYW CM12 .... 9 E5
Bellhouse Crs LOS SS9 .... 45 E1
Bellhouse La LOS SS9 .... 45 E2
Bellhouse Rd LOS SS9 .... 33 E5
Bellingham La RAYL SS6 .... 31 G1
Bellmaine Av SLH/COR SS17 .... 51 E5 1
Bells Hill Rd VGE SS16 .... 38 C4
Bell Wk WOS/PRIT SS0 .... 46 C2 1
Belmont Av WICKW SS12 .... 15 H2
Belmont Cl WICKW SS12 .... 16 A1
Belstedes LAIN SS15 .... 25 G5
Belton Br LOS SS9 .... 58 A1
Belton Gdns LOS SS9 .... 57 H1
Belton Wy East LOS SS9 .... 57 H1
Belton Wy West LOS SS9 .... 57 G1
Belvedere Av HOC/HUL SS5 .... 20 D2 2
Benderloch CVI SS8 .... 55 F5
Benfleet Park Rd SBF/HAD SS7 .... 41 G3
Benfleet Rd SBF/HAD SS7 .... 42 D4
Bentalls BSDN SS14 .... 26 B2
Bentalls Cl SOSN SS2 .... 47 F2
The Bentleys LOS SS9 .... 33 G4
Benton Gdns SLH/COR SS17 .... 51 E4 2
Benvenue Av LOS SS9 .... 33 G4
Berberis Cl VGE SS16 .... 36 C2 1
Berdens VGE SS16 .... 3 K4
Berens Cl WICKE SS11 .... 11 E4
Beresford Cl SBF/HAD SS7 .... 43 G2
Beresford Ct BCAYW CM12 .... 6 C5 1
Beresford Gdns SBF/HAD SS7 .... 43 F2
Beresford Rd SOS SS1 .... 5 G6
Berg Av CVI SS8 .... 56 C4 2
Berkeley Dr BCAYW CM12 .... 6 D5 1
Berkeley Gdns LOS SS9 .... 44 B5
Berkeley La CVI SS8 .... 69 H2
Berkley Hl SLH/COR SS17 .... 50 D5
Berkshire Cl LOS SS9 .... 44 D1
Berry Cl VGE SS16 .... 37 E1
WICKW SS12 .... 16 A2
Berry La VGE SS16 .... 37 E2
Berwood Rd SLH/COR SS17 .... 65 E1
Betjeman Cl RAYL SS6 .... 20 A5
Betony Crs BCAYW CM12 .... 6 C5
Betoyne Cl BCAYE CM11 .... 9 G3
Bett's La HOC/HUL SS5 .... 21 E2
Beveland Rd CVI SS8 .... 71 F1
Beverley Av CVI SS8 .... 69 G1
Beverley Gdns SOSN SS2 .... 46 D2
Beverley Ri BCAYE CM11 .... 9 F4
Bibby Cl SLH/COR SS17 .... 65 F1
Bickenhall SBN/FI SS3 .... 62 C1
Biddenden Ct PIT SS13 .... 28 B5 1
Bideford Cl WOS/PRIT SS0 .... 45 H1
Billet La SLH/COR SS17 .... 64 D3
Bilton Rd SBF/HAD SS7 .... 43 H3
Bircham Rd SOSN SS2 .... 47 F4
Birch Cl CVI SS8 .... 69 G1
RAYL SS6 .... 19 F5
SBF/HAD SS7 .... 29 G4
Birche Cl LOS SS9 .... 45 F2
The Birches SBF/HAD SS7 .... 29 H3
Birch Gn WICKW SS12 .... 16 C1
Birchwood SBF/HAD SS7 .... 29 G4
Birchwood Dr LOS SS9 .... 45 H4
Birchwood Rd SLH/COR SS17 .... 51 G4
Birs Cl WICKE SS11 .... 10 C4
Biscay SOSN SS2 .... 33 H4
Bishops Cl PIT SS13 .... 27 H1
Bishops Rd SLH/COR SS17 .... 65 E1
WICKW SS12 .... 16 C5
Bishopsteignton SBN/FI SS3 .... 62 B1
Blackgate Rd SBN/FI SS3 .... 63 F2
Blackmore Av CVI SS8 .... 70 A2 1
Blackmores LAIN SS15 .... 24 B5
Blacksmith Cl BCAYW CM12 .... 7 E5 1
Blackthorn Ct VGE SS16 .... 36 D2
Blackthorne Rd CVI SS8 .... 70 B1
Blackwater SBF/HAD SS7 .... 42 C2 1
Blackwater Cl SBN/FI SS3 .... 49 H5 2
Blake Hall Dr WICKE SS11 .... 17 F2
Blatches Cha LOS SS9 .... 33 G4
Blenheim Cha LOS SS9 .... 45 E3
Blenheim Crs LOS SS9 .... 45 F3
Blenheim Ms LOS SS9 .... 45 F3
Blenheim Park Cl LOS SS9 .... 45 G2
Blower Cl RAYL SS6 .... 20 A5
Bluebell Wd BCAYW CM12 .... 8 A1
Bluehouses VGE SS16 .... 2 C3
Blunts Wall Rd BCAYW CM12 .... 8 A4
Blyth Av SBN/FI SS3 .... 62 B2
Blythe Rd SLH/COR SS17 .... 50 D5 1
Blythe Wy SBF/HAD SS7 .... 29 H4
Blyton Cl WICKW SS12 .... 16 C3
Bobbing Cl RCFD SS4 .... 35 E1
Bockingham Gn PIT SS13 .... 27 H3
Bohemia Cha LOS SS9 .... 44 D1
Boleyn Cl BCAYW CM12 .... 6 D5 2
LOS SS9 .... 32 D4
Bolney Dr LOS SS9 .... 32 D4
Bommel Av CVI SS8 .... 71 F1
Bonchurch Av LOS SS9 .... 45 E4
Bonnygate BSDN SS14 .... 26 D4
Bootham Cl BCAYW CM12 .... 8 C4
Bootham Rd BCAYW CM12 .... 8 C4
Boreham Cl WICKE SS11 .... 17 G3 1
Borman Cl LOS SS9 .... 33 H5 1
Borrett Av CVI SS8 .... 55 H5
Borrowdale Cl SBF/HAD SS7 .... 30 C5
Borrowdale Rd SBF/HAD SS7 .... 30 C4
Borwick La BCAYE CM11 .... 15 F4
WICKW SS12 .... 16 A4
Boscombe Rd SOSN SS2 .... 5 F2
Boston Av RAYL SS6 .... 19 E4
SOS SS1 .... 4 B3
SOSN SS2 .... 4 A1
Boswell Av RCFD SS4 .... 22 C3
Bosworth Cl HOC/HUL SS5 .... 21 G4
Bosworth Rd LOS SS9 .... 32 D4
Botelers VGE SS16 .... 37 H2
Bouldrewood Rd SBF/HAD SS7 .... 41 G1
The Boulevard RCFD SS4 .... 23 E5
Boult Rd LAIN SS15 .... 25 F3
Boundary Rd LOS SS9 .... 32 C3
Bourne Av LAIN SS15 .... 24 D3
Bourne Cl LAIN SS15 .... 24 D3
Bournemouth Park Rd SOSN SS2 .... 47 G3
Bournes Green Cha SBN/FI SS3 .... 49 F4
SOS SS1 .... 49 E5
Bovinger Wy SOS SS1 .... 48 C5
Bower La BSDN SS14 .... 27 F3
Bowers Court Dr PIT SS13 .... 41 E1
Bowers Rd SBF/HAD SS7 .... 42 A1
Bowfell Dr VGE SS16 .... 36 D1
Bowman Av LOS SS9 .... 32 C5
Box Cl LAIN SS15 .... 25 G2 1
Boxford Cl RAYL SS6 .... 18 C5 2
Boyce Gn SBF/HAD SS7 .... 42 A4
Boyce Hill Cl LOS SS9 .... 44 C1
Boyce Rd SBN/FI SS3 .... 63 G1
SLH/COR SS17 .... 64 B1
Boyce View Dr SBF/HAD SS7 .... 41 G4
Boyd Ct WICKW SS12 .... 17 E3 1
Boyden Cl SOSN SS2 .... 48 C4
Boyton Cl SBF/HAD SS7 .... 42 C1
Boytons LAIN SS15 .... 25 H5
Bracelet Cl SLH/COR SS17 .... 51 E4 3
Brackendale BCAYE CM11 .... 9 G2
Brackendale Av PIT SS13 .... 40 B2
Brackendale Cl HOC/HUL SS5 .... 21 F1 1
Bracken Dell RAYL SS6 .... 31 H1
Bracken Wy SBF/HAD SS7 .... 30 D4
Brackley Crs PIT SS13 .... 27 H2
Bradbourne Wy PIT SS13 .... 40 B1 1
Bradford Bury LOS SS9 .... 32 D5
Bradley Av SBF/HAD SS7 .... 42 C2
Bradley Cl CVI SS8 .... 55 H4
SBF/HAD SS7 .... 42 C1
Bradley Link SBF/HAD SS7 .... 42 C1 1
Bradley Wy RCFD SS4 .... 34 D2
Braemar Crs LOS SS9 .... 44 B4
Braemore CVI SS8 .... 55 G4 1
Brairwood Cl LOS SS9 .... 45 E1
Braiswick Pl LAIN SS15 .... 25 E3
Bramble Cl LOS SS9 .... 32 C4
Bramble Crs SBF/HAD SS7 .... 44 B1
Bramble Rd CVI SS8 .... 56 B5
LOS SS9 .... 32 C4
SBF/HAD SS7 .... 32 A5
Bramble Tye LAIN SS15 .... 26 A2
Bramerton Rd HOC/HUL SS5 .... 21 E2
Bramfield Rd East RAYL SS6 .... 32 B1
Bramfield Rd West RAYL SS6 .... 32 A1 1
Bramley Gdns LAIN SS15 .... 25 F3 3
Bramleys SLH/COR SS17 .... 64 C1
The Bramleys RCFD SS4 .... 22 C3 1
Brampstead LAIN SS15 .... 24 D5 2
Brampton Cl SLH/COR SS17 .... 51 F4
WOS/PRIT SS0 .... 45 H2
Bramston Link LAIN SS15 .... 24 B4
Bramston Wy LAIN SS15 .... 24 B5
Branch Rd SBF/HAD SS7 .... 43 H4
Brandenburg Rd CVI SS8 .... 56 C4
Brandon Cl BCAYW CM12 .... 6 D5
Branksome Av SLH/COR SS17 .... 50 C5
WICKW SS12 .... 15 G1
Branksome Cl SLH/COR SS17 .... 64 B1
Branksome Rd SOSN SS2 .... 5 F2
Branscombe Gdns SOS SS1 .... 62 A1
Branscombe Sq SOS SS1 .... 49 E5
Branscombe Wk SOS SS1 .... 49 E5 1
Braxted Cl RCFD SS4 .... 22 B4
Braxteds LAIN SS15 .... 24 D5 3
Braybrooke BSDN SS14 .... 2 E1
Bray Ct SBN/FI SS3 .... 49 H4
Brayers Ms RCFD SS4 .... 35 E2 1
Brays La RCFD SS4 .... 22 D3
Break Egg Hl BCAYE CM11 .... 9 G2
Breams Fld VGE SS16 .... 37 F2
Brecon Cl PIT SS13 .... 28 B3 1
Brempsons BSDN SS14 .... 26 B4
Brendon Wy WOS/PRIT SS0 .... 45 H1
Brettenham Dr SOS SS1 .... 61 F1
Brewster Cl CVI SS8 .... 69 H1
Briar Cl BCAYE CM11 .... 13 G1 1
HOC/HUL SS5 .... 21 G4
Briar Md LAIN SS15 .... 25 E4
Briarswood CVI SS8 .... 55 H4
Briar Vw BCAYE CM11 .... 13 G1 2
Briarwood Dr LOS SS9 .... 45 E1
The Briary WICKW SS12 .... 16 A1 1
Briceway SLH/COR SS17 .... 51 E5 2
Brickfield Cl VGE SS16 .... 39 E4
Brickfield Rd VGE SS16 .... 39 E4
Brickfields Wy RCFD SS4 .... 35 F2
Bridge Cl SBN/FI SS3 .... 62 D2
Bridgecote La LAIN SS15 .... 26 A1
Bridge House Cl WICKW SS12 .... 16 B1 1
Bridge Rd WICKE SS11 .... 17 F1
Bridge St LAIN SS15 .... 25 H1
Bridgwater Dr LOS SS9 .... 45 G1
WOS/PRIT SS0 .... 45 H2
Bridleway BCAYE CM11 .... 7 G5
Brighton Av SOS SS1 .... 5 K2
Brightside BCAYW CM12 .... 8 B1
Brightside Cl BCAYW CM12 .... 8 B1
Brightwell Av WOS/PRIT SS0 .... 46 C4
Brimstone Av LAIN SS15 .... 25 E5
Brindles CVI SS8 .... 55 G5
Brinkworth Cl HOC/HUL SS5 .... 21 G2 1
Briscoe Rd PIT SS13 .... 28 A4
Bristol Cl RAYL SS6 .... 19 F3
Bristol Rd SOSN SS2 .... 34 C5
Britannia Gdns WOS/PRIT SS0 .... 59 F1
Britannia Rd WOS/PRIT SS0 .... 59 F1
Britten Cl VGE SS16 .... 36 D1
Brixham Cl RAYL SS6 .... 19 G3
Broad Cl HOC/HUL SS5 .... 21 F2
Broadclyst Av LOS SS9 .... 45 E1
Broadclyst Cl SOS SS1 .... 48 D5 1
Broadclyst Gdns SOS SS1 .... 49 E5
Broadhope Rd SLH/COR SS17 .... 64 B4
Broadlands SBF/HAD SS7 .... 30 C5
Broadlands Av HOC/HUL SS5 .... 21 G1
RAYL SS6 .... 19 G5
Broadlands Rd HOC/HUL SS5 .... 21 G2
Broadlawn LOS SS9 .... 44 D2
Broadmayne BSDN SS14 .... 2 D2
Broad Oaks WICKW SS12 .... 16 D2
Broad Oak Wy RAYL SS6 .... 31 H1
Broad Pde HOC/HUL SS5 .... 21 G2 2
Broad Wk HOC/HUL SS5 .... 21 G2
Broadwater Gn LAIN SS15 .... 24 C5 1
Broad Wy HOC/HUL SS5 .... 21 G1
Broadway LOS SS9 .... 58 B1
The Broadway SOS SS1 .... 61 H3
WICKW SS12 .... 10 C5
Broadway West LOS SS9 .... 58 A1 1
Brockenhurst Dr
SLH/COR SS17 .... 64 B4 1
Brock Hill Dr WICKE SS11 .... 10 B2
Brocksford Av RAYL SS6 .... 32 A2
Brodie Wk WICKW SS12 .... 17 E3 2
Bromfelde Rd BCAYE CM11 .... 14 D3
Bromfords Cl WICKW SS12 .... 16 A3
Bromfords Dr WICKW SS12 .... 16 A3
Bromley Ms RAYL SS6 .... 18 D5 1
Brompton Cl BCAYW CM12 .... 6 D5 3
Brook Cl RCFD SS4 .... 35 F3
Brook Dr SLH/COR SS17 .... 38 D5
WICKW SS12 .... 16 B2
Brookfields LOS SS9 .... 45 E1
Brookfields Cl LOS SS9 .... 45 E1
Brooklands WICKW SS12 .... 16 A1
Brooklands Av LOS SS9 .... 33 F5
Brooklands Pk LAIN SS15 .... 24 C5
Brooklands Sq CVI SS8 .... 69 F2
Brooklyn Dr RAYL SS6 .... 19 G3
Brook Md LAIN SS15 .... 25 E4
Brook Rd RAYL SS6 .... 31 F3
SBF/HAD SS7 .... 41 H5
Brookside BCAYE CM11 7
CVI SS8 .... 55 H4
HOC/HUL SS5 .... 21 G4
Broome Rd BCAYE CM11 7
Broomfield SBF/HAD SS7 43
Broomfield Av LOS SS9 45
RAYL SS6 .... 18 D5
Broomfield Gn CVI SS8 55
Broomfields PIT SS13 27
Broomfords Dr WICKW SS12 16
Broomhills Cha BCAYW CM12 12
Broughton Rd SBF/HAD SS7 44
Browning Av SOSN SS2 47
Brownlow Bend BSDN SS14 3
Brownlow Cross BSDN SS14 3
Brownlow Gn BSDN SS14 3
Browns Av WICKE SS11 11
Broxted Dr WICKW SS12 16
Bruce Gv WICKE SS11 17
Bruges Rd CVI SS8 .... 70 B2
Brundish PIT SS13 39
Brunel Rd LOS SS9 32
SBF/HAD SS7 30
Brunswick Pl RAYL SS6 18
Brunswick Rd SOS SS1 5
Brunwins Cl WICKE SS11 17
Brussum Rd CVI SS8 .... 70 C2
Bruton Av WOS/PRIT SS0 45
Bryant Av SOS SS1 61
Bryn Farm Cl BSDN SS14 26
Buchanan Gdns WICKW SS12 .... 16 D3
Buckerills PIT SS13 39
Buckingham Rd HOC/HUL SS5 21
LAIN SS15 .... 25 H3
Buckland SBN/FI SS3 49
Buckley Cl SLH/COR SS17 51
Buckwyns Cha BCAYW CM12 6
Buckwyns Ct BCAYW CM12 .... 8 C1
Budna Rd CVI SS8 55
Bull Cl VGE SS16 39
Buller Rd LAIN SS15 25
Bull La HOC/HUL SS5 20
RAYL SS6 31
Bullwood Ap HOC/HUL SS5 20
Bullwood Hall La HOC/HUL SS5 20
Bullwood Rd HOC/HUL SS5 21
Bulow Av CVI SS8 .... 70 A1
Bulphan Cl WICKW SS12 16
Bulwark Rd SBN/FI SS3 62
Bunters Av SBN/FI SS3 62
Bunting La BCAYE CM11 9
Burches LAIN SS15 25
Burches Md SBF/HAD SS7 30
Burches Rd SBF/HAD SS7 30
Burdett Av WOS/PRIT SS0 59
Burdett Rd SOS SS1 5
Buren Av CVI SS8 70
Burfield Cl LOS SS9 33
Burfield Rd LOS SS9 33
Burges Cl SOS SS1 62
Burges Rd SOS SS1 61
Burgess Av SLH/COR SS17 64
Burges Ter SOS SS1 61
Burghstead Cl BCAYW CM12 .... 8 D4
Burgundy Gdns PIT SS13 .... 28 A3
Burleigh Cl BCAYW CM12 7
Burleigh Sq SOS SS1 .... 62 A1
Burlescoombe Cl SOS SS1 .... 61 H1
Burlescoombe Leas SOS SS1 .... 49 E5
Burlescoombe Rd SOS SS1 49
Burlington Ct PIT SS13 28
Burlington Gdns SBF/HAD SS7 44
Burnaby Rd SOS SS1 5
Burne Av WICKW SS12 .... 16 A2
Burnham Rd LOS SS9 44
Burns Av PIT SS13 40
Burnside CVI SS8 .... 55 H4
Burnt Mills Rd PIT SS13 27
Burntwood Cl BCAYW CM12 8
Burr Cl VGE SS16 36
Burr Hill Cha WOS/PRIT SS0 46
Burrows Wy RAYL SS6 31
Burr's Wy SLH/COR SS17 51
Burstead Dr BCAYE CM11 13
Burton Cl SLH/COR SS17 51
Burwell Av CVI SS8 55
Bury Farm La BCAYE CM11 15
Bush Hall Rd BCAYW CM12 7
Bushy Md LAIN SS15 25
Butlers Gv VGE SS16 37
Butneys BSDN SS14 26
Buttercup Cl BCAYW CM12 .... 8 D1
Butterys SOS SS1 61
Buttsbury ING CM4 6
Butts La SLH/COR SS17 64
Butts Rd SLH/COR SS17 64
Buxton Av LOS SS9 44
Buxton Cl LOS SS9 44

uxton Link LAIN SS15 24 B5
uxton Sq LOS SS9 44 B3
uyl Av CVI SS8 56 A4
yfield LOS SS9 33 G4
yfletts VGE SS16 39 G2
yford Rd RAYL SS6 19 H5
yrd Ct LAIN SS15 25 F3
yrne Dr SOSN SS2 46 D1
yron Av SOSN SS2 47 G4
yron Cl CVI SS8 56 B5
yron Ct LAIN SS15 25 E5 1

C

abborns Crs SLH/COR SS17 64 C4
abinet Wy LOS SS9 32 D5
aernarvon Cl HOC/HUL SS5 21 E2 2
aister Dr PIT SS13 28 A5
aladonia La WICKW SS12 16 D3 3
aldwell Rd SLH/COR SS17 64 A3
alvert Dr PIT SS13 28 B2 1
alvina Cl LAIN SS15 26 A1
ambria Cl CVI SS8 68 D1 2
ambridge Cl VGE SS16 36 C1 3
ambridge Gdns RCFD SS4 22 B3 1
ambridge Rd CVI SS8 69 G1
WOS/PRIT SS0 4 A5
amelot Gdns PIT SS13 28 B3
ameron Cl LOS SS9 44 D4
SLH/COR SS17 50 D3
ameron Pl WICKW SS12 16 D3
amomile Dr WICKE SS11 10 D5
ampbell Cl WICKW SS12 16 C3 1
amperdown Rd CVI SS8 56 B4 1
amper Rd SOS SS1 5 J7
ampfield Rd SBN/FI SS3 62 D3
he Candlemakers SOSN SS2 47 F1
anewdon Cl WICKE SS11 10 C3 1
anewdon Gdns WICKE SS11 10 C3
anewdon Rd WOS/PRIT SS0 59 G1
anewdon View Rd RCFD SS4 22 C2
anon Cl SLH/COR SS17 65 E2
anonsleigh Crs LOS SS9 45 F5
anterbury Av SOSN SS2 48 B3
anterbury Cl BSDN SS14 27 G3 2
RAYL SS6 19 F3
he Canters SBF/HAD SS7 43 E1
anvey Rd CVI SS8 54 D5
LOS SS9 44 C5
PIT SS13 29 E5
anvey Wy CVI SS8 54 D2
SBF/HAD SS7 41 F3
apadocia St SOS SS1 61 F3
apel Cl SLH/COR SS17 64 D2
apel Ter SOS SS1 4 C5
ardigan Av WOS/PRIT SS0 46 B3
arisbrooke Cl PIT SS13 28 A5 1
arisbrooke Dr SLH/COR SS17 51 F5
arisbrooke Rd WOS/PRIT SS0 46 D5
arlingford Dr WOS/PRIT SS0 46 B3
arlisle Wy PIT SS13 28 A5
arlton Av WOS/PRIT SS0 46 B2
arlton Dr LOS SS9 45 G5
SBF/HAD SS7 43 F2
arlton Rd PIT SS13 28 D3
WICKE SS11 10 B3
arlyle Gdns BCAYW CM12 6 C5
WICKW SS12 16 D3
arnarvon Rd SOSN SS2 4 B1
arnival Cl BSDN SS14 26 C2
arol Cl LAIN SS15 25 G4
aroline's Cl SOSN SS2 46 D1 2
aro Rd CVI SS8 70 B1
arpenter Cl BCAYW CM12 8 C1
arruthers Dr WICKE SS11 10 C4
arson Rd BCAYE CM11 7 G5
arte Pl VGE SS16 36 D1
artlodge Av WICKE SS11 10 D5
artwright Rd SBF/HAD SS7 30 A4
arvers Wd BCAYE CM11 13 F1 1
ashiobury Ter SOS SS1 4 B5
ashmere Wy VGE SS16 39 E3
assel Av CVI SS8 56 B4
astle Av SBF/HAD SS7 43 G5
astle Cl RAYL SS6 31 F2
SBN/FI SS3 63 F1
astle Ct RAYL SS6 31 F2 1
astle Dr LOS SS9 57 G1
RAYL SS6 19 F5
astle La SBF/HAD SS7 43 H4
astle Rd RAYL SS6 31 F2
SBF/HAD SS7 43 H4
astle Ter RAYL SS6 31 F1 1
astleton Rd SOSN SS2 48 B5
astle View Rd CVI SS8 55 H3
aswell Cl SLH/COR SS17 51 F5

Cater Wd BCAYW CM12 9 E2
Cathedral Dr LAIN SS15 25 F4
Catherine Rd SBF/HAD SS7 42 A2
Cattawade End BSDN SS14 27 E4
Cattawade Link BSDN SS14 27 E4
Caulfield Rd SBN/FI SS3 62 B2
Caustonway RAYL SS6 19 G4
Cavell Rd BCAYE CM11 9 F4
Cavendish Gdns WOS/PRIT SS0 45 H4
Cavendish Wy LAIN SS15 25 G2
Caversham Av SBN/FI SS3 49 H5
Caversham Park Av RAYL SS6 19 F3 1
Cecil Wy RAYL SS6 32 A1
Cedar Av WICKW SS12 16 B3
Cedar Cl RAYL SS6 32 A3 1
SOSN SS2 47 F4
Cedar Hall Gdns SBF/HAD SS7 30 D5
Cedar Ms HOC/HUL SS5 20 D2
Cedar Park Cl SBF/HAD SS7 30 D5
Cedar Rd CVI SS8 55 G5
SBF/HAD SS7 30 D5
Cedars SLH/COR SS17 64 D2 1
Celandine Cl BCAYW CM12 8 C1 2
Central Av BCAYW CM12 7 F5
CVI SS8 55 F5 1
RCFD SS4 22 C3
SBF/HAD SS7 43 H1
SLH/COR SS17 50 D4
SOSN SS2 4 E1
Central Cl SBF/HAD SS7 43 H2
Central Rd SLH/COR SS17 64 C3
Central Wall CVI SS8 55 H3
Central Wall Rd CVI SS8 56 A4
Centurion Cl SBN/FI SS3 63 E1
Ceylon Rd WOS/PRIT SS0 59 G1
Chadacre Rd SOS SS1 49 E5
Chadwick Rd WOS/PRIT SS0 59 F1
Chaffinch Cl SBN/FI SS3 62 D1 1
Chaingate Av SOSN SS2 48 B4
Chalfont Cl LOS SS9 45 E2
Chalice Cl BSDN SS14 27 F5
Chalk End PIT SS13 27 H4
Chalk Rd CVI SS8 55 H3 3
Chalkwell Av WOS/PRIT SS0 59 E2
Chalkwell Esp WOS/PRIT SS0 59 E2
Chalkwell Park Dr LOS SS9 45 G4
Challacombe SBN/FI SS3 49 F5
Challock Lees PIT SS13 40 B1 2
Chalvedon Av PIT SS13 28 A4
Chamberlain Av CVI SS8 56 B5
SLH/COR SS17 51 F4
Champion Cl SLH/COR SS17 64 D1
WICKW SS12 16 C2 1
Champlain Av CVI SS8 55 G4
Chancel Cl LAIN SS15 25 F5
SBF/HAD SS7 29 H5
Chancellor Rd SOS SS1 4 D5
Chandlers Wy SOSN SS2 47 E1
Chandos Pde SBF/HAD SS7 44 A3
Chanton Cl LOS SS9 33 E4 1
Chantry Crs SLH/COR SS17 64 B3
Chantry Dr LAIN SS15 25 F4 2
Chantry Wy BCAYE CM11 9 E3
Chapel Ct BCAYE CM11 9 E3
Chapel La SBF/HAD SS7 43 F4
Chapel Rd SBN/FI SS3 63 E3
Chapel St BCAYW CM12 8 D3
Chaplin Cl LAIN SS15 25 H2
Chapman Rd CVI SS8 71 F1
Chapmans Cl LOS SS9 44 C5
Chapmans Wk LOS SS9 44 C5
Charfinch Crs BCAYE CM11 9 F4
Charfleets Cl CVI SS8 69 E1
Charfleets Rd CVI SS8 68 D1
Charfleets Service Rd CVI SS8 68 D1
Charity Farm Cha BCAYW CM12 8 C2
Charles Cl WOS/PRIT SS0 45 H1
Charleston Av PIT SS13 28 B2
Charleston Ct PIT SS13 28 B2 2
Charlotte Av WICKW SS12 16 B1 2
Charlton Cl PIT SS13 28 B4
Chase Cl SBF/HAD SS7 42 C1
Chase End RAYL SS6 32 A1
Chase Gdns WOS/PRIT SS0 46 C3
Chase Rd SLH/COR SS17 65 F1
SOS SS1 5 H3
Chaseside RAYL SS6 31 H3
The Chase BCAYE CM11 9 F3 2
LAIN SS15 25 E1
RAYL SS6 32 A2
RCFD SS4 22 A1
SBF/HAD SS7 42 C1
VGE SS16 37 H3
WICKE SS11 11 F2
WICKW SS12 15 H1
WICKW SS12 16 D4
Chaseway VGE SS16 39 G2
Chatsworth SBF/HAD SS7 30 C5 1

Chatsworth Gdns
HOC/HUL SS5 21 E2 3
Chatton Cl WICKW SS12 16 D3 4
Chaucer Wk WICKW SS12 16 B3
Cheapside East RAYL SS6 19 F4
Cheapside West RAYL SS6 19 E4
Cheddar Av WOS/PRIT SS0 45 H2
Chedington SBN/FI SS3 49 F5
Cheldon Barton SBN/FI SS3 62 B1
Chelmer Av RAYL SS6 31 F2
Chelmer Wy SBN/FI SS3 62 C2
Chelmsford Av SOSN SS2 4 A1
Chelmsford Rd WICKE SS11 18 B1
Chelsea Av SOS SS1 5 K7
Chelsworth Cl SOS SS1 61 G1 1
Chelsworth Crs SOS SS1 61 F1
Cheltenham Dr LOS SS9 45 G4
SBF/HAD SS7 31 E4
Cheltenham Rd HOC/HUL SS5 21 G1 1
SOS SS1 5 G4
Chenies Dr LAIN SS15 25 E2
Chepstow Cl BCAYE CM11 7 G5
The Cherries CVI SS8 70 A3 1
Cherrybrook SOS SS1 49 F5
Cherry Cl CVI SS8 55 F5
HOC/HUL SS5 21 F1
Cherrydown RAYL SS6 19 G4
Cherrydown East VGE SS16 2 D4
Cherrydown West VGE SS16 2 C4
Cherry Gdns BCAYW CM12 8 B1
Cherry La WICKE SS11 17 E1
Cherrymeade SBF/HAD SS7 42 D2
Cherry Orchard La RCFD SS4 34 A3
Cherry Orchard Wy RCFD SS4 34 A3
SOSN SS2 34 A4
Cherrytrees BCAYW CM12 8 C5
Chertsey Cl SBN/FI SS3 49 G5
Chesham Dr LAIN SS15 25 E2
Cheshunt Dr RAYL SS6 19 E2
Cheshunts PIT SS13 27 H5
Chester Av SOS SS1 5 K7
Chesterfield Av SBF/HAD SS7 30 A5
Chesterfield Crs LOS SS9 33 E5
Chesterford Gdns BSDN SS14 27 G3 3
Chester Hall La BSDN SS14 26 B2
Chestnut Av BCAYW CM12 8 C3
Chestnut Cl HOC/HUL SS5 21 G2
Chestnut Ct VGE SS16 39 H2
Chestnut Gv SBF/HAD SS7 41 G2
SOSN SS2 47 F4 1
Chestnut Rd VGE SS16 39 H2
The Chestnuts RAYL SS6 19 H4
Chestwood Cl BCAYW CM12 9 E1
Chevening Gdns HOC/HUL SS5 20 D2 3
Chevers Pawen PIT SS13 39 H1
Cheyne Ct WICKW SS12 16 D4 1
Chichester Cl BSDN SS14 27 G3
CVI SS8 69 H2 1
Chichester Rd SOSN SS2 4 D3
The Chignalls LAIN SS15 24 D5 4
Chilham Cl PIT SS13 40 B1
Chiltern Cl RAYL SS6 19 G5
The Chilterns CVI SS8 55 G5
The Chimes SBF/HAD SS7 42 B2
Chinchilla Rd SOS SS1 5 K2
Chisholm Ct WICKW SS12 16 D3 5
Chittock Ga BSDN SS14 27 F5
Chittock Md BSDN SS14 27 F5
Chorley Cl VGE SS16 36 C1
Christchurch Rd SOSN SS2 5 G2
Christopher Martin Rd
BSDN SS14 27 F1 1
Christy Wy LAIN SS15 24 B4
Church Cl CVI SS8 69 G1
SBN/FI SS3 62 C3
Church Cnr SBF/HAD SS7 42 A5
Church End Av WICKE SS11 10 D3
Church End La WICKE SS11 10 C3
Churchfields SBN/FI SS3 49 H4
Church Hl LAIN SS15 25 G4
SLH/COR SS17 64 B3
Churchill Crs SLH/COR SS17 50 D5
Church La BCAYE CM11 14 C2
PIT SS13 27 H1
Church Ms LAIN SS15 25 E4 1
Church Pde CVI SS8 55 F4
Church Park Rd PIT SS13 40 A1
Church Rd BSDN SS14 3 J3
BSDN SS14 26 D3
HOC/HUL SS5 20 C1
LAIN SS15 25 H2 1
PIT SS13 40 D1
RAYL SS6 31 H1
RCFD SS4 22 B1
SBF/HAD SS7 29 H5
SBF/HAD SS7 43 H3
SBN/FI SS3 62 B3
SLH/COR SS17 51 G5

SOS SS1 4 D5
VGE SS16 40 D3
WICKE SS11 18 A1
Church St BCAYE CM11 13 F3
BCAYW CM12 13 E3
Church View Rd SBF/HAD SS7 30 B5
Churchway SBF/HAD SS7 44 A4
Clare Av WICKE SS11 10 C3
Claremont Cl WOS/PRIT SS0 46 D5 3
Claremont Dr VGE SS16 39 G2
Claremont Rd LAIN SS15 25 E4
WOS/PRIT SS0 46 C5
Clarence Cl SBF/HAD SS7 42 A2
Clarence Rd PIT SS13 29 E4
RAYL SS6 32 B2
SBF/HAD SS7 42 A2
SLH/COR SS17 51 H5
SOS SS1 4 C5
Clarence Rd North SBF/HAD SS7 42 A2
Clarence St SOS SS1 4 C5
Clarendon Rd CVI SS8 56 B5
PIT SS13 28 B4
Clare Rd SBF/HAD SS7 29 F5
Claters Cl SOSN SS2 48 C4
Clatterfield Gdns WOS/PRIT SS0 45 H4
Clavering Ct RAYL SS6 19 E5 1
Claybrick Av HOC/HUL SS5 21 E3 1
Clayburn Cir BSDN SS14 3 J2
Claydon Crs BSDN SS14 26 D4
Claydons La SBF/HAD SS7 31 F3
Clay Hill Rd VGE SS16 2 E4
VGE SS16 39 F2 1
Clayspring Cl HOC/HUL SS5 21 E1
Clements Gdns HOC/HUL SS5 21 H3
Clements Hall La HOC/HUL SS5 21 H3
Clements Hall Wy HOC/HUL SS5 21 H4
Cleveland Dr WOS/PRIT SS0 46 C3
Cleveland Rd BSDN SS14 3 H2
CVI SS8 70 A2
Clickett End BSDN SS14 3 H2
Clickett Hl BSDN SS14 3 G2
Clickett Side BSDN SS14 3 G2
Clieveden Rd SOS SS1 61 G3
Cliff Av WOS/PRIT SS0 46 D5
WOS/PRIT SS0 58 D1
Cliff Gdns LOS SS9 58 D1
Clifford Cl LAIN SS15 37 G1
Cliff Pde LOS SS9 58 B1
Cliff Rd LOS SS9 58 D1
Cliffsea Gv LOS SS9 45 G5
Clifftown Pde SOS SS1 4 A6
Clifftown Rd SOS SS1 4 C5
Clifton Av SBF/HAD SS7 41 H2
Clifton Cl SBF/HAD SS7 42 A2
Clifton Dr WOS/PRIT SS0 59 G2
Clifton Ms SOS SS1 4 C6
Clifton Rd CVI SS8 70 A1
PIT SS13 29 E4
RCFD SS4 22 B1
Clifton Ter SOS SS1 4 C6
Clifton Wy SBF/HAD SS7 41 H2
Climmen Rd CVI SS8 56 A4 1
Clinton Rd CVI SS8 69 E1
Clock House Rd BCAYW CM12 12 B3
Cloisters SLH/COR SS17 64 D2
The Cloisters LAIN SS15 25 F5 1
Clova Rd LOS SS9 45 G4 1
Clovelly Gdns WICKE SS11 10 B5
Clover Cl VGE SS16 39 F3 1
Clover Wy VGE SS16 39 F3
Cluny Sq SOSN SS2 47 H3
Clyde Crs RAYL SS6 31 F2
Coach Ms BCAYE CM11 7 G5
Cobham Rd WOS/PRIT SS0 59 F2
Coburg La VGE SS16 36 C2
Cockerell Cl PIT SS13 28 A2
Cockethurst Cl WOS/PRIT SS0 45 H2
Codenham Gn VGE SS16 2 E5
Codenham Straight VGE SS16 2 E5
Cokefield Av SOSN SS2 47 H3
Coker Rd CVI SS8 69 E2
Colbert Av SOS SS1 61 F2
Colbourne Cl SLH/COR SS17 65 E1
Colchester Cl WOS/PRIT SS0 47 E4
Colchester Rd SOSN SS2 47 E4
Colemans Av WOS/PRIT SS0 46 C2
Coleman St SOSN SS2 4 D2
College Wy SOS SS1 4 C3
Collindale Cl CVI SS8 56 C5
Collingwood SBF/HAD SS7 42 B2 1
Collingwood Rd VGE SS16 3 J5
Collingwood Wk VGE SS16 3 K4
Collingwood Wy SBN/FI SS3 49 H5
Collins Cl SLH/COR SS17 64 D2
Collins Wy LOS SS9 33 H5
Colman Cl SLH/COR SS17 64 C1
Colne Dr SBN/FI SS3 49 H5
Colne Pl VGE SS16 3 G4

Coltishall Cl WICKE SS11 17 G2 1
Colville Cl SLH/COR SS17 51 E4
Colville Ms BCAYW CM12 6 C5 2
Colworth Cl SBF/HAD SS7 43 G2
Commercial Rd WOS/PRIT SS0 46 C3
Common Ap SBF/HAD SS7 30 D5
Commonhall La SBF/HAD SS7 43 G3
Common La SBF/HAD SS7 30 D4
The Common SBF/HAD SS7 30 D4
Compton Ct CVI SS8 70 C2 2
Concord Rd CVI SS8 55 G4
Conifers SBF/HAD SS7 43 H3
Coniston LOS SS9 33 H4
Coniston Cl RAYL SS6 31 H1 1
Coniston Rd CVI SS8 69 H1
SBF/HAD SS7 30 B4
Connaught Gdns SBN/FI SS3 62 B3
Connaught Rd RAYL SS6 32 B3
Connaught Wy BCAYW CM12 6 D5
Conrad Rd SLH/COR SS17 64 D2
Constable Wy SBN/FI SS3 63 E1
Constitution Hl SBF/HAD SS7 42 A3
Convent Cl LAIN SS15 25 F5 2
Convent Rd CVI SS8 70 A1
Con Wy SBF/HAD SS7 42 A3
Cookham Ct SBN/FI SS3 49 H4 1
Cooks Gn PIT SS13 28 B2 3
Coombe Dr VGE SS16 37 F5
Coombe Ri SLH/COR SS17 64 D2
Coombes Cl BCAYW CM12 8 C1
Coombes Gv RCFD SS4 35 F1
Coombewood Dr SBF/HAD SS7 42 B1
Coopersales LAIN SS15 24 C5
Coopers Dr BCAYE CM11 13 F2
Coopers Wy SOSN SS2 47 F1
Copdoek BSDN SS14 26 D4
Copelands RCFD SS4 22 C2 1
Copford Av RAYL SS6 32 A2
Copford Rd BCAYE CM11 9 F3 3
Copland Rd SLH/COR SS17 64 C3
Coppens Gn WICKW SS12 16 C2
Copper Beeches SBF/HAD SS7 31 E4 1
Copperfield BCAYE CM11 13 G2 2
Copperfields LAIN SS15 25 F4 3
Coppice La LAIN SS15 26 A2
The Copse BCAYW CM12 8 D1
Coptfold Cl SOS SS1 48 C5 1
Corasway SBF/HAD SS7 43 E1
Cordelia Crs RAYL SS6 19 F5
The Cordwainers SOSN SS2 47 F1
Corfe Cl PIT SS13 28 A5
Cornec Av LOS SS9 32 C5
Cornec Cha LOS SS9 32 D5
Corner Rd BCAYE CM11 15 E2
Cornflower Gdns BCAYW CM12 6 C5
Cornhill Av HOC/HUL SS5 21 F1
Cornwall Gdns RCFD SS4 22 B3
Cornwall Rd PIT SS13 29 E4
Cornwell Crs SLH/COR SS17 64 D1
Cornworthy SBN/FI SS3 62 B1
Corona Rd CVI SS8 56 B4
VGE SS16 37 E3
Corringham Rd SLH/COR SS17 64 C3
Corsel Rd CVI SS8 70 D1 1
Cosgrove Av LOS SS9 44 C3
Cossington Rd WOS/PRIT SS0 59 H2
Cotelands VGE SS16 39 G3
Cotswold Av RAYL SS6 19 G5
Cotswold Rd WOS/PRIT SS0 59 G1
Cottesmore Cl CVI SS8 69 H2
Cottesmore Gdns LOS SS9 44 B5
Cottis Cl VGE SS16 36 D3
Courtauld Rd PIT SS13 28 A1
Courtlands BCAYW CM12 8 B3
Courtney Park Rd VGE SS16 37 E1 1
The Courts RAYL SS6 19 H5
Coxbridge Ct BCAYW CM12 8 D3
Coxes Cl SLH/COR SS17 64 C1
Coxes Farm Rd BCAYE CM11 13 H1
Craftsmans Sq SOSN SS2 47 F1
Cranbrook Av SBF/HAD SS7 43 F2
Cranes Cl BSDN SS14 27 G2
Cranes Farm Rd BSDN SS14 26 B3
LAIN SS15 25 H3
Cranes La BSDN SS14 26 D3
Cranfield Park Av WICKW SS12 28 D1
Cranfield Park Rd WICKW SS12 16 C4
Cranleigh Dr LOS SS9 45 F4
Cranley Av WOS/PRIT SS0 46 C5
Cranley Gdns SBN/FI SS3 62 B3
Cranley Rd WOS/PRIT SS0 59 G1
Cranmer Cl BCAYW CM12 7 E4
Cranston Av WOS/PRIT SS0 46 C1
Craven Av CVI SS8 69 H1
Craven Cl RCFD SS4 22 C3
Crawford Cha WICKW SS12 16 D3
Crawford Cl BCAYW CM12 7 F5
Crawley Cl SLH/COR SS17 51 F4
Craylands BSDN SS14 27 G3
Crays Hl BCAYE CM11 14 C4
Crays Hill Rd BCAYE CM11 14 D3
Crays Vw BCAYW CM12 9 E5
Creek Rd CVI SS8 56 C5
Creek Vw VGE SS16 39 F3 2
Crescent Cl BCAYW CM12 8 C1 3
Crescent Gdns BCAYW CM12 8 C1 4
Crescent Rd BCAYW CM12 8 C1
CVI SS8 70 C2
LOS SS9 44 C5
SBF/HAD SS7 42 A4
The Crescent SBF/HAD SS7 44 A4
Cressells LAIN SS15 2 B3
Crest Av PIT SS13 28 B5
The Crest LOS SS9 33 E5
Creswick Av RAYL SS6 19 F5
Cricketers Wy PIT SS13 16 A5
Cricketfield Gv LOS SS9 45 G4
Croft Cl LOS SS9 45 F2
SBF/HAD SS7 41 H1
Crofton Av SLH/COR SS17 51 E5
Croft Rd SBF/HAD SS7 41 G1
The Crofts SBN/FI SS3 49 H2
The Croft RAYL SS6 32 A3
Cromer Av LAIN SS15 25 E3
Cromer Cl LAIN SS15 25 E3
Cromer Rd SOS SS1 5 F4
Cromwell Av BCAYW CM12 8 D2
Cromwell Rd HOC/HUL SS5 21 F2
SOSN SS2 47 F3
Cropenburg Wk CVI SS8 56 A4 2
Crosby Rd WOS/PRIT SS0 59 E1
Cross Av WICKW SS12 16 B2
Crossfell Rd SBF/HAD SS7 30 C4
Crossfield Rd SOSN SS2 48 A4
Cross Rd PIT SS13 29 E4
SBF/HAD SS7 43 E2
The Crossways WOS/PRIT SS0 58 D1
Crouch Dr WICKE SS11 10 C5
Crouch St LAIN SS15 25 H2
Crouchview Cl WICKE SS11 17 G1 2
Crowborough Rd SOSN SS2 47 E4
Crown Av PIT SS13 28 B4
Crown Cl PIT SS13 28 B5
Crown Gdns RAYL SS6 31 F1
Crown Hl RAYL SS6 31 F1
Crown Rd BCAYE CM11 9 E3
HOC/HUL SS5 20 C3
Crowstone Av WOS/PRIT SS0 59 F2
Crowstone Cl WOS/PRIT SS0 46 B5
Crowstone Rd WOS/PRIT SS0 59 F1
Culverdown BSDN SS14 2 D1
Cumberland Av SBF/HAD SS7 41 H3
SOSN SS2 47 H4
Cumberland Dr LAIN SS15 24 D5 5
Cunningham Dr WICKW SS12 16 D3
Curlew Crs VGE SS16 2 E7
Curlew Dr SBF/HAD SS7 41 H4
Curling Tye BSDN SS14 27 E4
Curling Wk BSDN SS14 27 E4
Curtisway RAYL SS6 19 H4

D

Daarle Av CVI SS8 69 H1
Daines Cl SOS SS1 62 A1
Daines Rd BCAYE CM11 9 E3
Daines Wy SOS SS1 49 E5
Dalen Av CVI SS8 69 H1
Dale Rd LOS SS9 44 C5
The Dales RCFD SS4 22 C5
The Dale SBF/HAD SS7 42 D2
Dalmatia Rd SOS SS1 5 K2
Dalmeney VGE SS16 37 E2
Daltons Fen PIT SS13 28 B3
Dalwood SBN/FI SS3 62 C1
Dalwood Gdns SBF/HAD SS7 43 H2
Dalys Rd RCFD SS4 34 D1
Danacre LAIN SS15 25 E5
Danbury Cl LOS SS9 45 G2
Danbury Down BSDN SS14 27 E3
Danbury Rd RAYL SS6 19 E5
Dandies Cha LOS SS9 33 E4
Dandies Cl LOS SS9 33 E4
Dandies Dr LOS SS9 33 E4
Dane's Av SBN/FI SS3 63 E3
Danescroft Cl LOS SS9 45 E2
Danescroft Dr LOS SS9 45 E2
Danesfield SBF/HAD SS7 41 G4
Danesleigh Gdns LOS SS9 45 E2
Dane St SBN/FI SS3 63 F3
Darell Wy BCAYE CM11 9 G4 1
Darenth Rd LOS SS9 44 C5
Dark La SBF/HAD SS7 30 D5
Darlinghurst Gv LOS SS9 45 H4
Dartmouth Cl RAYL SS6 19 G3 1
Datchet Dr SBN/FI SS3 49 H4
Davenants PIT SS13 28 A3
David Av WICKE SS11 10 C3
Davidson Gdns WICKW SS12 16 D3
David's Wk BCAYE CM11 9 F3 4
Dawlish Crs RAYL SS6 19 G3
Dawlish Dr LOS SS9 45 F5
Daws Heath Rd RAYL SS6 31 G2
SBF/HAD SS7 31 F5
Deacon Dr LAIN SS15 25 F4
Debden Gn VGE SS16 37 F2
Dedham Cl BCAYE CM11 9 F3
Dedham Rd BCAYE CM11 9 F3
Deepdale SBF/HAD SS7 30 C5
Deepdene Av RAYL SS6 19 F3
Deepwater Rd CVI SS8 69 F2
Deerbank Rd BCAYE CM11 9 F2
Deerhurst SBF/HAD SS7 31 E4
Deerhurst Cl SBF/HAD SS7 31 E4 2
Deirdre Av WICKW SS12 16 A1
Deirdre Cl WICKW SS12 16 A1
Delaware Crs SBN/FI SS3 62 C2
Delaware Rd SBN/FI SS3 62 B2
Delder Av CVI SS8 70 C2
Delft Rd CVI SS8 55 H5
Delfzul Rd CVI SS8 55 H5
Delgada Rd CVI SS8 70 C1
Delhi Rd PIT SS13 28 B5
Delimands LAIN SS15 2 A2
The Dell VGE SS16 3 F7
WICKE SS11 16 D1
Delmar Gdns WICKE SS11 10 B3
Delmores VGE SS16 37 F3
Delview CVI SS8 55 G4
Delvins PIT SS13 27 H3
Denbigh Rd LAIN SS15 37 E1
Dencourt Crs BSDN SS14 39 G1
Dene Cl RAYL SS6 19 G4 1
Dene Gdns RAYL SS6 19 G4
Denehurst Gdns VGE SS16 36 B2
Denesmere SBF/HAD SS7 41 H2 1
Deneway VGE SS16 39 E4
Dengayne BSDN SS14 3 K2
Denham Rd CVI SS8 55 H5
Denham V RAYL SS6 18 D5 3
Denton Ap WOS/PRIT SS0 46 B1 1
Denton Av WOS/PRIT SS0 46 B1
Denton Cl WOS/PRIT SS0 46 B1
Denver Dr PIT SS13 28 B2
Denys Dr BSDN SS14 27 G2
Derby Cl BCAYE CM11 7 G5
VGE SS16 36 C2 2
Derbydale RCFD SS4 22 B2
Derek Gdns SOSN SS2 46 D1
Dering Crs LOS SS9 33 E4
Derventer Av CVI SS8 55 H3
Derwent Av RAYL SS6 31 H1
Devereux Rd SOS SS1 4 C6
Devereux Wy BCAYW CM12 6 C5
Devon Gdns RCFD SS4 22 B3
Devonshire Cl LAIN SS15 24 D3
Devonshire Rd LAIN SS15 24 D3
Devon Wy CVI SS8 55 H4
Dewsgreen VGE SS16 39 F2
Dewyk Rd CVI SS8 56 B4
Dickens Cl SOSN SS2 47 G4
Dickens Dr LAIN SS15 25 F4
Digby Rd SLH/COR SS17 51 G4
Dinant Av CVI SS8 55 F4
Disraeli Rd RAYL SS6 32 C3
Ditton Court Rd WOS/PRIT SS0 59 G1
Dobsons Cl LOS SS9 45 G4
RAYL SS6 31 H2
Doeshill Dr WICKW SS12 16 D1
Doggetts Cha RCFD SS4 23 E2
Doggetts Cl RCFD SS4 23 E5
Dollant Av CVI SS8 69 H1
Dolphin Gdns BCAYW CM12 6 C5 3
Dolphins WOS/PRIT SS0 46 C1
Donald Thorn Cl WICKW SS12 16 C2 2
Dorchester Rd BCAYW CM12 6 D5 4
Doric Av RCFD SS4 22 C3
Dorothy Farm Rd RAYL SS6 32 B2 1
Dorothy Gdns SBF/HAD SS7 42 C1
Dorset Gdns RCFD SS4 22 B3
Dorset Wy BCAYW CM12 6 D5
Doublegate La WICKE SS11 17 H3
WICKW SS12 17 G4
Doublet Ms BCAYE CM11 7 G5
Douglas Dr WICKW SS12 16 C3
Douglas Rd SBF/HAD SS7 44 A3
Doulton Wy RCFD SS4 22 B2
Dovecote SBN/FI SS3 49 H5 3
Dovedale CVI SS8 56 C4 3
Dovedale Cl VGE SS16 36 D2 1
Dove Dr SBF/HAD SS7 41 G4
Dovercliff Rd CVI SS8 70 D1
Dovervelt Rd CVI SS8 56 A
Dover Wy PIT SS13 28 A
Dovesgate SBF/HAD SS7 41 G2
Doves Ms LAIN SS15 25 G2
Dowland Cl SLH/COR SS17 64 B1
Downer Rd SBF/HAD SS7 42 A
Downer Rd North SBF/HAD SS7 42 B
Downesway SBF/HAD SS7 42 A
Downey Cl BSDN SS14 26 D
Downhall Cl RAYL SS6 19 G
Downhall Park Wy RAYL SS6 19 F
Down Hall Rd RAYL SS6 19 F
Downham Rd CVI SS8 69 H
WICKE SS11 10 B
Downs Gv VGE SS16 39 F
Drake Cl SBF/HAD SS7 43 F
Drake Rd LAIN SS15 25 G
WOS/PRIT SS0 59 F
The Drakes SBN/FI SS3 62 D
Drakes Wy RAYL SS6 19 H
Drewsteignton SBN/FI SS3 62 C
Driftway VGE SS16 39 G
The Drive RAYL SS6 32 C
RCFD SS4 35 E
WOS/PRIT SS0 59 E
The Driveway CVI SS8 70 A
Droitwich Av SOSN SS2 5 K
Drummond Pl WICKW SS12 16 D3
Dryden Av SOSN SS2 47 G
Dry St VGE SS16 37 F
Dubarry Cl SBF/HAD SS7 42 C
Duke Pl LAIN SS15 25 H
Dukes Farm Cl BCAYW CM12 7 F
Dukes Farm Rd BCAYW CM12 9 E
Dukes Rd BCAYE CM11 9 F
Dulverton Av WOS/PRIT SS0 45 H
Dulverton Cl WOS/PRIT SS0 45 H
Dunbar Pl WICKW SS12 16 D
Duncan Cl WICKW SS12 17 E3
Dundee Av LOS SS9 44 C
Dundee Cl LOS SS9 44 D
Dundee Ct BSDN SS14 27 G
Dundonald Dr LOS SS9 45 G
Dunfane BCAYW CM12 7 F
Dungannon Cha SOS SS1 62 A
Dungannon Dr SOS SS1 62 A
Dunstable Rd SLH/COR SS17 64 B
Dunster Av WOS/PRIT SS0 45 H
Dunton Rd RBRW/HUT CM13 24 A
Durban La LAIN SS15 26 A1
The Durdans VGE SS16 37 E
Durham Rd LAIN SS15 24 B
RCFD SS4 22 A
SOSN SS2 48 A
Durham Wy RAYL SS6 19 G
Durley Cl SBF/HAD SS7 42 B
Durrington Cl VGE SS16 3 G
Duxford WICKE SS11 17 F
Dyke Crs CVI SS8 55 E
Dynevor Gdns LOS SS9 44 C

E

Eagle Wy SBN/FI SS3 62 D
Earl Mountbatten Dr
BCAYW CM12 8 C2
Earls Hall Av SOSN SS2 46 D
Earls Hall Pde SOSN SS2 46 D
Earlswood SBF/HAD SS7 42 A
Eastbourne Gv WOS/PRIT SS0 46 B
Eastbrooks PIT SS13 28 A
Eastbury Av RCFD SS4 22 C
Eastcheap RAYL SS6 19 F
Eastcote Gv SOSN SS2 48 A
East Crs CVI SS8 55 G
Eastern Av SBF/HAD SS7 41 H
SOSN SS2 47 G
Eastern Cl SOSN SS2 47 F
Eastern Esp CVI SS8 70 C
SOS SS1 5 G
Eastern Rd RAYL SS6 31 E
Eastfield Rd CVI SS8 56 C
LAIN SS15 26 A
East Glebe Dr RAYL SS6 19 F
Eastleigh Rd SBF/HAD SS7 55 F
Eastley VGE SS16 2 B
East Mayne BSDN SS14 27 H
PIT SS13 27 G
Easton End LAIN SS15 24 D5
East Philbrick Crs RAYL SS6 19 F5
East St LOS SS9 58 B
RCFD SS4 35 E
SOSN SS2 47 E
East Thorpe BSDN SS14 3 G
Eastview Dr RAYL SS6 19 G
Eastways CVI SS8 55 G

stwood Bvd WOS/PRIT SS0 45 H3
stwoodbury Cl SOSN SS2 34 C5
stwoodbury Crs SOSN SS2 34 D5
stwoodbury La SOSN SS2 34 A5
stwood La South
WOS/PRIT SS0 46 A4
stwood Old Rd LOS SS9 44 D1
SBF/HAD SS7 32 B4
stwood Park Dr LOS SS9 33 F5
stwood Ri LOS SS9 32 D4
stwood Rd LOS SS9 45 E3
RAYL SS6 31 H2
stwood Rd North LOS SS9 45 E2
ton Cl BCAYW CM12 6 D5
ton Rd LOS SS9 44 D4
cleston Gdns BCAYW CM12 6 D5 5
gecotts VGE SS16 37 H2 1
inburgh Av LOS SS9 44 C4
SLH/COR SS17 51 E5
inburgh Cl RAYL SS6 19 E3 1
inburgh Wy PIT SS13 28 A5
ith Cl CVI SS8 69 F1
ith Rd CVI SS8 69 E1
SOSN SS2 47 E4
ith Wy SLH/COR SS17 51 F4
ward Cl BCAYW CM12 6 C5 4
RCFD SS4 22 B2 2
ward Gdns WICKE SS11 10 C5
bert Gdns WICKE SS11 10 C4
erton Dr VGE SS16 36 B1
senhower Rd LAIN SS15 24 D5 7
dbert Cl SOSN SS2 48 B4 1
deland LAIN SS15 25 H4
der Av WICKW SS12 16 A2
derberry Cl VGE SS16 37 E1 2
derstep Av CVI SS8 70 D1 2
derton Rd WOS/PRIT SS0 59 G1
der Wy WICKW SS12 16 B2
don Wy HOC/HUL SS5 21 E2
eanor Cha WICKW SS12 16 B1
ectric Av WOS/PRIT SS0 46 B4
gar Cl LAIN SS15 25 G3
SBF/HAD SS7 29 G5
ham Dr PIT SS13 40 B1
zabeth Av RAYL SS6 31 F3 1
zabeth Cl HOC/HUL SS5 21 F4
zabeth Dr WICKW SS12 10 A5
zabeth Rd SOS SS1 5 K7
zabeth Wy LAIN SS15 37 G1
SBF/HAD SS7 43 F2 1
enbrook Cl LOS SS9 45 F3
esmere Rd CVI SS8 69 F1
m Cl RAYL SS6 19 G5
SBN/FI SS3 62 D2
m Dr RAYL SS6 19 G5
mer Ap SOS SS1 4 C4
mer Av SOS SS1 4 C4
m Gn PIT SS13 39 H1
m Gv SOS SS1 61 H1
mhurst Av SBF/HAD SS7 41 G2
m Rd CVI SS8 70 B1
LOS SS9 45 F5
PIT SS13 28 D2
SBF/HAD SS7 43 G4
SBN/FI SS3 62 D2
WICKE SS11 10 C5
msleigh Dr LOS SS9 45 F3
mstead Cl SLH/COR SS17 51 G4
mtree Rd VGE SS16 39 G2
m Vw Rd SBF/HAD SS7 41 G3
mwood Av HOC/HUL SS5 21 F4
ounda Ct SBF/HAD SS7 42 A2
senham Ct RAYL SS6 19 E5 2
senham Crs BSDN SS14 27 G5
sinor Av CVI SS8 55 H3
verston Cl LAIN SS15 25 G3 1
y Cl RAYL SS6 19 F4
y Rd SOSN SS2 47 G4
nanuel Rd VGE SS16 37 E2
ndeavour Dr BSDN SS14 26 C2
ndway SBF/HAD SS7 43 H4
nfield Rd WICKE SS11 17 H1
nglefield Cl HOC/HUL SS5 21 H4
nnismore Gdns SOSN SS2 47 F3
nsign Cl LOS SS9 45 H5 1
nterprise Wy WICKW SS12 17 E2
pping Cl LOS SS9 33 F4 1
ric Rd PIT SS13 29 E5
rskine Pl WICKW SS12 16 D2 3
splanade Gdns WOS/PRIT SS0 59 E1
ssex Cl CVI SS8 69 H2
LAIN SS15 25 E5
RAYL SS6 32 A2
ssex Gdns LOS SS9 45 F2
ssex Rd CVI SS8 56 B5
ssex St SOSN SS2 4 D3
ssex Wy SBF/HAD SS7 42 B5
state Rd SBF/HAD SS7 44 A3
Ethelred Gdns WICKE SS11 10 C4
Ethel Rd RAYL SS6 32 C3
Eton Cl CVI SS8 56 A4
Eton Wk SBN/FI SS3 49 H5
Evelyn Rd HOC/HUL SS5 21 F3
Everard Rd BSDN SS14 27 G3
Everest RAYL SS6 19 G3
Everest Ri BCAYW CM12 8 C4
Eversley Rd PIT SS13 40 C1
SBF/HAD SS7 29 G4
Ewan Cl LOS SS9 44 B3 1
Ewan Wy SBF/HAD SS7 44 B3
Exeter Cl BSDN SS14 27 G4
Exford Av WOS/PRIT SS0 45 H1
Exmouth Dr RAYL SS6 19 G3
Eynesham Wy PIT SS13 27 H2 2

F

Fairburn Cl SOS SS1 5 F3
Fairfax Av PIT SS13 28 B3
Fairfax Dr WOS/PRIT SS0 46 A4
Fairfield Crs LOS SS9 33 G4
Fairfield Gdns LOS SS9 33 F4
Fairfield Ri BCAYW CM12 8 C5
Fairfield Rd LOS SS9 33 F4
Fairland Cl RAYL SS6 19 H3
Fairlawn Gdns SOSN SS2 46 D1
Fairleigh Av PIT SS13 40 C1
Fairleigh Dr LOS SS9 45 E5
Fairleigh Rd PIT SS13 40 C1
Fairlight Rd SBF/HAD SS7 43 F3
Fairlop Av CVI SS8 55 H5
Fairlop Gdns BSDN SS14 3 J1
Fair Md BSDN SS14 26 D3
Fairmead RAYL SS6 19 E4
Fairmead Av SBF/HAD SS7 43 H1
WOS/PRIT SS0 46 B4
Fairview BCAYW CM12 8 D4 2
CVI SS8 55 G4
Fairview Av SLH/COR SS17 64 B3
Fairview Cha SLH/COR SS17 64 B4
Fairview Cl SBF/HAD SS7 29 H4
Fairview Crs SBF/HAD SS7 29 H4
Fairview Dr WOS/PRIT SS0 46 B2
Fairview Gdns LOS SS9 44 D4
Fairview Rd BSDN SS14 3 J2
Fairway WICKW SS12 16 D5
Fairway Gdns LOS SS9 44 D1
Fairway Gardens Cl LOS SS9 44 D1 1
The Fairway LOS SS9 44 D1
SBF/HAD SS7 29 H4
Falbro Crs SBF/HAD SS7 43 G3
Falbro Cresent SBF/HAD SS7 43 G2
Falcon Cl LOS SS9 45 F1
RAYL SS6 19 E5
Falcon Pk BSDN SS14 26 A3
Falcon Wy VGE SS16 3 G5
Falkenham End BSDN SS14 26 D4
Falkenham Ri BSDN SS14 26 D3
Falkenham Rw BSDN SS14 26 D4
Fallowfield SBN/FI SS3 49 G5
The Fallows CVI SS8 55 G3
Falstones LAIN SS15 25 G5
Fambridge Dr WICKW SS12 16 D2
Fane Rd SBF/HAD SS7 30 A3
Fanton Av WICKW SS12 17 E5
Fanton Cha WICKE SS11 17 F2
Fanton Gdns WICKE SS11 17 G2
Fanton Wk WICKE SS11 17 G1
Faraday Rd LOS SS9 32 D5
Farm Rd CVI SS8 56 A4
Farm Vw RAYL SS6 19 G3
Farm Wy SBF/HAD SS7 31 E5
Farnes Av WICKW SS12 16 B1 3
Farriers Dr BCAYW CM12 6 D5 6
Farriers Wy SOSN SS2 47 E1
Farringdon Service Rd SOS SS1 4 C4
Fastnet SOSN SS2 33 H4
Fauners VGE SS16 2 C4
Featherby Wy RCFD SS4 35 F2
Feeches Rd SOSN SS2 46 C1
Feering Dr BSDN SS14 39 G1
Feering Gn BSDN SS14 39 G1
Feering Rd BCAYE CM11 9 F3
Feering Rw BSDN SS14 39 G1 1
Felmores PIT SS13 27 H3
Felstead Cl SBF/HAD SS7 42 A2
Felstead Rd SBF/HAD SS7 42 A2
Felsted Rd BCAYE CM11 9 F3 5
Fenners Wy PIT SS13 27 H1 1
Fenton Wy LAIN SS15 24 C4
Fenwick Wy CVI SS8 55 H3
Fermoy Rd SOS SS1 61 H2
Fernbank BCAYW CM12 8 C4
Fernbrook Av SOS SS1 5 K3
Fern Cl BCAYW CM12 9 E1
Ferndale Cl LAIN SS15 25 E5 2
Ferndale Crs CVI SS8 70 A2
Ferndale Rd RAYL SS6 19 G2
SOSN SS2 47 H4
Fern Hl VGE SS16 37 F2
Fernlea Rd SBF/HAD SS7 42 B3
Fernleigh Dr LOS SS9 45 H5
Fernside Cl SLH/COR SS17 51 G4 1
Fern Wk VGE SS16 36 B2
Fernwood SBF/HAD SS7 43 H2
Ferrymead CVI SS8 55 G4
Ferry Rd SBF/HAD SS7 55 E1
Festival Link BSDN SS14 26 C3
Festival Wy BSDN SS14 26 C2
Fetherston Rd SLH/COR SS17 64 C2
The Fielders CVI SS8 69 G2
Fieldfare BCAYW CM12 9 F5
Fieldway PIT SS13 40 A2
WICKW SS12 16 C5
Fifth Av CVI SS8 55 F5
WICKE SS11 17 F2
Fillebrook Av LOS SS9 45 H4
Finches Cl SLH/COR SS17 51 H4
The Finches SBF/HAD SS7 30 D4
Finchfield RAYL SS6 31 G2 1
Finchingfield Wy WICKW SS12 16 B3 1
Finchley Rd WOS/PRIT SS0 59 F1
Firfield Rd SBF/HAD SS7 31 F5
The Firle VGE SS16 37 F3
Firmans VGE SS16 37 E3
First Av BCAYW CM12 12 B1
CVI SS8 69 E1
SLH/COR SS17 64 C1
WICKE SS11 17 F2
WOS/PRIT SS0 59 E1
The Firs CVI SS8 55 G4
Fitzroy Cl BCAYW CM12 8 D1
Fitzwarren SBN/FI SS3 49 G5
Fitzwilliam Rd SBF/HAD SS7 43 F4
Five Oaks SBF/HAD SS7 43 E2
Flamboro Cl LOS SS9 33 E5
Fleethall Rd RCFD SS4 35 F3
Fleet Rd SBF/HAD SS7 42 A4
Fleetwood Av WOS/PRIT SS0 46 B4
Flemings Farm Rd LOS SS9 33 E3
Flemming Av LOS SS9 45 E3
Flemming Crs LOS SS9 45 E3
Fletcher Dr WICKW SS12 16 C2
Fletchers VGE SS16 37 H2
Fletchers Sq SOSN SS2 47 F1
Flint Cl VGE SS16 36 C1 4
Florence Cl SBF/HAD SS7 43 G3
Florence Gdns SBF/HAD SS7 43 F3
Florence Rd CVI SS8 56 B5
Florence Wy VGE SS16 37 E1
Flower Cl SOS SS1 5 G3
Fobbing Rd SLH/COR SS17 51 H5
Fodderwick BSDN SS14 2 D2
Foksville Rd CVI SS8 70 B1
Folly Cha HOC/HUL SS5 20 C2
Folly La HOC/HUL SS5 20 C2
Fonteyn Cl LAIN SS15 25 F3
Ford Cl LAIN SS15 24 D5
Forest Gld VGE SS16 36 C2 3
Fore St LAIN SS15 25 H1
Forest View Dr LOS SS9 44 B3
Forfar Cl LOS SS9 44 C4
Fortescue Cha SOS SS1 48 C5
Fort William Rd SLH/COR SS17 38 C4
Fossetts Wy SOSN SS2 47 H3
Fostal Cl LOS SS9 45 F3
Foster Rd CVI SS8 56 B5
Fountain La HOC/HUL SS5 20 C3
Four Sisters Cl LOS SS9 45 G1 1
Four Sisters Wy LOS SS9 33 G5
Fourth Av SLH/COR SS17 50 D4
WICKE SS11 17 F2
Fowler Cl SOS SS1 5 G3
Fox Cl SBF/HAD SS7 30 C5
Foxfield Cl HOC/HUL SS5 21 H2 1
Foxfield Dr SLH/COR SS17 50 D4 2
The Foxgloves BCAYW CM12 8 C1 5
Foxhatch WICKW SS12 16 D2
Foxleigh BCAYW CM12 8 D5 1
Foxleigh Cl BCAYW CM12 8 D5
Foxmeadows SBF/HAD SS7 30 C5 2
Foxwood Pl LOS SS9 45 E4
Foys Wk BCAYE CM11 13 F1 2
Frampton Rd BSDN SS14 27 H2 3
Francis Wk RAYL SS6 31 F1
Franklins Wy WICKE SS11 10 D5 1
Fraser Cl LAIN SS15 24 B5
Freeman Ct SLH/COR SS17 65 E1
Fremantle SBN/FI SS3 62 C4
The Fremnells BSDN SS14 27 E4
Frerichs Cl WICKW SS12 16 C3
Freshwater Dr VGE SS16 39 G3
Frettons BSDN SS14 39 F1
Friars Cl LAIN SS15 25 F5 3
Friars St SBN/FI SS3 63 E2
Friern Gdns WICKW SS12 16 A1
Friern Pl WICKW SS12 16 A2
Friern Wk WICKW SS12 16 A1
Frithwood Cl BCAYW CM12 12 C1
Frithwood La BCAYW CM12 8 C5
Frobisher Wy SBN/FI SS3 49 H5
Froden Brook BCAYE CM11 13 F1
Froden Ct BCAYE CM11 13 F2 1
The Fryth BSDN SS14 27 F3
Fulford Dr LOS SS9 33 H5
Fulmar Wy WICKE SS11 17 F3
Fulton Rd SBF/HAD SS7 30 A4
Furlongs VGE SS16 3 J5
Furrowfelde VGE SS16 2 D6
Furtherwick Rd CVI SS8 56 A5
Furze Gld VGE SS16 37 E1 3
Fyefields PIT SS13 28 B3
Fyfield Av WICKW SS12 16 B3

G

The Gables PIT SS13 28 A3
SBF/HAD SS7 32 B4
Gafzelle Dr CVI SS8 70 D1
Gainsborough Av CVI SS8 70 D1
Gainsborough Cl BCAYW CM12 9 E4
Gainsborough Dr WOS/PRIT SS0 46 D3
Gains Cl CVI SS8 56 C5
Galleydene SBF/HAD SS7 43 F3
The Gallops VGE SS16 37 E1
Galton Rd WOS/PRIT SS0 59 E1
Gambleside VGE SS16 39 F3
Ganels Cl BCAYE CM11 13 F1 3
Ganels Rd BCAYE CM11 13 F1
Gardiners Cl BSDN SS14 27 E2
Gardiners La North BCAYE CM11 15 E3
Gardiners La South BSDN SS14 27 F1
Gardiners Link BSDN SS14 27 E1
Gardiners Wy BSDN SS14 27 E1
Gardner Av SLH/COR SS17 51 E4
Gascoigne Wy BCAYE CM11 9 G3 1
Gate Lodge Sq LAIN SS15 26 A1 2
Gate Lodge Wy LAIN SS15 26 A1
Gateway BSDN SS14 3 F2
Gatscombe Cl HOC/HUL SS5 21 E2 4
The Gattens RAYL SS6 20 A4
Gatwick Vw BCAYW CM12 9 E5
Gay Bowers BSDN SS14 27 E4
HOC/HUL SS5 20 C2
Gayleighs RAYL SS6 19 G4
Gaynesford VGE SS16 37 H2
Gayton Rd SOSN SS2 47 F4
Gaywood LAIN SS15 24 D4
The Geerings SLH/COR SS17 65 F1
Geesh Rd CVI SS8 56 B4 2
Genesta Rd WOS/PRIT SS0 59 F1
Genk Cl CVI SS8 56 A4
Gennep Rd CVI SS8 56 A4
Gentry Cl SLH/COR SS17 64 B2 1
George Cl CVI SS8 55 G3
George St SBN/FI SS3 63 F3
Gernons VGE SS16 2 B5
Geylen Rd CVI SS8 56 C5
Ghyllgrove BSDN SS14 26 C4
Ghyllgrove Cl BSDN SS14 26 C3
Gibcracks BSDN SS14 27 F5
Gideons Wy SLH/COR SS17 64 C1
Gifford Gn PIT SS13 40 A1 1
Gifford Rd SBF/HAD SS7 42 A1
Giffords Cross Av SLH/COR SS17 51 F5
Giffords Cross Rd SLH/COR SS17 65 F1
Gifhorn Rd CVI SS8 70 D1
Gilbert Cl RAYL SS6 32 A1
Gilbert Dr VGE SS16 36 D1
Gildborne Cl SLH/COR SS17 52 A4
Gills Av CVI SS8 56 B5
The Gill SBF/HAD SS7 43 G1
Gilman Dr SBN/FI SS3 62 B2
Gilmour Ri BCAYW CM12 8 C4
Gippeswyck BSDN SS14 26 D4
Gipson Park Cl LOS SS9 33 E5
The Glade VGE SS16 3 G6
Gladstone Gdns RAYL SS6 31 E2
Gladstone Rd HOC/HUL SS5 21 F3
Glanmire BCAYE CM11 7 G4
Glasseys La RAYL SS6 31 F3
Glastonbury Cha WOS/PRIT SS0 46 A1
Glebe BSDN SS14 26 D3
Glebe Cl RAYL SS6 19 F5
SOS SS1 61 F1
Glebe Dr RAYL SS6 19 F5
Glebelands SBF/HAD SS7 29 G4
Glebe Rd WICKE SS11 16 D1

Glebe Wy SBF/HAD SS7 44 A3
Glenbervie Dr LOS SS9 45 G4
Glencoe Dr WICKE SS11 11 F5 1
Glencree BCAYE CM11 7 G4
Glen Cft HOC/HUL SS5 21 G3
Glendale Gdns LOS SS9 45 E5
Gleneagles SBF/HAD SS7 41 G1
Gleneagles Rd LOS SS9 44 D1 2
Glenfield Rd SLH/COR SS17 51 G4 2
Glenhurst Rd SOSN SS2 47 F4
Glenmere VGE SS16 39 E4
Glenmere Park Av SBF/HAD SS7 43 E3
Glenmore St SOSN SS2 5 J2
Glenridding SBF/HAD SS7 42 A1 1
Glen Rd LOS SS9 58 D1
SBF/HAD SS7 42 B1
Glenside BCAYE CM11 9 G3
The Glen RAYL SS6 31 H3
SLH/COR SS17 65 E1
VGE SS16 39 H2
Glenwood Av HOC/HUL SS5 21 G3 1
LOS SS9 32 C4
WOS/PRIT SS0 46 C4
Glenwood Gdns VGE SS16 36 B2
Gleten Rd CVI SS8 56 C5
Gloucester Av RAYL SS6 32 B3
Gloucester Pl BCAYW CM12 6 D5
Gloucester Ter SOS SS1 61 G3
Glynde Wy SOSN SS2 48 C5
Goatsmoor La BCAYE CM11 7 H5
Gobions VGE SS16 2 C5
Goirle Av CVI SS8 56 B5
Goldcrest Dr BCAYE CM11 9 F4
Golden Cross Rd RCFD SS4 22 C2
Golden Manor Dr SBF/HAD SS7 42 C1
Goldfinch La SBF/HAD SS7 30 D4
Goldhanger Cl RAYL SS6 18 D5 4
Goldhanger Cross BSDN SS14 27 F4
Golding Crs SLH/COR SS17 64 D1
Goldings Crs VGE SS16 39 F3
Goldington Crs BCAYW CM12 6 C5
Goldmer Cl SBN/FI SS3 62 B1
Goldsmith Dr RAYL SS6 19 E1
Goldsmiths Av SLH/COR SS17 65 F1
Golf Ride SBF/HAD SS7 42 A3
Goodview Rd LAIN SS15 26 B1
Goodwood Cl SBF/HAD SS7 30 D4
Gordon Cl BCAYW CM12 8 C2
Gordon Pl SOS SS1 4 B4
Gordon Rd BSDN SS14 3 K3
LOS SS9 44 C4
SLH/COR SS17 65 E1
SOS SS1 4 B3
Gordons PIT SS13 39 H1 1
The Gore BSDN SS14 2 D1
Gosfield Cl RAYL SS6 18 D5 5
The Goslings SBN/FI SS3 63 F2
Gowan Brae SBF/HAD SS7 41 G1 1
Gowan Cl SBF/HAD SS7 41 G1
Goya Ri SBN/FI SS3 63 F1
Grafton Rd CVI SS8 70 B2
Graham Cl BCAYW CM12 7 E5
HOC/HUL SS5 21 F1
SLH/COR SS17 50 C5
Grainger Cl SOSN SS2 47 F4 2
Grainger Rd SOSN SS2 4 D1
Grand Dr LOS SS9 58 C1
Grand Pde LOS SS9 58 C1
Grandview Rd SBF/HAD SS7 30 C4
Grange Av LOS SS9 44 B1
WICKW SS12 16 A2
Grange Cl LOS SS9 45 F3
Grange Gdns RAYL SS6 19 E5
SOS SS1 4 E4
Grange Park Dr LOS SS9 45 G4
Grange Rd BCAYE CM11 13 F1
LOS SS9 45 E5
PIT SS13 28 D3
SBF/HAD SS7 30 B3
WICKE SS11 10 B3
Grangeway SBF/HAD SS7 30 D5 1
Granites Cha BCAYE CM11 14 A2
Grant Cl WICKW SS12 16 D3 7
Granville Cl BCAYW CM12 6 C5 5
SBF/HAD SS7 42 B2
Grapnells VGE SS16 39 G2
Grasmead Av LOS SS9 45 G4
Grasmere Rd CVI SS8 69 F1
SBF/HAD SS7 30 B5
Gratmore Gn VGE SS16 39 F3
Gravel Rd LOS SS9 32 C3
Grays Av VGE SS16 37 F5
Graysons Cl RAYL SS6 31 H1
Great Berry Farm Cha
VGE SS16 36 D2 2
Great Berry La VGE SS16 36 D2
Great Burches Rd SBF/HAD SS7 30 D4
Great Eastern Rd HOC/HUL SS5 21 F3
Great Hays LOS SS9 44 D1
Greathouse Cha SLH/COR SS17 51 H3
Great Knightleys LAIN SS15 2 A2
Great Leighs Wy PIT SS13 28 B2 4
Great Mistley VGE SS16 3 H3
Great Oaks BSDN SS14 2 D2
Great Ranton PIT SS13 28 B3
Great Saling WICKE SS11 17 F2 1
Great Spenders BSDN SS14 27 E3
Great Wheatley Rd RAYL SS6 30 D2
Greenacre La ING CM4 7 H2
Greenacre Ms LOS SS9 45 F4
Greenacres SBF/HAD SS7 43 H3
Green Av CVI SS8 69 F1
Greenbanks LOS SS9 45 H4
Greendyke CVI SS8 55 G4 2
Greenfields BCAYW CM12 8 D5
Greenfields Cl BCAYW CM12 8 C5
Greenlands RCFD SS4 22 C4
Green La BCAYW CM12 12 D5
CVI SS8 69 G1
LOS SS9 33 E4
VGE SS16 37 G2
Greenleas SBF/HAD SS7 31 E5
Greenoaks SBF/HAD SS7 42 B3
Green Rd SBF/HAD SS7 42 A5
Greens Farm La BCAYE CM11 9 F4
Greensted Cl BSDN SS14 39 G1
The Greensted BSDN SS14 39 G1
Greensward La HOC/HUL SS5 21 G2
The Green LOS SS9 33 F4
SLH/COR SS17 64 C3 1
Greenway BCAYE CM11 9 G4
Greenways CVI SS8 55 G4 3
RCFD SS4 35 E1
SBF/HAD SS7 41 G4
SOS SS1 61 F2
The Greenway WICKE SS11 10 B2
Greenwood Av SBF/HAD SS7 42 A5
Gregory Cl HOC/HUL SS5 21 G4 2
Greyhound Wy SOSN SS2 4 D1
Griffin Av CVI SS8 56 B4
Grimston Rd BSDN SS14 27 G2
Grosvenor Gdns BCAYW CM12 8 D1
Grosvenor Ms WOS/PRIT SS0 59 F2
Grosvenor Rd RAYL SS6 19 E4 2
SBF/HAD SS7 42 B5
WOS/PRIT SS0 59 F2
Grove Av VGE SS16 37 E3
Grove Cl RAYL SS6 32 A1
Grove Ct RAYL SS6 32 B2
Grove Hl LOS SS9 32 C4
Grovelands Rd WICKW SS12 16 C2
Grove Rd BCAYW CM12 8 C3
CVI SS8 56 B5
RAYL SS6 32 A1
SBF/HAD SS7 42 A4
SLH/COR SS17 64 C4
Grover St SOS SS1 4 D4
The Grove BCAYE CM11 7 F5
SOSN SS2 47 G4
Grove Wk SBN/FI SS3 62 D2 1
Grovewood Av LOS SS9 32 C4
Grovewood Cl LOS SS9 32 C4
Guernsey Gdns WICKE SS11 10 B4
Guildford Rd SOSN SS2 4 D2
Gun Hill Pl VGE SS16 3 F4
Gunners Rd SBN/FI SS3 63 F2
Gustedhall La HOC/HUL SS5 33 F1
Gwendalen Av CVI SS8 56 C5

H

Haarlem Rd CVI SS8 55 E5
Haarle Rd CVI SS8 70 C2 3
Haase Cl CVI SS8 55 H3
Hackamore SBF/HAD SS7 43 E1
Haddon Cl RAYL SS6 18 D5
Hadfield Rd SLH/COR SS17 64 C3
Hadleigh Park Av SBF/HAD SS7 43 F3
Hadleigh Rd LOS SS9 44 D5
WOS/PRIT SS0 59 H2
Hainault Av RCFD SS4 22 B4
WOS/PRIT SS0 46 C4
Hainault Cl SBF/HAD SS7 43 H2
Hallam Ct BCAYW CM12 8 C1 6
Hall Cl SLH/COR SS17 50 D5
Hall Crs SBF/HAD SS7 43 G3
Hallet Rd CVI SS8 70 D1
Hall Farm Cl SBF/HAD SS7 42 A5
Hall Farm Rd SBF/HAD SS7 42 A4
Hall Park Av WOS/PRIT SS0 59 E1
Hall Rd HOC/HUL SS5 33 H1
RCFD SS4 34 C2
Halstead Ct WICKW SS12 16 B3 2
Halstow Wy PIT SS13 40 B1
Hamboro Gdns LOS SS9 44 C5
Hambro' Av RAYL SS6 19 G4
Hambro Cl RAYL SS6 19 H4
Hambro Hl RAYL SS6 19 H3
Hamilton Cl LOS SS9 44 B4
Hamilton Gdns HOC/HUL SS5 21 F1
Hamilton Ms RAYL SS6 20 A5
Hamlet Court Ms
WOS/PRIT SS0 46 D5 4
Hamlet Court Rd WOS/PRIT SS0 59 G1
Hamlet Rd WOS/PRIT SS0 4 A5
Hamley Cl SBF/HAD SS7 29 G5
Hammonds La BCAYE CM11 13 F1 4
Hampstead Gdns HOC/HUL SS5 21 G1
Hampton Cl SOSN SS2 46 D2
Hampton Ct HOC/HUL SS5 21 E2 5
Hampton Gdns SOSN SS2 46 D2
Hamstel Rd SOSN SS2 48 A3
Handel Rd CVI SS8 70 C2
Handleys Cha LAIN SS15 26 A1
Hannah Cl CVI SS8 55 H3 4
Hannett Rd CVI SS8 70 D1
Hanningfield Cl RAYL SS6 18 D5 6
Hanover Cl BSDN SS14 39 F1 1
Hanover Dr BSDN SS14 39 F1
Hanover Ms HOC/HUL SS5 21 E2 6
Harberts Wy RAYL SS6 19 F3
Harcourt Av SOSN SS2 4 A1
Hardie Rd SLH/COR SS17 64 C2
Harding's Elms Rd BCAYE CM11 14 C4
Hardwick Cl RAYL SS6 31 G2
Hardys Wy CVI SS8 55 H3
Harebell Cl BCAYW CM12 8 C1
Hares Cha BCAYW CM12 8 C2
Haresland Cl SBF/HAD SS7 44 A1
Harewood Av RCFD SS4 22 B3
Harlech Rd PIT SS13 40 A1
Harley St LOS SS9 44 D5
Harold Gdns WICKE SS11 10 C4
Haron Cl CVI SS8 70 A1
Harper Wy RAYL SS6 19 F5 2
Harridge Cl LOS SS9 45 F3
Harridge Rd LOS SS9 45 F3
Harris Cl SLH/COR SS17 51 G5
WICKW SS12 17 E3
Harrods Ct BCAYE CM11 9 H3 1
Harrogate Rd HOC/HUL SS5 21 G1
Harrow Cl HOC/HUL SS5 21 H3
Harrow Gdns HOC/HUL SS5 21 H3
Harrow Rd CVI SS8 56 A4
WICKW SS12 29 F1
Hart Cl SBF/HAD SS7 30 D5
Hartford Cl RAYL SS6 18 D4
Hartford End PIT SS13 39 H1
Hartington Pl SOS SS1 5 F6
Hartington Rd SOS SS1 4 E5
Hartland Cl LOS SS9 33 E4
Hart Rd SBF/HAD SS7 30 C5
Harvest Rd CVI SS8 56 A4
Harvey Rd PIT SS13 28 A1
Haskins SLH/COR SS17 65 E2 1
Haslemere Rd WICKE SS11 10 B3
Hassell Rd CVI SS8 70 C1
Hassenbrook Rd SLH/COR SS17 64 C2
Hastings Rd SOS SS1 5 F4
The Hastings WICKE SS11 10 C4
Hatches Farm Rd BCAYW CM12 12 A3
Hatfield Dr BCAYE CM11 9 G3 2
Hatfield Rd RAYL SS6 19 E5
The Hatherley BSDN SS14 27 E4
Hatley Gdns SBF/HAD SS7 41 H1
Hatterill LAIN SS15 37 F1
Havana Dr RAYL SS6 19 E2
Haven Cl CVI SS8 69 E1
VGE SS16 39 F3
Havengore PIT SS13 28 B3
Haven Ri BCAYE CM11 13 G2
Haven Rd CVI SS8 69 E2
Havenside SBN/FI SS3 49 H1
Havis Rd SLH/COR SS17 50 D5
Hawkbush Gn PIT SS13 28 A2 1
Hawkesbury Bush La VGE SS16 38 B4
Hawkesbury Cl CVI SS8 69 F2
Hawkesbury Rd CVI SS8 69 F1
Hawk Hl WICKE SS11 11 H2
Hawkins Cl WICKE SS11 17 E1 1
Hawkridge SBN/FI SS3 62 B1
Hawks La HOC/HUL SS5 21 F3
Hawksway VGE SS16 3 F6
Hawkwell Cha HOC/HUL SS5 21 F4
Hawkwell Park Dr HOC/HUL SS5 21 G3
Hawkwell Rd HOC/HUL SS5 21 F2
Hawthorn Cl HOC/HUL SS5 21 G3 2
Hawthorne Gdns HOC/HUL SS5 20 C3
Hawthorne Rd SLH/COR SS17 51 E5
Hawthorn Rd CVI SS8 70 B1
Hawthorns LOS SS9 45 F2
SBF/HAD SS7 41 H2 2
The Hawthorns SLH/COR SS17 51
Hawthorn Wy RAYL SS6 32 A3
Hawtree Cl SOS SS1 5
Hayes Barton SOS SS1 62
Hayes La CVI SS8 69
Hazel Cl LAIN SS15 26
LOS SS9 44
SBF/HAD SS7 44
Hazelmere PIT SS13 39
Hazelwood HOC/HUL SS5 21
SBF/HAD SS7 29 G4
Hazelwood Gv LOS SS9 45
Hazlemere Rd SBF/HAD SS7 42
Headcorn Cl PIT SS13 40
Headley Rd BCAYE CM11 9
Hearsall Av SLH/COR SS17 64
Heath Cl BCAYW CM12 8
Heather Bank BCAYE CM11 9 F3
Heathercroft Rd WICKE SS11 17 F2
Heather Dr SBF/HAD SS7 44
Heathfield SBF/HAD SS7 31
Heathleigh Dr VGE SS16 37
Heath Rd BCAYE CM11 9
Hedgehope Av RAYL SS6 19
Hedge La SBF/HAD SS7 43
Heeswyk Rd CVI SS8 56 C4
Heideburg Rd CVI SS8 56
Heilsburg Rd CVI SS8 56
Helden Av CVI SS8 56
Helena Cl HOC/HUL SS5 21
Helena Rd RAYL SS6 31
Hellendoorn Rd CVI SS8 70
Helmores LAIN SS15 24
Helmsdale CVI SS8 55 G4
Helpeston BSDN SS14 3
Hemmells LAIN SS15 25
Henderson Gdns WICKW SS12 16
Hendon Cl WICKW SS12 16
Hengist Gdns WICKE SS11 10
Henham Cl BCAYE CM11 9 G3
Henley Crs WOS/PRIT SS0 46
Henry Dr LOS SS9 44
Henson Av CVI SS8 70
Herbert Gv SOS SS1 4
Herbert Rd CVI SS8 56 B5
SBN/FI SS3 62
Herd La SLH/COR SS17 51
Hereward Gdns WICKE SS11 10
Heritage Wy RCFD SS4 34
Hermes Wy SBN/FI SS3 63
Hermitage Av SBF/HAD SS7 42
Hermitage Cl SBF/HAD SS7 42
Hermitage Dr LAIN SS15 25
Hermitage Rd WOS/PRIT SS0 59
Hernen Rd CVI SS8 56
Heron Av WICKE SS11 17
Heron Cl RAYL SS6 31
Heron Dl BSDN SS14 3
Heron Gdns RAYL SS6 19
Herongate SBF/HAD SS7 41
SBN/FI SS3 62
Herschell Rd LOS SS9 44
Hertford Dr SLH/COR SS17 38
Hertford Rd CVI SS8 69
Hetzand Rd CVI SS8 71
Hever Cl HOC/HUL SS5 21
Heybridge Dr WICKW SS12 16
Heycroft Rd HOC/HUL SS5 21
LOS SS9 33
Heygate Av SOS SS1 4
Hickling Cl LOS SS9 32
Hickstars La BCAYE CM11 13 F1
Highams Rd HOC/HUL SS5 21
High Bank VGE SS16 36 C2
Highbank Cl LOS SS9 45
High Beeches SBF/HAD SS7 41
Highcliff Crs RCFD SS4 22
High Cliff Dr LOS SS9 58
Highcliffe Cl WICKE SS11 11 E5
Highcliffe Rd WICKE SS11 17
Highcliffe Wy WICKE SS11 17
Highcliff Rd SBF/HAD SS7 42
High Cloister BCAYE CM11 9 E3
Highfield Ap BCAYE CM11 9 G5
Highfield Av SBF/HAD SS7 43
Highfield Cl WOS/PRIT SS0 46 C4
Highfield Crs RAYL SS6 31
WOS/PRIT SS0 46
Highfield Dr WOS/PRIT SS0 46 C4
Highfield Gdns WOS/PRIT SS0 46
Highfield Gv WOS/PRIT SS0 46
Highfield Rd BCAYE CM11 13
Highfield Wy WOS/PRIT SS0 46
Highland Gv BCAYE CM11 9
Highland Rd SLH/COR SS17 38 C5
Highlands Av VGE SS16 3
Highlands Bvd LOS SS9 44
Highlands Crs PIT SS13 29

ghlands Rd PIT SS13 .... 29 E5
gh Md HOC/HUL SS5 .... 21 F3
ghmead RAYL SS6 .... 31 E1
gh Meadow BCAYE CM11 .... 9 F3 7
gh Oaks VGE SS16 .... 37 E3
gh Rd HOC/HUL SS5 .... 20 B3
LAIN SS15 .... 25 E3
RAYL SS6 .... 31 F3
SBF/HAD SS7 .... 41 G1
SLH/COR SS17 .... 38 D5
VGE SS16 .... 37 E3
gh Rd North LAIN SS15 .... 25 F2
gh St BCAYW CM12 .... 8 D3
CVI SS8 .... 56 B5
LOS SS9 .... 57 H1
RAYL SS6 .... 31 F2
SBF/HAD SS7 .... 42 A5
SBF/HAD SS7 .... 43 G3
SBN/FI SS3 .... 63 F2
SLH/COR SS17 .... 64 C3
SOS SS1 .... 4 C4
WICKW SS12 .... 16 C1
ghview Av VGE SS16 .... 36 B2
gh View Ri BCAYE CM11 .... 14 D3
ghview Rd SBF/HAD SS7 .... 30 D4
ghwood Cl LOS SS9 .... 45 G2
lary Cl RCFD SS4 .... 22 D3
lary Crs RAYL SS6 .... 31 H1
lbery Rd CVI SS8 .... 70 B1
ldaville Dr WOS/PRIT SS0 .... 46 B4
llary Mt BCAYW CM12 .... 8 C4
ll Av WICKE SS11 .... 17 E1
llborough Rd WOS/PRIT SS0 .... 46 C3
ll Cl SBF/HAD SS7 .... 42 B2
llcrest Rd HOC/HUL SS5 .... 21 F3
SOS SS1 .... 4 E4
llcrest Vw VGE SS16 .... 39 E3
llhouse Cl BCAYW CM12 .... 9 E1
llhouse Dr BCAYW CM12 .... 9 E1
ll La HOC/HUL SS5 .... 21 G3
ll Rd SBF/HAD SS7 .... 42 B3
SOSN SS2 .... 47 E3
llside Av HOC/HUL SS5 .... 21 F3
llside Cl BCAYE CM11 .... 9 E4 1
llside Crs LOS SS9 .... 58 D1 1
llside Rd BCAYW CM12 .... 9 E4
HOC/HUL SS5 .... 20 C3
LOS SS9 .... 32 D3
SBF/HAD SS7 .... 42 A5
ll Ter SLH/COR SS17 .... 51 H4
ll Top Av SBF/HAD SS7 .... 42 C4
lltop Cl RAYL SS6 .... 31 F2
ll Top Ri VGE SS16 .... 36 C2
llview Gdns SLH/COR SS17 .... 51 E4 4
llview Rd RAYL SS6 .... 31 F1
llway BCAYE CM11 .... 9 G3
WOS/PRIT SS0 .... 58 D1
llwood Gv WICKW SS12 .... 16 D1
lton Rd CVI SS8 .... 55 H4
lton Wk CVI SS8 .... 55 H4
lversum Wy CVI SS8 .... 56 A4 3
ndles Rd CVI SS8 .... 56 C5
nguar St SBN/FI SS3 .... 63 E3
obhouse Rd SLH/COR SS17 .... 50 C5 2
obleythick La WOS/PRIT SS0 .... 46 C3
ockley Cl BSDN SS14 .... 3 J1
ockley Gn BSDN SS14 .... 27 F5
ockley Ri HOC/HUL SS5 .... 21 F3
ockley Rd BSDN SS14 .... 3 K1
RAYL SS6 .... 19 H5
odgson Ct WICKW SS12 .... 17 F3
odgson Wy WICKW SS12 .... 17 E2
e Hoe BCAYW CM12 .... 13 E4
ogarth Dr SBN/FI SS3 .... 63 F1
ogarth Wy RCFD SS4 .... 22 B2
olbech Rd BSDN SS14 .... 27 G3
olbek Rd CVI SS8 .... 70 D1
olbrook Cl BCAYE CM11 .... 9 G3 4
olden Gdns BSDN SS14 .... 27 G2
olden Rd BSDN SS14 .... 27 F2
olgate PIT SS13 .... 28 B3
olland Av CVI SS8 .... 55 E4
olland Rd WOS/PRIT SS0 .... 59 G2
ollands Wk VGE SS16 .... 39 E4
e Hollies SLH/COR SS17 .... 64 B3 2
ollyford BCAYE CM11 .... 7 F5
olly Gv VGE SS16 .... 36 C1
ollymead SLH/COR SS17 .... 50 D5
ollytree Gdns RAYL SS6 .... 31 E3
olme Wk WICKW SS12 .... 17 E3
olmsdale Cl WOS/PRIT SS0 .... 46 A3
olmswood CVI SS8 .... 56 D4 1
olst Av LAIN SS15 .... 25 F3
olst Cl SLH/COR SS17 .... 64 B1
olt Farm Wy RCFD SS4 .... 22 C4
olton Rd CVI SS8 .... 71 E1
RAYL SS6 .... 32 B2 2
oltynge SBF/HAD SS7 .... 41 H2

Holyoak La HOC/HUL SS5 .... 21 F4
Holyrood Dr WOS/PRIT SS0 .... 46 A4
Homefield Cl BCAYE CM11 .... 13 G2 3
Homefields Av SBF/HAD SS7 .... 41 G1
Home Md LAIN SS15 .... 25 E3
Home Mdw BCAYW CM12 .... 8 D3 1
Homestead Dr VGE SS16 .... 37 F4
Homestead Gdns SBF/HAD SS7 .... 43 G3
Homestead Rd PIT SS13 .... 28 D4
SBF/HAD SS7 .... 43 G4 1
Homestead Wy SBF/HAD SS7 .... 43 G4
Honeypot La BSDN SS14 .... 3 F1
ING CM4 .... 7 F1
Honiley Av WICKW SS12 .... 28 D1
Honington Cl WICKE SS11 .... 17 G2 2
Honiton Rd SOS SS1 .... 5 G4
Honywood Rd BSDN SS14 .... 15 G5
Hood Cl WICKW SS12 .... 16 D2
Hooley Dr RAYL SS6 .... 19 F2
Hoover Dr LAIN SS15 .... 24 C5
Hope Av SLH/COR SS17 .... 50 D4
Hope Rd BCAYE CM11 .... 14 D3
CVI SS8 .... 70 C1
SBF/HAD SS7 .... 41 H5
Horace Rd BCAYE CM11 .... 9 E1
SOS SS1 .... 4 E5
Horkesley Wy WICKW SS12 .... 16 D2 4
Hornbeams SBF/HAD SS7 .... 29 G3
Hornbeam Wy LAIN SS15 .... 25 G2
Hornby Av WOS/PRIT SS0 .... 46 B1
Hornby Cl WOS/PRIT SS0 .... 46 C1
Hornchurch Cl WICKE SS11 .... 17 F2 3
Hornsby Sq LAIN SS15 .... 24 B4
Hornsby Wy LAIN SS15 .... 24 C4
Hornsland Rd CVI SS8 .... 70 D1
Horseshoe Cl BCAYW CM12 .... 6 D5
Horsley Cross BSDN SS14 .... 26 C4
Hospital Rd SBN/FI SS3 .... 63 E3
Hovefields Av PIT SS13 .... 28 C1
WICKW SS12 .... 16 C5
Hovefields Dr WICKW SS12 .... 16 C5
Howard Cha BSDN SS14 .... 26 A3
Howard Crs PIT SS13 .... 40 B1
Howard Pl CVI SS8 .... 70 A2 2
Howards Cha WOS/PRIT SS0 .... 46 D4
Howell Rd SLH/COR SS17 .... 51 E3
Hudson Crs LOS SS9 .... 33 F5
Hudson Rd LOS SS9 .... 33 E5
Hudsons Cl SLH/COR SS17 .... 64 C1 1
Hudson Wy CVI SS8 .... 55 H3
Humber Cl RAYL SS6 .... 31 F2
Hunter Dr WICKW SS12 .... 16 D3
Hunters Av BCAYW CM12 .... 13 E1
Huntingdon Rd SOS SS1 .... 5 K4
Hunts Md BCAYW CM12 .... 8 C4
Hurlock Rd BCAYE CM11 .... 9 E3 2
Hurricane Cl WICKE SS11 .... 17 G3
Hurricane Wy WICKE SS11 .... 17 F3
Hurst Wy LOS SS9 .... 45 G2
The Hyde VGE SS16 .... 37 F2
Hydeway SBF/HAD SS7 .... 42 C1
Hyde Wy WICKW SS12 .... 16 C2
Hyde Wood La RCFD SS4 .... 23 E1
The Hylands HOC/HUL SS5 .... 21 E3

I

Ian Rd BCAYW CM12 .... 8 C1
Ilfracombe Av PIT SS13 .... 40 C1
SOS SS1 .... 5 J3
Ilfracombe Rd SOSN SS2 .... 5 H2
Ilgars Rd WICKE SS11 .... 10 D4
Ilmington Dr PIT SS13 .... 27 H2
Imperial Av WOS/PRIT SS0 .... 46 A5
Ingatestone Rd ING CM4 .... 6 C1
Ingaway VGE SS16 .... 2 A4
Inglefield Rd SLH/COR SS17 .... 51 G1
Ingrave Cl WICKW SS12 .... 16 D2 5
Innes Cl WICKW SS12 .... 16 C3
Inverness Av WOS/PRIT SS0 .... 46 C4
Invicta Ct BCAYW CM12 .... 8 B1
Iona Wy WICKW SS12 .... 17 E3
Ipswich Ms VGE SS16 .... 36 C1 5
Ironwell La HOC/HUL SS5 .... 21 H5
RCFD SS4 .... 34 C1
Irvine Pl WICKW SS12 .... 17 E3 4
Irvine Wy BCAYW CM12 .... 8 D4 3
Irvington Cl LOS SS9 .... 45 E2
Irvon Hill Rd WICKW SS12 .... 16 B1
Irye Md VGE SS16 .... 37 F2
Ivy Rd SBF/HAD SS7 .... 29 F5

J

Jackdaw Cl BCAYE CM11 .... 9 F5
SBN/FI SS3 .... 62 D1
Jacks Cl WICKE SS11 .... 17 E1
Jacksons La BCAYE CM11 .... 9 E2
Jacksons Ms BCAYE CM11 .... 9 F3 8
Jacqueline Gdns BCAYW CM12 .... 9 E1
Janette Av CVI SS8 .... 69 F1
Jardine Rd PIT SS13 .... 28 B3
Jarvis Rd CVI SS8 .... 55 H3
SBF/HAD SS7 .... 42 B2
Jasmine Cl VGE SS16 .... 36 C2
Jason Cl CVI SS8 .... 56 A4
Jefferson Av LAIN SS15 .... 24 D5
Jena Cl SBN/FI SS3 .... 62 D2
Jermayns LAIN SS15 .... 25 H5
Jersey Gdns WICKE SS11 .... 10 C5
Jesmond Rd CVI SS8 .... 70 A2
Johnson Cl RCFD SS4 .... 22 C3
WICKW SS12 .... 16 C3 2
Johnstone Rd SOS SS1 .... 61 H2
John St SBN/FI SS3 .... 63 F3
Jones Cl SOSN SS2 .... 46 D3
Josselin Ct PIT SS13 .... 28 B1 1
Josselin Rd PIT SS13 .... 28 B1
Jotmans La SBF/HAD SS7 .... 41 F3
Journeymans Wy SOSN SS2 .... 47 F1
Jubilee Cl HOC/HUL SS5 .... 21 F3
Jubilee Dr WICKW SS12 .... 10 B5
Jubilee Rd BCAYE CM11 .... 14 C4
RAYL SS6 .... 31 H1
Juliers Cl CVI SS8 .... 70 C1
Juliers Rd CVI SS8 .... 70 C1
Junction Rd VGE SS16 .... 40 A2
Juniper Cl BCAYE CM11 .... 9 F1
Juniper Rd LOS SS9 .... 45 G2

K

Kale Rd SBF/HAD SS7 .... 42 B2
Kamerwyk Av CVI SS8 .... 56 B5
Karen Cl SBF/HAD SS7 .... 55 E1
SLH/COR SS17 .... 64 B3 3
WICKW SS12 .... 16 B2
Katherine Cl RAYL SS6 .... 32 B2
Katherine Rd PIT SS13 .... 28 D4
Kathleen Cl SLH/COR SS17 .... 50 C5
Kathleen Dr LOS SS9 .... 45 G4
Kathleen Ferrier Crs LAIN SS15 .... 25 F3
Keats Wy WICKW SS12 .... 16 B1
Keegan Pl CVI SS8 .... 56 B5 3
Keer Av CVI SS8 .... 70 C2
Keighley Ms SBN/FI SS3 .... 49 G4
Keith Av WICKE SS11 .... 10 C4
Keith Wy SOSN SS2 .... 46 D1
Kellington Rd CVI SS8 .... 56 B4 3
Kelly Rd PIT SS13 .... 28 D5
Kelvedon Cl RAYL SS6 .... 18 D5 7
Kelvedon Rd BCAYE CM11 .... 9 F3 9
Kelvin Rd SBF/HAD SS7 .... 30 A4
Kelvinside SLH/COR SS17 .... 50 D4
Kembles RAYL SS6 .... 19 H3
Kempton Cl SBF/HAD SS7 .... 31 E3
Kendal Cl RAYL SS6 .... 31 H1
Kendal Ct WICKE SS11 .... 17 F3
Kendal Wy LOS SS9 .... 33 F4
Kenholme LOS SS9 .... 45 F2
Kenilworth Cl BCAYW CM12 .... 8 B3 1
Kenilworth Gdns RAYL SS6 .... 19 F5
WOS/PRIT SS0 .... 45 H3
Kenilworth Pl LAIN SS15 .... 25 H2 2
Kenley Cl WICKE SS11 .... 17 F2
Kenmore Cl CVI SS8 .... 70 D2 1
Kennedy Av LAIN SS15 .... 24 C5
Kennedy Cl RAYL SS6 .... 32 B3
SBF/HAD SS7 .... 29 G4
Kennel La BCAYW CM12 .... 13 E1
Kenneth Gdns SLH/COR SS17 .... 51 E4 5
Kenneth Rd PIT SS13 .... 28 B4
SBF/HAD SS7 .... 42 C1
Kennington Av SBF/HAD SS7 .... 41 H1
Kensington Gdns BCAYW CM12 .... 8 D1 2
Kensington Rd SOS SS1 .... 5 J5
Kent Av CVI SS8 .... 56 A4 4
LOS SS9 .... 45 G4
Kent Cl LAIN SS15 .... 25 E5
Kent Elms Cl SOSN SS2 .... 45 G1
Kent Green Cl HOC/HUL SS5 .... 21 G3
Kenton Wy VGE SS16 .... 36 C1
Kents Hill Rd SBF/HAD SS7 .... 42 A3
Kents Hill Rd North SBF/HAD SS7 .... 42 A1
Kent View Av LOS SS9 .... 58 D1
Kent View Rd VGE SS16 .... 39 G1
Kent Wy RAYL SS6 .... 32 B3
Kenway SOSN SS2 .... 47 F4
Kenwood Rd SLH/COR SS17 .... 51 G5
Kersbrooke Wy SLH/COR SS17 .... 51 G4
Kershaws Cl WICKW SS12 .... 16 B3
Kestrel Gv RAYL SS6 .... 19 E5
Keswick Cl RAYL SS6 .... 31 H1 2
Keswick Rd SBF/HAD SS7 .... 30 B5
Kevin Cl BCAYE CM11 .... 13 G1
Keyes Cl SBN/FI SS3 .... 49 H5
Keysland SBF/HAD SS7 .... 31 E4
Kibcaps VGE SS16 .... 2 A5
Kiln Rd SBF/HAD SS7 .... 42 D2
Kilnwood Av HOC/HUL SS5 .... 21 E3
Kilowan Cl VGE SS16 .... 36 C2
Kilworth Av SOS SS1 .... 5 F4
Kimberley Rd SBF/HAD SS7 .... 41 H3
Kimberly Dr LAIN SS15 .... 26 A1
King Edward Rd LAIN SS15 .... 25 E3
King Edward's Rd SLH/COR SS17 .... 64 C4
Kingfisher Cl SBN/FI SS3 .... 49 H5
Kingfisher Crs RAYL SS6 .... 19 E5 3
Kingfisher Dr SBF/HAD SS7 .... 41 H4
Kingfishers VGE SS16 .... 3 G5
King George's Cl RAYL SS6 .... 31 G2
King Henry's Dr RCFD SS4 .... 35 E4
Kingley Cl WICKW SS12 .... 16 A1
Kingley Dr WICKW SS12 .... 16 A1
Kings Cl CVI SS8 .... 68 D1
RAYL SS6 .... 31 H1
Kings Crs LAIN SS15 .... 25 E2
Kingsdown Cl PIT SS13 .... 28 B5
Kings Farm RAYL SS6 .... 19 H3
Kingshawes SBF/HAD SS7 .... 31 E5
Kingsley Crs SBF/HAD SS7 .... 31 E3
Kingsley La SBF/HAD SS7 .... 31 E3
Kingsman Rd SLH/COR SS17 .... 64 A3
Kingsmere SBF/HAD SS7 .... 43 F1
Kings Pk SBF/HAD SS7 .... 42 C1
Kings Rd CVI SS8 .... 68 D1
LAIN SS15 .... 25 E2
RAYL SS6 .... 31 H1
SBF/HAD SS7 .... 42 B4
WOS/PRIT SS0 .... 46 A5
Kingsteignton SBN/FI SS3 .... 49 F5
Kingston Av SBN/FI SS3 .... 49 H4
Kingston Hl VGE SS16 .... 37 G4
Kingston Wy SBF/HAD SS7 .... 42 B1
King St SLH/COR SS17 .... 64 B3
Kings Wy BCAYE CM11 .... 13 G2
Kingsway WOS/PRIT SS0 .... 45 H4
Kingsway Ms WOS/PRIT SS0 .... 46 A4 1
Kingswood Cha LOS SS9 .... 45 E3
Kingswood Cl BCAYE CM11 .... 9 F2
Kingswood Crs RAYL SS6 .... 31 E2
Kingswood Rd VGE SS16 .... 3 G4
Kirby Rd BSDN SS14 .... 27 F5
Kitkatts Rd CVI SS8 .... 69 H1
The Knares VGE SS16 .... 37 H2 2
Knightbridge Wk BCAYW CM12 .... 8 D2
Knights LAIN SS15 .... 25 G4
Knightswick Rd CVI SS8 .... 56 A5
Knivet Cl RAYL SS6 .... 31 H2
Knollcroft SBN/FI SS3 .... 62 C4
The Knoll BCAYW CM12 .... 9 E1
RAYL SS6 .... 31 G1 1
The Knowle VGE SS16 .... 3 H5
Knox Ct WICKW SS12 .... 17 E3 5
Kolburg Rd CVI SS8 .... 70 C2 4
Kollum Rd CVI SS8 .... 71 E1
Koln Cl CVI SS8 .... 68 D1
Komberg Crs CVI SS8 .... 56 B4
Konnybrook SBF/HAD SS7 .... 42 D2
Korndyk Av CVI SS8 .... 56 B5
Kursaal Wy SOS SS1 .... 5 G5
Kynoch Ct SLH/COR SS17 .... 64 D3

L

Laars Av CVI SS8 .... 56 B5
Laburnum Av WICKW SS12 .... 16 B2
Laburnum Cl HOC/HUL SS5 .... 20 D2 4
WICKW SS12 .... 16 B1 4
Laburnum Dr SLH/COR SS17 .... 65 F1
Laburnum Gv CVI SS8 .... 69 E1
HOC/HUL SS5 .... 20 C3
Laburnum Wy RAYL SS6 .... 19 E2 1
Labworth Rd CVI SS8 .... 70 B2
Ladram Cl SOS SS1 .... 62 B1
Ladram Rd SOS SS1 .... 62 A1
Ladram Wy SOS SS1 .... 62 A1
Ladysmith Wy LAIN SS15 .... 26 A2 1
Laindon Common Rd
BCAYW CM12 .... 12 C3
Laindon Link LAIN SS15 .... 25 F5
Laindon Rd BCAYW CM12 .... 8 D5

Laindon West LAIN SS15 24 B5 1
Lake Av BCAYW CM12 8 D2
Lake Dr SBF/HAD SS7 42 B1
Lakeside RAYL SS6 19 G4 2
Lakeside Crs CVI SS8 56 C4 5
Lakeview CVI SS8 55 H4
Lake Vw VGE SS16 36 C2
Lambeth Ms HOC/HUL SS5 20 D2 5
Lambeth Rd LOS SS9 33 F5
SBF/HAD SS7 29 H5
Lambourne CVI SS8 69 H2
Lambourne Crs BSDN SS14 39 G1
Lambourni Cl SBN/FI SS3 49 H4 2
Lamont Cl WICKW SS12 16 D3 8
Lampern Crs BCAYW CM12 7 F4
Lampits Hl SLH/COR SS17 51 F3
Lampits Hill Av SLH/COR SS17 51 F4
Lampits La SLH/COR SS17 51 F4
Lancaster Dr VGE SS16 36 C1 6
Lancaster Gdns RAYL SS6 32 B3 1
SOS SS1 4 E3
Lancaster Rd RAYL SS6 32 B2
Lancer Wy BCAYW CM12 8 C2
Landermere BSDN SS14 26 B4
Landsburg Rd CVI SS8 56 C4
Langdon Rd RAYL SS6 19 E5
Langdon Wy SLH/COR SS17 51 G4
Langemore Wy BCAYE CM11 9 E3
Langenhoe WICKW SS12 16 D2
Langford Crs SBF/HAD SS7 30 C5
Langford Gv PIT SS13 28 B3
Langham Crs BCAYW CM12 9 E5
Langham Dr RAYL SS6 18 D5 8
Langland Cl SLH/COR SS17 51 F5 1
Langley Cl LOS SS9 32 C4
SOS SS1 5 G3
Langleys VGE SS16 2 E5
Langport Dr WOS/PRIT SS0 45 H2
Langside Cl LAIN SS15 25 E3 1
Lanhams PIT SS13 28 A3
Lansdown Av SBF/HAD SS7 32 A5
Lansdowne Av LOS SS9 45 H5
Lansdowne Dr RAYL SS6 19 F5
Lappmark Rd CVI SS8 70 C1
Lapwater Cl LOS SS9 44 D4
Lapwing Rd WICKE SS11 10 B3 1
Larch Cl LAIN SS15 25 F2
The Larches SBF/HAD SS7 29 G3
Larchwood Cl LOS SS9 32 C5
Larke Ri WOS/PRIT SS0 46 C2
Larkfield SLH/COR SS17 51 G4
Larkfield Cl RCFD SS4 22 C4
Larkswood Rd SLH/COR SS17 51 G5
Larup Av CVI SS8 56 B4
Lascelles Gdns RCFD SS4 22 B3
Latchetts Shaw VGE SS16 2 E5
Latchingdon Cl RAYL SS6 18 D5 9
Latimer Dr LAIN SS15 25 E2
Laurel Av WICKW SS12 16 B1
Laurel Cl LOS SS9 58 A1
The Laurels RAYL SS6 32 A3
Lavender Gv WOS/PRIT SS0 46 C3
Lavender Ms WOS/PRIT SS0 46 C2
Lavender Wy WICKW SS12 16 B1 5
Lawn Av SOSN SS2 47 G4
Lawnscourt SBF/HAD SS7 29 G4 3
The Lawns SBF/HAD SS7 29 H4
Lawrence Rd PIT SS13 29 E3
Laxtons SLH/COR SS17 64 C1 2
The Laxtons RCFD SS4 22 C3 2
Leamington Rd HOC/HUL SS5 21 G1
SOS SS1 5 G4
Lea Rd SBF/HAD SS7 41 H1
Leas Cl WOS/PRIT SS0 59 E1
Leas Gdns WOS/PRIT SS0 59 E1
The Leas WOS/PRIT SS0 59 F2
Leasway RAYL SS6 31 F1
WICKW SS12 16 A2
The Leasway WOS/PRIT SS0 59 E1
Lea Wy BCAYW CM12 9 E5
Lede Rd CVI SS8 56 A5 1
Lee Chapel La VGE SS16 37 F3
Leecon Wy RCFD SS4 22 C5
Lee Rd PIT SS13 29 E5
Lee Woottens La VGE SS16 2 C4
Leicester Av RCFD SS4 35 E3
Leige Av CVI SS8 55 H3 5
Leigham Court Dr LOS SS9 45 G4
Leigh Beck La CVI SS8 70 D2
Leigh Beck Rd CVI SS8 71 E1
Leigh Cliff Rd LOS SS9 58 C1
Leighcroft Gdns LOS SS9 45 F2
Leigh Fells PIT SS13 28 B5
Leighfields SBF/HAD SS7 31 E5
Leighfields Av LOS SS9 33 E5
Leighfields Rd LOS SS9 32 D5
Leigh Gdns LOS SS9 44 D5
Leigh Hall Rd LOS SS9 45 F5
Leigh Hts SBF/HAD SS7 44 A3
Leigh Hl LOS SS9 58 B1
Leigh Hill Cl LOS SS9 58 B1
Leigh Park Cl LOS SS9 44 D5
Leigh Park Rd LOS SS9 58 A1
Leigh Rd CVI SS8 70 A2
LOS SS9 45 G5
Leighton Av LOS SS9 45 G4
Leighton Rd SBF/HAD SS7 29 H4
Leigh View Dr LOS SS9 45 G2
Leighville Gv LOS SS9 45 E5
Leighwood Av LOS SS9 45 E1
Leinster Rd LAIN SS15 25 F4
Leitrim Av SBN/FI SS3 62 B3
Lekoe Rd CVI SS8 55 G3 1
Lenham Wy PIT SS13 28 B5
Lennox Dr WICKW SS12 17 E3
Leonard Dr RAYL SS6 18 D4 1
Leonard Rd VGE SS16 38 C4
WOS/PRIT SS0 59 G2
Leon Dr VGE SS16 39 E4
Leslie Cl LOS SS9 33 E5
Leslie Dr LOS SS9 33 E5
Leslie Gdns RAYL SS6 32 A2
Leslie Rd RAYL SS6 31 H2
Lesney Gdns RCFD SS4 22 C5
Letzen Rd CVI SS8 55 H5
Lever La RCFD SS4 35 E2
Levett Rd SLH/COR SS17 64 D2
Lewes Rd SOSN SS2 47 H3
Lewes Wy SBF/HAD SS7 31 E4
Leysings VGE SS16 37 H2
The Leys VGE SS16 3 H5
The Lichfields BSDN SS14 27 G4
Lifstan Wy SOS SS1 61 F1
Lilac Av CVI SS8 56 B4
WICKW SS12 16 B1
Lilford Rd BCAYE CM11 9 F1
Lilian Pl RAYL SS6 32 B3
Lillyville Wk RAYL SS6 32 B2 3
Limburg Rd CVI SS8 55 E5
Lime Av LOS SS9 44 D4
Lime Pl LAIN SS15 25 F2
Lime Rd SBF/HAD SS7 42 B2
Limeslade Cl SLH/COR SS17 51 F5 2
The Limes RAYL SS6 32 A3
Limetree Av SBF/HAD SS7 41 G2
Limetree Rd CVI SS8 56 C5
Lincefield VGE SS16 37 E3 1
Lincoln Cha SOSN SS2 48 B3
Lincoln Rd BSDN SS14 27 G4
RCFD SS4 22 A2
Lincoln Wy CVI SS8 55 F5
RAYL SS6 19 F3
Linda Gdns BCAYW CM12 8 B1
Linden Cl RAYL SS6 32 A2
SBF/HAD SS7 41 H1
Linden Leas SBF/HAD SS7 29 H5 1
Linden Rd SBF/HAD SS7 29 H5
The Lindens VGE SS16 36 D1 1
Linden Wy CVI SS8 55 G5
Linde Rd CVI SS8 56 A5
Lindisfarne Av LOS SS9 45 H4
Lindon Rd WICKE SS11 10 B2
Lindsell Gn BSDN SS14 39 F1 2
Lindsell La BSDN SS14 39 F1 3
Linford Dr BSDN SS14 39 F1
Lingcroft VGE SS16 2 D6
Lingfield Dr RCFD SS4 23 F5
Linkdale BCAYW CM12 9 E5
Link Rd CVI SS8 55 F5
RAYL SS6 19 G5
SLH/COR SS17 64 C1
The Links BCAYW CM12 8 B1
Linksway LOS SS9 44 D2
Links Wy SBF/HAD SS7 44 A3
Linkway BSDN SS14 2 E1
Linnet Cl SBN/FI SS3 49 H5
Linnet Dr SBF/HAD SS7 41 H4
Linnets VGE SS16 2 D7
Linroping Av CVI SS8 71 E1
Linton Rd SBN/FI SS3 62 D3
Lionel Rd CVI SS8 69 H1
Lion Hl SLH/COR SS17 52 A5
Lion La BCAYW CM12 8 D3
Lippits Hl VGE SS16 37 F3
Lisa Cl BCAYW CM12 7 E4
Little Bentley BSDN SS14 26 C4
Little Berry La VGE SS16 36 D2 3
Littlebury Ct PIT SS13 27 H3
Littlebury Gn PIT SS13 27 H3
Little Charlton PIT SS13 28 B5
Little Chittock BSDN SS14 27 F5
Little Garth PIT SS13 39 H1
Little Gypps Cl CVI SS8 55 G5
Little Gypps Rd CVI SS8 69 G1
Little Hays LOS SS9 32 C5
Littlehurst La LAIN SS15 26 A1
Little Lullaway LAIN SS15 25 H4
Little Norsey Rd BCAYW CM12 9 F1
Little Oaks BSDN SS14 2 D1
Little Oxcroft LAIN SS15 37 F1 1
Little Searles PIT SS13 28 A4
Little Spenders BSDN SS14 27 E3
Little Stambridge Hall Rd
RCFD SS4 35 G1
Little Thorpe SOS SS1 48 D5
Littlethorpe VGE SS16 39 G2 1
Little Wheatley Cha RAYL SS6 18 D5
Lloyd Wise Cl SOSN SS2 48 A3
Locarno Av WICKE SS11 10 D4
Locke Cl SLH/COR SS17 64 B1
Locks Hl RCFD SS4 35 E2 2
Locksley Cl SOSN SS2 48 C4
Lodge Cl RAYL SS6 31 H2
SBF/HAD SS7 42 D1
Lodge Farm Cl LOS SS9 45 E1 1
Lodgelands Cl RAYL SS6 32 A2 1
Lodwick SBN/FI SS3 62 B4
Logan Link WICKW SS12 17 E3
London Hl RAYL SS6 19 F5
London Rd BCAYE CM11 15 F2
BCAYW CM12 8 B3
PIT SS13 40 C1
RAYL SS6 18 D4
SBF/HAD SS7 41 F1
SLH/COR SS17 64 A3
SOS SS1 4 C3
VGE SS16 39 E4
WICKE SS11 18 A2
WOS/PRIT SS0 46 C5
Longborough Cl PIT SS13 27 H2 4
Longfield Cl WICKE SS11 17 F1
Longfield Rd WICKE SS11 17 F1
Long Meadow Dr WICKE SS11 10 D5
Long Riding BSDN SS14 3 G2
Longrise BCAYW CM12 9 E5
Long Rd CVI SS8 69 F1
Longsands SBN/FI SS3 62 C2 1
Longtail BCAYE CM11 7 F5
Longwick VGE SS16 37 F2
Lonsdale Rd SOSN SS2 48 A4
Lord Roberts Av LOS SS9 45 G5
Lornes Cl SOSN SS2 48 A3
Lorraine Cl BCAYE CM11 13 G2 4
Lorrimore Cl BCAYW CM12 6 C5 6
Loten Rd SBF/HAD SS7 41 G4
Lottem Rd CVI SS8 70 C2
Louisa Av SBF/HAD SS7 29 G5
Louis Dr RAYL SS6 18 D4
Louis Dr East RAYL SS6 19 E5
Louis Dr West RAYL SS6 18 D4
Louise Rd RAYL SS6 31 H1
Louvaine Av WICKW SS12 16 A1
Lovelace Av SOS SS1 5 J3
Lovelace Gdns SOSN SS2 5 J2
Love La RAYL SS6 31 F1
Lovell Ri LOS SS9 33 H5 2
Lovens Cl CVI SS8 70 B2
Lower Av PIT SS13 28 D3
Lower Church Rd SBF/HAD SS7 29 G5
Lower Cloister BCAYE CM11 9 E3 3
Lower Dunton Rd
RBRW/HUT CM13 24 A5
Lower Lambricks RAYL SS6 19 G4
Lower Park Rd WICKW SS12 16 B4
Lower Southend Rd WICKE SS11 10 C5
Lower St LAIN SS15 25 H2
Loxford PIT SS13 27 H3
Lubbards Cl RAYL SS6 19 G3
Lucerne Dr WICKE SS11 17 F1
Lucerne Wk WICKE SS11 17 F1
Luckyn La BSDN SS14 26 A3
Lucy Rd SOS SS1 4 E6
Luker Rd SOS SS1 4 C4
Lulworth Cl SLH/COR SS17 64 A4
Luncies Rd BSDN SS14 39 F1
Lundy Cl SOSN SS2 34 A4
Lutea Cl LAIN SS15 25 G2
Lych Ga LAIN SS15 25 F5 4
Lydford Rd WOS/PRIT SS0 59 H2 1
Lylt Rd CVI SS8 69 H1 1
Lyme Rd SOSN SS2 5 G1
Lymington Av LOS SS9 45 F4
Lympstone Cl WOS/PRIT SS0 45 H1
Lyndale Av SOSN SS2 47 G3
Lyndene SBF/HAD SS7 41 G1
Lyndhurst Rd SLH/COR SS17 51 E5
Lynfords Av WICKE SS11 11 E2
Lynfords Dr WICKE SS11 11 E2
Lynn View Cl SBF/HAD SS7 41 H1
Lynstede BSDN SS14 39 H1
Lynton Rd SBF/HAD SS7 43 F3
SOS SS1 61 G3
Lynwood Gn RAYL SS6 32 B3

M

Macaulay Rd VGE SS16 36 D1
Macdonald Av WOS/PRIT SS0 46
Macgregor Dr WICKW SS12 16
Macintyres Wk RCFD SS4 22
Mackenzie Cl WICKW SS12 16 D2
Mackley Dr SLH/COR SS17 51
Maclaren Wy WICKW SS12 16 D3
Macmurdo Cl LOS SS9 33
Macmurdo Rd LOS SS9 33
Madeira Av LOS SS9 45
Madrid Av RAYL SS6 18
Magazine Rd SBN/FI SS3 62
Magenta Cl BCAYW CM12 8
Magnolia Rd HOC/HUL SS5 22
Magnolias BCAYE CM11 13 F2
Magnolia Wy RCFD SS4 35
Mahonia Dr VGE SS16 36
Maine Crs RAYL SS6 19
Main Rd HOC/HUL SS5 21
Maitland Pl SBN/FI SS3 49
Maitland Rd WICKW SS12 16
Maldon Rd SOSN SS2 4
Malgraves PIT SS13 28
Malgraves Pl PIT SS13 28
Mallards SBN/FI SS3 49
Mallory Wy BCAYW CM12 8 D4
Mallow Gdns BCAYW CM12 6
Malmsmead SBN/FI SS3 62
Malting Villas Rd RCFD SS4 35
Malvern Av CVI SS8 69
Malvern Cl RAYL SS6 19
Malwood Dr SBF/HAD SS7 41
Malwood Rd SBF/HAD SS7 41
Malyon Court Cl SBF/HAD SS7 43
Malyons PIT SS13 28
Malyons Cl PIT SS13 28
Malyons Gn PIT SS13 28
Malyons Ms PIT SS13 28
Malyons Pl PIT SS13 28
The Malyons SBF/HAD SS7 43
Manchester Dr LOS SS9 45
Mandeville Wy SBF/HAD SS7 29 H4
VGE SS16 36
Manilla Rd SOS SS1 5
Mannering Gdns WOS/PRIT SS0 46
Manners Wy SOSN SS2 46
Manning Gv VGE SS16 37
Manns Wy RAYL SS6 19
Manor Av PIT SS13 28
Manor Cl RAYL SS6 31
Manor Rd HOC/HUL SS5 20
LAIN SS15 25
SBF/HAD SS7 29
SLH/COR SS17 64
WOS/PRIT SS0 59
The Manorway SLH/COR SS17 64
Mansel Cl LOS SS9 33
Mansted Gdns RCFD SS4 22
Maple Av LOS SS9 58
Maple Dr RAYL SS6 19
Mapleford Sweep VGE SS16 3
Mapleleaf Cl HOC/HUL SS5 21 G1
Mapleleaf Gdns WICKW SS12 16
Maple Md BCAYW CM12 9 F5
Maplesfield SBF/HAD SS7 43
Maple Sq SOSN SS2 47
Maplestead BSDN SS14 27
Maple Tree La VGE SS16 36 C1
Maple Wy CVI SS8 69
Maplin Cl SBF/HAD SS7 29
Maplin Gdns BSDN SS14 39
Maplin Wy SOS SS1 62
Maplin Wy North SBN/FI SS3 62
Marcos Rd CVI SS8 70
Marcus Av SOS SS1 62
Marcus Cha SOS SS1 62
Marcus Gdns SOS SS1 62
Marden Ash LAIN SS15 24 D5
Margarite Wy WICKW SS12 10
Margeth Rd BCAYW CM12 13
Margraten Av CVI SS8 70
Marguerite Dr LOS SS9 45
Marigold La ING CM4 7
Marina Av RAYL SS6 19
Marina Cl SOSN SS2 46
Marine Ap CVI SS8 70
Marine Av CVI SS8 70
LOS SS9 45
WOS/PRIT SS0 59
Marine Cl LOS SS9 44
Marine Pde CVI SS8 71
LOS SS9 44
SOS SS1 4
Mariskals PIT SS13 39

rket Av WICKW SS12 10 B5
rket Pl SOS SS1 4 D5
rket Rd WICKW SS12 16 B1
rket Sq BSDN SS14 2 D3
rkhams SLH/COR SS17 65 E1
rkhams Cha LAIN SS15 25 G4 1
AIN SS15 25 H4 1
rks Cl BCAYW CM12 8 B1
rlborough Cl SBF/HAD SS7 30 A4
rlborough Rd SOS SS1 5 K4
rlborough Wk
HOC/HUL SS5 20 D2 6
rlborough Wy BCAYW CM12 6 D5
rlin Cl SBF/HAD SS7 31 H5
rlowe Cl BCAYW CM12 7 E5
rlow Gdns SOSN SS2 46 D2
rney Dr BSDN SS14 39 G1
rshall Cl LOS SS9 44 B3
rshalls RCFD SS4 22 C4
rshalls Cl RAYL SS6 32 A1
rsh La SLH/COR SS17 52 A3
rsh View Ct VGE SS16 39 F3 3
rtin Cl BCAYE CM11 9 E4
rtindale Av LAIN SS15 25 G1
rtingale SBF/HAD SS7 43 E1
rtingale Cl BCAYE CM11 7 G5 1
rtingale Rd BCAYE CM11 7 G5
rtins Cl SLH/COR SS17 64 C1
rtins Ms SBF/HAD SS7 41 H2
rtin Wk HOC/HUL SS5 21 G4
rtock Av WOS/PRIT SS0 45 H1
rtyns Gv WOS/PRIT SS0 46 A4
rylands Av HOC/HUL SS5 21 E1
tching Gn BSDN SS14 27 E2
tlock Rd CVI SS8 69 G1
ugham Cl WICKW SS12 16 C3
urice Rd CVI SS8 70 C1 1
ya Cl SBN/FI SS3 62 D2
y Av CVI SS8 56 B5
ydells PIT SS13 40 A1
yfair Av PIT SS13 28 B3
yfield Av SOSN SS2 46 D2
yflower Cl SOSN SS2 34 A5
yflower Rd BCAYE CM11 9 E3 4
yflowers SBF/HAD SS7 29 G4 4
yland Av CVI SS8 69 G2
e Maze LOS SS9 33 E4
calmont Dr RAYL SS6 19 F1
divitt Wk LOS SS9 33 H5 3
ade Rd BCAYE CM11 7 G5
adgate PIT SS13 28 B3 2
adow Cl SBF/HAD SS7 31 E5
adow Ct WICKE SS11 10 D5
adow Dr SOS SS1 61 F1
GE SS16 50 A1
adowland Rd WICKE SS11 17 F2
adow La WICKE SS11 10 D2
adow Ri BCAYE CM11 9 F3
adow Rd SBF/HAD SS7 43 H4
adowside RAYL SS6 31 G1 2
adow Vw VGE SS16 36 B2
adow Wy HOC/HUL SS5 21 F3
VICKW SS12 16 C5
e Meadow Wy BCAYE CM11 9 F3
e Meads VGE SS16 39 H3
e Mead LAIN SS15 25 E3
adway CVI SS8 70 B2
AYL SS6 32 A2
BF/HAD SS7 29 H4
e Meadway WOS/PRIT SS0 59 E1
akins Cl LOS SS9 33 G5
doc Cl PIT SS13 28 B3
dway Crs LOS SS9 44 C5
esons Md RCFD SS4 22 C5
ggison Wy SBF/HAD SS7 41 H3
lcombe Rd SBF/HAD SS7 41 H3
llow Purgess Cl LAIN SS15 25 F5
llow Purgess End LAIN SS15 25 F5
lville Dr WICKW SS12 16 C3
ndip Cl RAYL SS6 19 G5
VICKE SS11 16 D1 1
ndip Crs WOS/PRIT SS0 45 H1
ndip Rd LOS SS9 45 H2
ntmore VGE SS16 37 E2
nzies Av LAIN SS15 24 C5
ppel Av CVI SS8 55 H3
rcer Rd BCAYE CM11 7 G5
rcury Cl WICKE SS11 11 E5
redene BSDN SS14 39 G1
rilies Cl WOS/PRIT SS0 46 A3
rilies Gdns WOS/PRIT SS0 46 A3
rlin Ct CVI SS8 70 A1 2
rlin Wy WICKE SS11 10 C4
rricks La VGE SS16 39 F4
rrivale SBF/HAD SS7 41 H4
rryfield Ap LOS SS9 45 F2
rryfields Av HOC/HUL SS5 21 E1
rrylands LAIN SS15 24 D4
Mersea Crs WICKW SS12 17 E2
Merton Rd SBF/HAD SS7 41 H2
Mess Rd SBN/FI SS3 63 E4
Meteor Rd WOS/PRIT SS0 59 G1
Methersgate BSDN SS14 26 D4
Metz Av CVI SS8 55 H5
The Mews HOC/HUL SS5 20 D2
Meyel Av CVI SS8 56 B4
Meynell Av CVI SS8 70 B2
Mey Wk HOC/HUL SS5 20 D2
Middle Dr SLH/COR SS17 38 C5
Middle Md RCFD SS4 35 E1 1
Middlesburg CVI SS8 55 F4
Middlesex Av LOS SS9 45 G4
Midhurst Av WOS/PRIT SS0 46 C2
Midsummer Meadow
SBN/FI SS3 49 H5 4
Milbanke Cl SBN/FI SS3 49 H5 5
Mildmayes VGE SS16 37 F2
Miles Gray Rd BSDN SS14 25 H2
Millfield Cl RAYL SS6 19 H5
Mill Gn PIT SS13 27 H5
Mill Green Pl PIT SS13 27 H4
Millhead Wy RCFD SS4 35 G2
Mill Hl SBF/HAD SS7 42 B5
Mill Hill Dr BCAYW CM12 7 E5
Mill La RCFD SS4 35 G2
SLH/COR SS17 51 G2
Mill Rd BCAYE CM11 13 G2
Mills Ct PIT SS13 28 B2
Millview Mdw RCFD SS4 35 E2
Milner Pl BCAYW CM12 6 C5
Milton Av VGE SS16 36 B2
WOS/PRIT SS0 59 H2
Milton Cl RAYL SS6 32 A1
Milton Pl SOS SS1 4 B5
Milton Rd SLH/COR SS17 51 E3
WOS/PRIT SS0 59 H1
Milton St SOSN SS2 4 C2
Miltsin Av CVI SS8 56 B4
Minster Rd LAIN SS15 25 F5
Minton Hts RCFD SS4 22 B2
Miramar Av CVI SS8 69 F1
Mistley End VGE SS16 3 H4
Mistley Pth VGE SS16 3 H4
Mistley Side VGE SS16 3 H3
Mitchells Av CVI SS8 56 C5
Moat Edge Gdns BCAYW CM12 8 D1
Moat End SOS SS1 49 E5
Moat Fld BSDN SS14 26 D3
Moat Ri RAYL SS6 31 G2
Mollands VGE SS16 39 G2
Monastery Rd LAIN SS15 25 F5
Monks Hvn SLH/COR SS17 64 D1
Monmouth Ms VGE SS16 36 C1 8
Monoux Cl BCAYE CM11 9 G4
Mons Av BCAYE CM11 9 G3
Montague Av LOS SS9 44 C4
Montague Pl CVI SS8 69 F1
Montague Wy BCAYW CM12 6 D5
Montfort Av SLH/COR SS17 51 F5
Montgomery Ct SBN/FI SS3 49 H5 6
Montpelier Cl BCAYW CM12 6 D5 7
Montsale PIT SS13 28 B3
Moons Cl RCFD SS4 22 C1
Moorcroft RCFD SS4 22 B2
Moorcroft Av SBF/HAD SS7 31 H5
Moore Cl BCAYE CM11 7 G5 2
Moores Av SLH/COR SS17 38 D5
Moor Park Cl LOS SS9 44 D1
Moor Park Gdns LOS SS9 44 D1
Mopsies Rd BSDN SS14 27 F5
Moreland Av SBF/HAD SS7 29 H4
Moreland Cl SBF/HAD SS7 29 H5
Moreland Rd WICKE SS11 10 B3
Moretons PIT SS13 27 H5
Morley Hl SLH/COR SS17 51 E3
Morley Link SLH/COR SS17 51 E4 6
Mornington Av RCFD SS4 35 F1
Mornington Crs CVI SS8 56 B5 4
SBF/HAD SS7 44 A3
Mornington Rd CVI SS8 56 A4
Morrells VGE SS16 2 A6
Morris Av BCAYE CM11 9 G4
Morris Ct LAIN SS15 25 E4
Mortimer Rd RAYL SS6 19 G3
Moseley St SOSN SS2 5 K1
Moss Cl VGE SS16 39 F3
Moss Dr VGE SS16 39 F3
Motehill VGE SS16 37 F2
Mountain Ash Cl SBF/HAD SS7 32 C5
Mount Av HOC/HUL SS5 21 E2
RAYL SS6 19 F5
WOS/PRIT SS0 58 D1
Mountbatten Dr SBN/FI SS3 49 H5
Mount Bovers La HOC/HUL SS5 21 F5
Mount Cl RAYL SS6 31 F1
WICKE SS11 10 D5
Mount Crs HOC/HUL SS5 21 F2
SBF/HAD SS7 42 B2
Mountdale Gdns LOS SS9 45 G2
Mountfield Cl SLH/COR SS17 64 D1
Mountfields PIT SS13 40 A2
Mountnessing SBF/HAD SS7 43 G4
Mountnessing Rd BCAYW CM12 6 A3
Mount Rd SBF/HAD SS7 42 C2
WICKE SS11 10 D5
The Mount BCAYE CM11 9 H2
SLH/COR SS17 65 E1
Mount Vw BCAYE CM11 9 H3
Mountview Cl VGE SS16 39 F3
Mount Wy WICKE SS11 10 D5
Mucking Wharf Rd SLH/COR SS17 64 B5
Muirway SBF/HAD SS7 29 G4
Mulberry Rd CVI SS8 68 D1
Mullberry Gdns VGE SS16 37 E1 4
The Mullions BCAYW CM12 8 C2
Munro Ct WICKW SS12 16 D3 10
Munsterburg Rd CVI SS8 56 C4
Murrels La HOC/HUL SS5 20 B1
Musket Gv LOS SS9 32 C4
Mynchens LAIN SS15 25 H5

N

Namur Rd CVI SS8 56 B4
Nansen Av RCFD SS4 22 C2
Napier Av SOS SS1 4 B4
Napier Crs WICKW SS12 16 D3
Napier Gdns SBF/HAD SS7 31 F5
Napier Rd RAYL SS6 20 A5
Navestock Cl RAYL SS6 18 D5 10
Navestock Gdns SOS SS1 48 C5
Nayland Cl WICKW SS12 16 D1 2
The Nazeing BSDN SS14 27 F5
Neil Armstrong Wy LOS SS9 33 H4
Nelson Cl RAYL SS6 20 A4
Nelson Dr LOS SS9 45 G5
Nelson Gdns RAYL SS6 20 A4
Nelson Ms SOS SS1 4 C5
Nelson Rd BSDN SS14 3 K2
RAYL SS6 20 A5
RCFD SS4 22 C2
WOS/PRIT SS0 45 H4
Nelson St SOS SS1 4 C5
Ness Rd SBN/FI SS3 62 C2
Nestuda Wy WOS/PRIT SS0 34 A5
Netherfield SBF/HAD SS7 42 D2
Nether Mayne LAIN SS15 2 C3
VGE SS16 2 C7
Nether Priors BSDN SS14 3 F2
Nevada Rd CVI SS8 56 B4
Nevendon Ms PIT SS13 27 H1 2
Nevendon Rd PIT SS13 27 H1
WICKW SS12 16 A4
Nevern Cl RAYL SS6 32 A3
Nevern Rd RAYL SS6 31 H3
Neville Shaw BSDN SS14 26 C4
New Av VGE SS16 36 D2
New Century Rd LAIN SS15 25 E5
Newell Av SBN/FI SS3 63 F1
Newhall RCFD SS4 22 B2
Newhouse Av WICKW SS12 15 G1
Newington Av SOSN SS2 48 B4
Newington Cl SOSN SS2 48 C4
Newlands Cl BCAYW CM12 9 E1 1
Newlands End LAIN SS15 25 E3
Newlands Rd BCAYW CM12 9 E1
CVI SS8 56 C4 6
WICKW SS12 16 C4
New Park Rd SBF/HAD SS7 41 H1
New Rd BCAYW CM12 12 D5
CVI SS8 69 F1
LOS SS9 58 A1
SBF/HAD SS7 43 G3
Newsum Gdns RAYL SS6 18 D5 11
Newton Hall Gdns RCFD SS4 22 C2
Newton Park Rd SBF/HAD SS7 31 E4
New Waverley Rd LAIN SS15 25 H2
Nicholl Rd LAIN SS15 25 E4
Nicholson Crs SBF/HAD SS7 43 E3 1
Nicholson Gv WICKW SS12 16 D3 11
Nicholson Rd SBF/HAD SS7 43 E3
Nightingale Cl RAYL SS6 19 E5 4
SOSN SS2 34 D5
Nightingale Rd CVI SS8 70 B1 1
Nightingales VGE SS16 36 C1
Niven Cl WICKW SS12 16 D3
Noak Hill Cl BCAYW CM12 13 F5
Noak Hill Rd BCAYW CM12 13 E3
Nobel Sq PIT SS13 28 B1
Nobles Green Cl LOS SS9 33 F4
Nobles Green Rd LOS SS9 33 F4
Nordland Rd CVI SS8 56 C5
Noredale SBN/FI SS3 62 C3
Nore Rd LOS SS9 32 D3
Norfolk Av LOS SS9 45 G3
Norfolk Cl CVI SS8 55 H4 3
LAIN SS15 24 D5
Norfolk Wy CVI SS8 55 G4
Norman Crs RAYL SS6 19 H3 1
Normans Rd CVI SS8 56 C5
Norsey Cl BCAYE CM11 9 E2
Norsey Dr BCAYE CM11 9 F2
Norsey Rd BCAYE CM11 9 E2
Norsey View Dr BCAYW CM12 7 E4
Northampton Gv VGE SS16 36 C2
North Av CVI SS8 55 G5
SOSN SS2 4 E1
North Benfleet Hall Rd
WICKW SS12 29 E2
North Colne VGE SS16 3 J5
North Crs SOSN SS2 46 B1
WICKW SS12 16 C1
North Crockerford VGE SS16 39 F1
Northern Av SBF/HAD SS7 41 H1
Northfalls Rd CVI SS8 71 E1
Northfield Cl BCAYE CM11 9 F3 10
North Gunnels BSDN SS14 2 E2
Northlands Ap VGE SS16 37 F5
Northlands Cl SLH/COR SS17 50 D4
Northlands Farm Cha
SLH/COR SS17 50 D2
North Rd BCAYE CM11 15 E3
WOS/PRIT SS0 46 D5
North Shoebury Rd SBN/FI SS3 49 G5
North St LOS SS9 58 B1
RCFD SS4 35 E1
Northumberland Av LAIN SS15 37 F1 2
SOS SS1 5 H6
Northumberland Crs SOS SS1 5 J6
Northview Dr WOS/PRIT SS0 46 C4
Northville Dr WOS/PRIT SS0 46 B2
North Weald Cl WICKE SS11 17 G2 3
Northwick Rd CVI SS8 54 B5
Norton Av CVI SS8 70 D1
Norton Cl SLH/COR SS17 51 E5
Norwich Av SOSN SS2 47 H3
Norwich Cl SOSN SS2 47 H4 1
Norwich Crs RAYL SS6 19 F3
Norwood Dr SBF/HAD SS7 42 B5
Norwood End BSDN SS14 27 E4
Nottage Cl SLH/COR SS17 51 E5 3
Nottingham Wy VGE SS16 36 C1
Nursery Cl RAYL SS6 31 G2
Nursery Gdns LAIN SS15 25 F3
Nursery Rd SLH/COR SS17 64 C1
Nutcombe Crs RCFD SS4 22 C4
Nuthatch Cl BCAYE CM11 9 F5

O

Oak Av BCAYE CM11 14 D4
WICKE SS11 17 H1
Oak Cha WICKW SS12 15 H1
Oakdene Rd PIT SS13 28 A3
Oaken Grange Dr SOSN SS2 46 D1
Oakfield Cl SBF/HAD SS7 41 H3
Oakfield Rd SBF/HAD SS7 41 H3
Oakham Cl VGE SS16 36 C1 9
Oakhurst Cl WICKW SS12 16 B3
Oakhurst Dr WICKW SS12 16 A2
Oakhurst Rd RAYL SS6 32 A3
SOSN SS2 47 F4
Oaklands Ms RCFD SS4 22 B4 1
Oak La BCAYE CM11 14 D5
Oakleigh Av SOS SS1 5 K3
Oakleigh Park Dr LOS SS9 45 F5
Oakleighs SBF/HAD SS7 41 H2
Oakley Av RAYL SS6 18 C5
Oakley Dr BCAYW CM12 6 C5 7
Oak Rd BCAYE CM11 14 D4
CVI SS8 70 B1
RCFD SS4 34 C1
Oak Rd North SBF/HAD SS7 43 H4
Oak Rd South SBF/HAD SS7 43 H4
The Oaks BCAYE CM11 13 F2
Oak Wk HOC/HUL SS5 21 F1
SBF/HAD SS7 29 G3
Oakwood Av LOS SS9 45 F2
Oakwood Cl SBF/HAD SS7 41 G1 2
Oakwood Dr BCAYW CM12 7 F5
Oakwood Gv PIT SS13 28 A5
Oakwood Rd RAYL SS6 19 F4
SLH/COR SS17 51 G5
Oast Wy RCFD SS4 35 E1
Oban Ct WICKE SS11 17 G3
Oban Rd SOSN SS2 5 G2
Odessa Rd CVI SS8 70 B1
Ogilvie Ct WICKW SS12 16 D3 12

Old Church Hl VGE SS16 36 C5
Old Church Rd PIT SS13 41 E1
Old Hill Av VGE SS16 50 A1
Old Jenkins Cl SLH/COR SS17 64 A3 1
Old Leigh Rd LOS SS9 45 H5
Old London Rd WICKE SS11 18 A2
Old Md LOS SS9 33 H4
Old School Meadow SBN/FI SS3 49 H2
Old Ship La RCFD SS4 35 E1 2
Old Southend Rd SOS SS1 5 F5
Oldwyk VGE SS16 39 F2
Olive Av LOS SS9 44 B4
Olivia Dr LOS SS9 45 G4
One Tree Hl SLH/COR SS17 38 A5
Orange Rd CVI SS8 56 C5
Orchard Av BCAYW CM12 7 F5
HOC/HUL SS5 21 F1
RAYL SS6 31 F3
Orchard Cl HOC/HUL SS5 21 G1 3
Orchard Gv LOS SS9 33 G5
Orchard Md LOS SS9 45 F1
Orchard Rd SBF/HAD SS7 29 G5
Orchard Side LOS SS9 33 G5
The Orchard WICKW SS12 16 A1
Orchill Dr SBF/HAD SS7 43 H2
Orlando Dr PIT SS13 28 B2 5
Ormonde Av RCFD SS4 22 D5 1
SBF/HAD SS7 44 B4
Ormonde Gdns LOS SS9 44 B4
Ormsby Rd CVI SS8 69 E2
Orrmo Rd CVI SS8 71 E1
Orsett Av LOS SS9 44 D1
Orsett End BSDN SS14 26 D4
Orwell Ct WICKE SS11 17 G3
Osborne Rd PIT SS13 28 D3
VGE SS16 3 H3
WOS/PRIT SS0 46 D5
Osbourne Av HOC/HUL SS5 20 D2
Osprey Cl SBN/FI SS3 49 H5 7
Osterley Dr VGE SS16 36 C1 10
Ouida Rd CVI SS8 70 C1
Outing Cl SOS SS1 5 G5
Outwood Common Rd
BCAYE CM11 9 H1
Outwood Farm Cl BCAYE CM11 9 H3
Outwood Farm Rd BCAYE CM11 9 H5
Overton Cl SBF/HAD SS7 29 H5
Overton Dr SBF/HAD SS7 29 H5
Overton Rd SBF/HAD SS7 29 G4 5
Overton Wy SBF/HAD SS7 29 G5
Ovington Gdns BCAYW CM12 6 D5
Oxford Cl VGE SS16 36 C1 11
Oxford Rd CVI SS8 56 B5
RCFD SS4 22 D4
SLH/COR SS17 64 A4
Oxley Gdns SLH/COR SS17 50 C5
Oxwich Cl SLH/COR SS17 51 F5
Ozonia Av WICKW SS12 16 B3
Ozonia Cl WICKW SS12 16 A3
Ozonia Wy WICKW SS12 16 B3

P

Paarl Rd CVI SS8 55 H5
Paddock Cl BCAYE CM11 13 F1 6
LOS SS9 33 F4
The Paddocks RAYL SS6 32 A1
Page Rd PIT SS13 29 E4
Paget Dr BCAYW CM12 6 D5
Paignton Cl RAYL SS6 19 G3 2
Painswick Av SLH/COR SS17 51 E4
Palace Gv LAIN SS15 25 H3 2
Palatine Pk LAIN SS15 24 C5 2
Pall Ml LOS SS9 45 F5
Palmeira Av WOS/PRIT SS0 59 G2
Palmer Cl LAIN SS15 25 G5 1
Palmers SLH/COR SS17 65 E1 1
Palmerstone Rd CVI SS8 69 E1 1
Palmerston Rd WOS/PRIT SS0 59 G2
Palm Ms LAIN SS15 25 G2
Panadown LAIN SS15 2 B2
Panfields LAIN SS15 24 D5
Pantile Av SOSN SS2 47 H3
Papenburg Rd CVI SS8 55 H3
Paprills VGE SS16 37 H1
Pargat Dr LOS SS9 32 D4
Pargetters Hyam
HOC/HUL SS5 21 G2 3
Parish Wy LAIN SS15 25 F4
Parkanaur Av SOS SS1 62 A3
Park Av CVI SS8 71 E2
LOS SS9 45 F1
Park Cha SBF/HAD SS7 43 H4
Park Cl WICKW SS12 16 B2 1
Park Crs WOS/PRIT SS0 4 A4
Park Dr WICKW SS12 16 C2
Parkfields SBF/HAD SS7 43 F2
Park Gdns HOC/HUL SS5 21 G3
Park Gate Rd SLH/COR SS17 51 F1
Parkhurst Dr RAYL SS6 19 F2
Parkhurst Rd PIT SS13 40 A1
Parklands BCAYE CM11 9 E2 1
CVI SS8 55 H4 4
RCFD SS4 22 C4
Parklands Av RAYL SS6 31 H1
Park La CVI SS8 71 E1
SOS SS1 5 H4
WOS/PRIT SS0 4 A4
Parkmill Cl SLH/COR SS17 51 F5
Park Rd CVI SS8 71 E2
LOS SS9 44 C5
SBF/HAD SS7 30 C5
SLH/COR SS17 64 A3
SLH/COR SS17 65 F1
WOS/PRIT SS0 4 A3
Park Side BCAYE CM11 9 F3 11
PIT SS13 27 H4
WOS/PRIT SS0 45 H5
Parkstone Av SBF/HAD SS7 43 E2
Parkstone Dr SOSN SS2 46 D3
Park St WOS/PRIT SS0 4 A4
Park Ter WOS/PRIT SS0 4 A4
Park View Dr LOS SS9 44 C1
Parkway RAYL SS6 31 H3
SLH/COR SS17 51 H4
Parkway Cl LOS SS9 33 G4
The Parkway CVI SS8 70 A2
Parry Cl SLH/COR SS17 64 C1
Parsonage La LAIN SS15 25 F5
Parsons Lawn SBN/FI SS3 49 G5
Parsons Rd SBF/HAD SS7 30 A4
Paslowes VGE SS16 39 G2
Passingham Av BCAYE CM11 13 F2
Passingham Cl BCAYE CM11 13 F1 7
Pathways BSDN SS14 39 F1 4
Patricia Dr SLH/COR SS17 51 H3
Patricia Gdns BCAYE CM11 13 G1 3
Patterdale SBF/HAD SS7 29 G4
Pattiswick Cnr BSDN SS14 27 F4 1
Pattiswick Sq BSDN SS14 27 F4
Pattocks BSDN SS14 3 K2
Pauline Gdns BCAYW CM12 8 C1 7
Paul's Rd LAIN SS15 25 F3
Pavilion Cl SOSN SS2 5 K2
SOSN SS2 48 B5 1
Pavilion Dr LOS SS9 45 G4
Pavillion Pl BCAYW CM12 8 C1 8
Paxfords LAIN SS15 24 C5 3
Paycocke Cl BSDN SS14 27 G1
Paycocke Rd BSDN SS14 27 F1
Paynters Md VGE SS16 39 F3
Peach Av HOC/HUL SS5 21 F1
Pearmain Cl WICKE SS11 10 C4
Pearsons SLH/COR SS17 65 E1 2
Pearsons Av RAYL SS6 19 E4
Peartree Cl SOSN SS2 47 H3
Pear Trees SBF/HAD SS7 42 C2 2
Pebmarsh Dr WICKW SS12 16 D2
Peel Av SBN/FI SS3 63 F2
Peldon Pavement BSDN SS14 27 E3 1
Pelham Pl SLH/COR SS17 50 D5
Pelham Rd SOSN SS2 48 B5
Pembroke Av SLH/COR SS17 51 F5
Pembroke Cl BCAYW CM12 6 D5 8
Pembroke Ms PIT SS13 28 B3 3
Pembury Rd WOS/PRIT SS0 59 F2
Pendle Cl BSDN SS14 27 H2
Pendle Dr BSDN SS14 27 G2
Pendlestone SBF/HAD SS7 43 F2
Pendower RAYL SS6 31 E3
Penhurst Av SOSN SS2 47 E4 1
Pennial Rd CVI SS8 55 H5
Pentland Av SBN/FI SS3 62 B3
Percy Cottis Rd RCFD SS4 22 D5
Percy Rd LOS SS9 45 E4
Peregrine Cl SBN/FI SS3 49 H5
VGE SS16 3 F5
Peregrine Dr SBF/HAD SS7 41 H4
Peregrine Gdns RAYL SS6 19 E5 5
Perry Gn BSDN SS14 26 C3
Perry Rd SBF/HAD SS7 41 G3
Perry St BCAYW CM12 8 C2
Peterborough Wy BSDN SS14 27 G3
Petworth Gdns SOSN SS2 48 C4
Pevensey Wy PIT SS13 28 A5 2
Philbrick Crs West RAYL SS6 19 E5
Philmead Rd SBF/HAD SS7 41 G4
Philpott Av SOSN SS2 48 A4
Phoenix Wy SBF/HAD SS7 31 F4
Picketts CVI SS8 55 E5
Picketts Av LOS SS9 45 F2
Picketts Cl LOS SS9 45 F2
Pickwick Cl LAIN SS15 25 G4 2
Picton Cl RAYL SS6 31 H2
Picton Gdns RAYL SS6 31 G2
Piercys PIT SS13 39 H1
Pier Hl SOS SS1 4 D6
Pilgrims Cl BCAYE CM11 9 E3 5
SOS SS1 48 B5
Pilgrims Wy SBF/HAD SS7 44 A3 1
Pilgrim Wy LAIN SS15 25 F5
Pine Cl CVI SS8 69 F1
LOS SS9 44 C1
Pine Rd SBF/HAD SS7 43 G4
The Pines LAIN SS15 25 F2
Pinetrees SBF/HAD SS7 43 F3
Pinewood Av LOS SS9 45 E1
Pipps Hill La BSDN SS14 26 C2
Pipps Hill Rd North BCAYE CM11 14 C5
Pipps Hill Rd South BSDN SS14 26 C3
Pitmans Cl SOS SS1 4 D4
Pitsea Hall La VGE SS16 40 A3
Pitsea Rd PIT SS13 27 H5
Pitsea View Rd BCAYE CM11 15 E4
Pitseaville Gv VGE SS16 39 F1
Pittfields VGE SS16 36 D1
Plaistow Cl SLH/COR SS17 64 C2
Plas Newydd SOS SS1 61 F3
Pleasant Dr BCAYW CM12 8 B1
Pleasant Ms SOS SS1 5 F6
Pleasant Rd SOS SS1 5 F5
Pleshey Cl SOS SS1 61 G1
WICKW SS12 16 D2 7
Plowmans RAYL SS6 19 H4 1
Plumberow Av HOC/HUL SS5 21 F1
Plumleys PIT SS13 28 A4
Plymtree SOS SS1 49 F5
Point Cl CVI SS8 71 E1
Point Rd CVI SS8 70 D1
Poley Rd SLH/COR SS17 64 B3
Pollards Cl RCFD SS4 34 D1
Polstead Cl RAYL SS6 18 D5
Polsteads VGE SS16 39 F3
Pomfret Md BSDN SS14 2 D1
Poors La SBF/HAD SS7 43 H2
Poors La North SBF/HAD SS7 44 B1
Popes Crs PIT SS13 39 H1
Popes Wk RAYL SS6 32 A1
Poplar Rd CVI SS8 70 B1
RAYL SS6 32 A3
Poplars Av HOC/HUL SS5 21 F4
Poppyfield Cl LOS SS9 33 E5
Porchester Rd BCAYW CM12 6 D5
Porlock Av WOS/PRIT SS0 45 H2
Porters PIT SS13 28 B3
Portland Av SOS SS1 4 E5
Portman Dr BCAYW CM12 7 E5
Post Meadow BCAYE CM11 13 G2
Potash Rd BCAYE CM11 7 G4
Potters Wy SOSN SS2 47 E1
Pound La LAIN SS15 25 G3
PIT SS13 29 E5
WICKW SS12 29 E2
Pound Lane Central LAIN SS15 25 G2
Pound La North LAIN SS15 25 G1
Powell Rd LAIN SS15 25 E4
Poynings Av SOSN SS2 5 K1
Poyntens RAYL SS6 31 F2
Poynters La SBN/FI SS3 49 G4
Prentice Cl RCFD SS4 35 E1
Prescott VGE SS16 37 F3
Preston Gdns RAYL SS6 19 G4
Preston Rd WOS/PRIT SS0 59 G1
Prestwood Cl SBF/HAD SS7 30 C5
Prestwood Dr SBF/HAD SS7 30 D4
Pretoria Cl LAIN SS15 26 A2 2
Primrose Cl CVI SS8 55 H3
VGE SS16 37 E2
Prince Av WOS/PRIT SS0 45 G1
Prince Cl WOS/PRIT SS0 46 B1
Prince Edward Rd BCAYE CM11 9 F3
Princes Av SBF/HAD SS7 30 C5
SLH/COR SS17 65 F1
Princes Cl BCAYW CM12 7 F4
LAIN SS15 25 H3
Princes Ct BCAYW CM12 7 F4 1
Princes Ms BCAYW CM12 7 F4 2
Princes Rd CVI SS8 69 G1
Princess Gdns RCFD SS4 22 B3
Princess Rd RAYL SS6 20 A5
Princes St WOS/PRIT SS0 4 B3
Prince William Av CVI SS8 55 G3
Priors Cl BSDN SS14 3 G1
Priors East BSDN SS14 3 G2
Priory Av SOSN SS2 47 E3
Priory Crs SOSN SS2 46 D2
Priory Rd SLH/COR SS17 64 D1
The Priory BCAYW CM12 7 F4
Priory View Rd LOS SS9 45 F1 1
Priory Wood Crs LOS SS9 45 F1
Prittle Cl SBF/HAD SS7 43 F1
Prittlewell Cha WOS/PRIT SS0 46 B3
Prittlewell Sq SOS SS1 4
Prittlewell St SOSN SS2 4
Progress Rd LOS SS9 32
Prospect Av SLH/COR SS17 64
Prospect Cl SOS SS1 5
Protea Wy CVI SS8 56
Prower Cl BCAYE CM11 9
Puckleside VGE SS16 37 F
Puffin Pl SBN/FI SS3 49
Pugh Pl SLH/COR SS17 50
Pulpits Cl HOC/HUL SS5 21
Purcell Cl LAIN SS15 25
SLH/COR SS17 64
Purdeys Wy RCFD SS4 35
Purleigh Cl PIT SS13 28
Purleigh Rd RAYL SS6 19
Purley Wy WOS/PRIT SS0 46

Q

Quebec Av SOS SS1 4
Quebec Cl SOS SS1 4
Queen Anne's Dr WOS/PRIT SS0 46
Queen Elizabeth Cha RCFD SS4 35
Queen Elizabeth Dr
SLH/COR SS17 51
Queen's Av LOS SS9 45
Queen's Gate Ms BCAYW CM12 6 C
Queensland Av RCFD SS4 35
Queensmere SBF/HAD SS7 43
Queens Park Av BCAYW CM12 6
Queens Rd BCAYE CM11 14
LAIN SS15 25
LOS SS9 58
RAYL SS6 31
SBF/HAD SS7 42
WOS/PRIT SS0 4
Queensway SOS SS1 4
SOSN SS2 4
Quendon Rd BSDN SS14 27
Quilters Cl BSDN SS14 27 E
Quilters Dr BCAYW CM12 8
Quilters Straight BSDN SS14 27
Quorn Gdns LOS SS9 44

R

Rachael Clarke Cl
SLH/COR SS17 50 D
Rackenford SBN/FI SS3 62 C
Radford Ct BCAYW CM12 9 E
Radford Crs BCAYW CM12 8
Radford Wy BCAYW CM12 8
Radstocks BCAYW CM12 9
Radwinter Av WICKW SS12 16
Railway Ap LAIN SS15 24
Railway Ter SOSN SS2 47
Rainbow Av CVI SS8 56 B
Rainbow La SLH/COR SS17 65
Rainbow Rd CVI SS8 56
Raliegh Dr LAIN SS15 37
The Ramparts RAYL SS6 31
Rampart St SBN/FI SS3 63
Rampart Ter SBN/FI SS3 63
Ramsay Dr VGE SS16 39
Ramsden View Rd WICKW SS12 15
Ramsey Cha WICKW SS12 17
Ramuz Dr WOS/PRIT SS0 46
Randolph Cl LOS SS9 45
Randway RAYL SS6 31 G
Rantree Fold VGE SS16 2
Raphael Dr SBN/FI SS3 63
Raphaels LAIN SS15 37
Rat La SBF/HAD SS7 31
Rattwick Dr CVI SS8 71
Raven Cl BCAYW CM12 8
Raven Crs BCAYW CM12 8
Ravendale Wy SBN/FI SS3 49
Raven Dr SBF/HAD SS7 41
Raven La BCAYW CM12 8
Ravenscourt Dr VGE SS16 39
Ravensdale VGE SS16 3
Ravensfield BSDN SS14 27
Ravenswood Cha RCFD SS4 35
Rawreth La RAYL SS6 19
WICKE SS11 18
Ray Cl CVI SS8 69
LOS SS9 44
Rayleigh Av LOS SS9 32
WOS/PRIT SS0 46
Rayleigh Downs Rd RAYL SS6 32
Rayleigh Dr LOS SS9 45
Rayleigh Rd LOS SS9 32
SBF/HAD SS7 31

SLH/COR SS17 64 A3
yment Av CVI SS8 70 C1
ymonds Dr SBF/HAD SS7 30 C5
yside BSDN SS14 3 H2
y Wk LOS SS9 44 C5
ad Cl HOC/HUL SS5 21 H4
ading Cl VGE SS16 36 C1 12
bels La SBN/FI SS3 48 C2
creation Av LOS SS9 45 G4
SLH/COR SS17 51 G4
ctory Av RCFD SS4 22 B2
ctory Cha SOS SS1 48 B5
ctory Cl SBF/HAD SS7 43 H3
ctory Gdns PIT SS13 40 B1
ctory Garth RAYL SS6 19 G6
ctory Gv LOS SS9 58 A1
WICKE SS11 17 E1
ctory Park Dr PIT SS13 40 A1
ctory Rd BCAYW CM12 12 C4
HOC/HUL SS5 21 H5
PIT SS13 28 B4
SBF/HAD SS7 43 H3
SLH/COR SS17 64 B3
dcliff Dr LOS SS9 58 C1
dgate Cl WICKE SS11 11 F5
dgrave Rd VGE SS16 39 F2
e Redinge BCAYE CM11 13 G1
dlie Cl SLH/COR SS17 50 C5
dstock Rd SOSN SS2 47 F4
dwing Dr BCAYE CM11 9 F5
dwood Dr LAIN SS15 25 G2
e Redwoods CVI SS8 69 F1 2
ed Pond Wk VGE SS16 37 E2 1
eds Wy WICKW SS12 10 B5
eves Cl VGE SS16 36 C2 5
gan Cl SLH/COR SS17 50 D5
gency Cl RCFD SS4 34 D1
WICKE SS11 10 C3
gency Gn SOSN SS2 47 E4
gent Cl RAYL SS6 19 E4
mbrandt Cl CVI SS8 69 H1
SBN/FI SS3 63 F1
nacres VGE SS16 2 A5
pton Cl PIT SS13 27 H2
pton Gv LOS SS9 33 H4
treat Rd HOC/HUL SS5 21 F2
WOS/PRIT SS0 59 H2
ttendon Cl RAYL SS6 18 D5 12
ttendon Gdns WICKE SS11 10 D4
ttendon Vw WICKE SS11 11 E5
oda Rd SBF/HAD SS7 42 A2
oda Rd North SBF/HAD SS7 42 B1
hmond Av SBF/HAD SS7 41 H4
SBN/FI SS3 62 C3
WOS/PRIT SS0 59 H1 1
hmond Dr RAYL SS6 31 G3
WOS/PRIT SS0 46 B2
hmond Rd WICKE SS11 10 B3
hmond St SOSN SS2 5 J1
ketts Dr BCAYW CM12 8 C2
kling VGE SS16 39 G2
gemount SBF/HAD SS7 42 B2 2
geway BCAYW CM12 8 D5
RAYL SS6 31 F2
geway Gdns WOS/PRIT SS0 59 E1 1
e Ridgeway LOS SS9 58 D1
WOS/PRIT SS0 59 E1
e Ridings CVI SS8 55 H4 5
RCFD SS4 35 E2
ley Rd PIT SS13 28 B2
fams Ct PIT SS13 28 B3 4
fams Dr PIT SS13 28 B3
gwood Dr LOS SS9 32 C4
pleside BSDN SS14 39 G1
e Pk LAIN SS15 2 A2
e Rising BCAYE CM11 9 F4
enhall SBF/HAD SS7 31 E3
WICKE SS11 17 F2
erdale LOS SS9 33 E4
erside Wk WICKW SS12 10 A5
ertons VGE SS16 39 G2
erview VGE SS16 39 H2
er View Rd SBF/HAD SS7 42 A4
iera Dr SOS SS1 5 H3
ach Av RAYL SS6 31 F2
ach V LOS SS9 33 G4
ach Valley Wy HOC/HUL SS5 20 D5
RCFD SS4 33 H3
bert Cl BCAYW CM12 8 C3
bertson Dr WICKW SS12 16 D3 13
berts Rd LAIN SS15 25 E4 2
bin Cl BCAYW CM12 7 F4
binia Cl LAIN SS15 25 G2
che Av RCFD SS4 34 D1
chefort Dr RCFD SS4 35 E3
chehall Wy RCFD SS4 35 G3
chester Dr WOS/PRIT SS0 46 B2
chester Ms WOS/PRIT SS0 46 B2
Rocheway RCFD SS4 35 F1
Rochford Av WOS/PRIT SS0 46 D5
Rochford Cl WICKE SS11 17 E2 2
Rochford Garden Wy RCFD SS4 22 D5
Rochford Hall Cl RCFD SS4 35 E2
Rochford Rd CVI SS8 70 C1
SOSN SS2 46 C2
Rockall SOSN SS2 33 H4
Rockleigh Av LOS SS9 45 H5
Rodbridge Dr SOS SS1 61 G1
Rodings Av SLH/COR SS17 50 C5
The Rodings LOS SS9 33 E4
Roding Wy WICKW SS12 16 D1
Roedean Cl SOSN SS2 48 C5
Roedean Gdns SOSN SS2 48 C4
Roggel Rd CVI SS8 70 C2
Rokells BSDN SS14 26 B4
Rokescroft PIT SS13 39 H1
Roland La CVI SS8 56 A5 2
Romainville Wy CVI SS8 68 D1
Roman Wy BCAYW CM12 8 D5
Romney Rd BCAYW CM12 8 C4
Romsey Cl HOC/HUL SS5 21 E2
SLH/COR SS17 64 A3 2
Romsey Crs SBF/HAD SS7 41 G1
Romsey Dr SBF/HAD SS7 41 F1
Romsey Rd SBF/HAD SS7 41 F1
Romsey Wy SBF/HAD SS7 41 G1
Ronald Dr RAYL SS6 18 D4
Ronald Hill Gv LOS SS9 45 E5
Ronald Park Av WOS/PRIT SS0 46 B4
Roodegate BSDN SS14 2 C1
Rookery Cl RAYL SS6 31 F1
SLH/COR SS17 64 A3
Rookery Hl SLH/COR SS17 65 G1
Rookyards VGE SS16 39 F1 5
Roosevel Av CVI SS8 55 H5
Roosevelt Rd LAIN SS15 24 D5 9
Roots Hall Av SOSN SS2 47 E4
Roots Hall Dr SOSN SS2 46 D4
Rosary Gdns WOS/PRIT SS0 46 A2
Rosbach Rd CVI SS8 70 C1
Rosberg Rd CVI SS8 70 D1 3
Roscommon Wy CVI SS8 54 D5
Rose Acre BSDN SS14 27 G6
Rosebay Av BCAYW CM12 6 C5
Roseberry Av SBF/HAD SS7 29 H5
VGE SS16 37 E2
Rose Cl WICKW SS12 16 D3 14
Rosecroft Cl VGE SS16 36 D2
Roselaine BSDN SS14 26 C4
Rose La BCAYW CM12 8 D3
Rosemead SBF/HAD SS7 29 H4
Roserna Rd CVI SS8 70 C1
Rose Rd CVI SS8 69 H1
Rose Valley Crs SLH/COR SS17 50 C5
Rose Wy RCFD SS4 35 F3
Rosewood La SBN/FI SS3 63 E3
Rossiter Rd SBN/FI SS3 63 G1
Rosslyn Cl HOC/HUL SS5 21 F1
Rosslyn Rd BCAYW CM12 8 C3
HOC/HUL SS5 21 F2
Ross Wy VGE SS16 37 E3
Rothwell Cl LOS SS9 32 D5
Roundacre LAIN SS15 2 C3
Round Hill Rd SBF/HAD SS7 42 D4
Rowan Cl RAYL SS6 19 E2 2
The Rowans BCAYE CM11 9 G5
Rowans Wy WICKE SS11 10 D5
Rowan Wk LOS SS9 33 E5
Rowenhall LAIN SS15 24 C5
Rowhedge Cl PIT SS13 28 C1 1
The Rowlands SBF/HAD SS7 42 B2 3
Royal Artillery Wy SOSN SS2 48 B3
Royal Cl RCFD SS4 22 C3
Royal Ms SOS SS1 4 C6
Royal Oak Dr WICKE SS11 11 F5
Royal Ter SOS SS1 4 C6
Roydon Br BSDN SS14 27 E3
Royer Cl HOC/HUL SS5 21 H4 1
Royston Av LAIN SS15 25 G2
SOSN SS2 47 G3
Rubens Cl SBN/FI SS3 63 F1
Rubicon Av WICKE SS11 11 E5
Ruffles Cl RAYL SS6 19 H5
Rumbullion Dr BCAYW CM12 8 C2 2
Rundells Wk BSDN SS14 27 F4 2
The Rundels SBF/HAD SS7 42 D1
Runnymede Cha SBF/HAD SS7 42 D2
Runnymede Rd CVI SS8 70 A1
SLH/COR SS17 64 B3
Runwell Gdns WICKE SS11 10 C3
Runwell Rd WICKE SS11 10 C5
Runwell Ter SOS SS1 4 B5
Rushbottom La SBF/HAD SS7 29 G5
WICKW SS12 29 G3
Rush Cl SBF/HAD SS7 29 G5
Rushdene Rd BCAYW CM12 8 C5
Rushley PIT SS13 28 C3
Ruskin Av SOSN SS2 47 F4
Ruskin Dene BCAYW CM12 8 D2
Ruskin Rd SLH/COR SS17 64 B3
Ruskoi Rd CVI SS8 55 G4
Russell Cl LAIN SS15 25 E5
Russell Gdns WICKE SS11 16 D1
Russell Gv RCFD SS4 35 F1
Russet Cl SLH/COR SS17 64 C1
The Russets RCFD SS4 22 C3 3
Russetts VGE SS16 36 D1
Rutherford Cl BCAYW CM12 6 D5 9
LOS SS9 32 D5
Ruthven Cl WICKW SS12 16 C2
Rutland Av SOS SS1 61 F1
Rutland Cl LAIN SS15 24 D5
Rutland Dr RAYL SS6 19 E1
Rutland Gdns RCFD SS4 22 B3
Rydal Cl RAYL SS6 31 H1
Ryde Cl LOS SS9 44 C1
Ryde Dr SLH/COR SS17 64 B4
Ryder Wy PIT SS13 28 C1
The Ryde LOS SS9 44 C1
Ryedene VGE SS16 39 F3
Ryedene Cl VGE SS16 39 F3 4
Ryedene Pl VGE SS16 39 F3 5
Rylands Rd SOSN SS2 47 H4

S

Sackville Rd SOSN SS2 48 B5
Sadlers SBF/HAD SS7 29 G4
Sadlers Cl BCAYE CM11 7 G6
Saffory Cl LOS SS9 32 D4
Saffron Wk BCAYE CM11 9 E3 6
St Agnes Dr CVI SS8 69 E1
St Agnes Rd BCAYW CM12 13 F5
St Andrews Cl CVI SS8 55 E5 1
St Andrews La LAIN SS15 25 F4
St Andrew's Rd RCFD SS4 34 D1
SBN/FI SS3 62 B3
St Annes Rd CVI SS8 70 C1
St Ann's Rd SOSN SS2 4 D2
St Augustine's Av SOS SS1 62 A3
St Benet's Rd SOSN SS2 47 E3
St Catherines Cl WICKE SS11 11 E5 2
St Chads Cl LAIN SS15 25 F4 4
St Charles Dr WICKE SS11 16 D1
St Christophers Cl CVI SS8 55 E5
St Clare Meadow RCFD SS4 23 E5
St Clement's Av LOS SS9 45 F4
St Clements Cl HOC/HUL SS5 21 H4
SBF/HAD SS7 41 H1 1
St Clement's Crs SBF/HAD SS7 42 A1
St Clement's Dr LOS SS9 45 F3
St Clement's Rd SBF/HAD SS7 41 H1
St Cleres Crs WICKE SS11 17 E1
St Davids Dr SBF/HAD SS7 44 B3
St David's Rd VGE SS16 37 E2
St Davids Ter LOS SS9 44 B3
St David's Wy WICKE SS11 17 E1 2
St Edith's Cl BCAYW CM12 8 D4 5
St Ediths La BCAYW CM12 8 D4 6
St Edmund's Cl SOSN SS2 47 H3 1
St Gabriels Ct PIT SS13 40 A1 2
St George's Dr WOS/PRIT SS0 46 D3
St George's La SBN/FI SS3 63 E3
St George's Park Av
WOS/PRIT SS0 46 A4
St Georges Wk SBF/HAD SS7 29 G6 1
St Guiberts Rd CVI SS8 55 F4
St Helen's Rd WOS/PRIT SS0 59 H1
St Helens Wk BCAYW CM12 8 C1 9
St James Av SOS SS1 62 A3
St James Av East SLH/COR SS17 64 D1
St James Av West SLH/COR SS17 64 D1
St James Cl CVI SS8 55 E5 2
WOS/PRIT SS0 45 H3
St James Gdns WOS/PRIT SS0 45 H3
St James Ms BCAYW CM12 8 D3 2
St James Rd VGE SS16 3 K3
St James's Wk HOC/HUL SS5 20 D2 7
St Johns Cl LAIN SS15 25 F4 5
St Johns Crs CVI SS8 55 E5
St Johns Dr RAYL SS6 18 C4
St Johns Ms SLH/COR SS17 51 E5 4
St John's Rd BCAYE CM11 9 E2
SBF/HAD SS7 43 F3
WOS/PRIT SS0 59 H1
St John's Wy SLH/COR SS17 51 E5
St Lawrence Gdns LOS SS9 33 F5
St Leonard's Rd SOS SS1 4 E5
St Lukes Cl CVI SS8 55 E5 3
St Luke's Rd SOSN SS2 47 H3
St Margaret's Av SLH/COR SS17 64 B4
St Mark's Fld RCFD SS4 35 E1
St Marks Rd CVI SS8 55 E5
SBF/HAD SS7 43 F3
St Martin's Cl RAYL SS6 31 F3
SBF/HAD SS7 29 G4
St Mary's Av BCAYW CM12 8 D3
St Marys Cl SBF/HAD SS7 42 A5 1
SBN/FI SS3 49 G6
St Mary's Crs PIT SS13 28 B4
St Mary's Dr SBF/HAD SS7 42 B5
St Mary's Rd SBF/HAD SS7 55 E1
SOSN SS2 47 E4
WICKW SS12 16 A3
St Michaels Av PIT SS13 40 A2
St Michaels Rd CVI SS8 69 E1
SBF/HAD SS7 32 A5
St Nicholas La LAIN SS15 25 G4
St Omar Cl WICKW SS12 16 C2 3
St Pauls Gdns BCAYW CM12 8 D1 3
St Pauls Rd CVI SS8 55 E5
St Peter's Pavement
BSDN SS14 27 G2 1
St Peters Rd CVI SS8 55 E5 4
HOC/HUL SS5 20 C1
St Peter's Ter WICKW SS12 16 B1
St Peters Wk BCAYW CM12 8 C1
St Vincent's Rd WOS/PRIT SS0 59 H2
Sairard Cl LOS SS9 33 E4
Sairard Gdns LOS SS9 33 E4
Salcott Crs WICKW SS12 16 D1
Salesbury Dr BCAYE CM11 9 G3
Saling Gn LAIN SS15 26 A1 3
Salisbury Av SLH/COR SS17 64 C3 2
WOS/PRIT SS0 46 D5
Salisbury Rd LOS SS9 44 D5
The Saltings SBF/HAD SS7 43 G3
Samuel Rd VGE SS16 37 E2
Samuels Dr SOS SS1 62 A1
Sanctuary Gdn SLH/COR SS17 64 D2 2
Sanctuary Rd LOS SS9 44 B3
Sandbanks SBF/HAD SS7 43 G4
Sanderlings SBF/HAD SS7 41 H4 1
Sanders Rd CVI SS8 55 H3
Sandhill Rd LOS SS9 32 C3
Sandhurst CVI SS8 68 D1
Sandhurst Cl LOS SS9 45 G2
Sandhurst Crs LOS SS9 45 G2
Sandleigh Rd LOS SS9 45 H5
Sandon Cl BSDN SS14 39 G1
RCFD SS4 22 C5 1
Sandon Ct BSDN SS14 39 G1 2
Sandon Rd BSDN SS14 39 G1
Sandown Av WOS/PRIT SS0 46 A4
Sandown Cl WICKE SS11 17 F1 2
Sandown Rd SBF/HAD SS7 31 E4
WICKE SS11 17 F1
Sandpiper Cl SBN/FI SS3 62 D1
Sandpit Rd SBN/FI SS3 63 G1
Sandringham Av
HOC/HUL SS5 20 D2 8
Sandringham Cl SLH/COR SS17 64 D1
Sandringham Rd LAIN SS15 25 H3
SOS SS1 5 K4
San Remo Pde WOS/PRIT SS0 59 H2
San Remo Rd CVI SS8 70 C1
Satanita Rd WOS/PRIT SS0 59 F1
Savoy Cl VGE SS16 36 D1
Saxon Cl RAYL SS6 19 H3
WICKE SS11 10 D4
Saxon Gdns SBN/FI SS3 62 B2
Saxonville SBF/HAD SS7 41 G2
Saxon Wy SBF/HAD SS7 41 H4
Sayers SBF/HAD SS7 30 D5
Scaldhurst PIT SS13 28 B3 5
Scarborough Rd LOS SS9 45 F4
Scarletts BSDN SS14 26 D3
School La SBF/HAD SS7 55 E1
WICKW SS12 29 F1
School Rd BCAYW CM12 9 E5 1
School Wy LOS SS9 45 G3
Scimitar Pk PIT SS13 28 C1
Scott Dr WICKW SS12 16 C3
Scratton Rd SLH/COR SS17 64 C2
SOS SS1 4 B5
Scrub La SBF/HAD SS7 43 H3
Scrub Ri BCAYW CM12 8 C5
Seaforth Av SOSN SS2 47 H4
Seaforth Gv SOSN SS2 48 A4
Seaforth Rd WOS/PRIT SS0 59 G2
Seamore Av SBF/HAD SS7 29 H5
Seamore Cl SBF/HAD SS7 29 G5
Sea Reach LOS SS9 58 B1 2
Seaview Av VGE SS16 39 E3
Seaview Rd CVI SS8 70 D2
LOS SS9 58 B1
SBN/FI SS3 62 C3
Seaview Ter SBF/HAD SS7 43 G5
Seaway CVI SS8 70 A2
SOS SS1 4 E6

Seax Ct LAIN SS15 24 C4
Seax Wy LAIN SS15 24 C4
Sebert Cl BCAYE CM11 13 G1 4
Second Av BCAYW CM12 12 B1
CVI SS8 55 E5
SLH/COR SS17 64 C1
WICKE SS11 17 F2
WOS/PRIT SS0 59 E2
Seddons Wk HOC/HUL SS5 21 F2 1
Sedgemoor SBN/FI SS3 49 G5
Selbourne Rd HOC/HUL SS5 21 F2
SBF/HAD SS7 42 A1
SOSN SS2 47 H4 2
Seldon Cl WOS/PRIT SS0 46 A3
Selworthy Cl BCAYE CM11 13 F1
Selwyn Rd SOSN SS2 47 H4
Semples SLH/COR SS17 65 E2 2
Seven Acres WICKE SS11 10 D5
Seventh Av CVI SS8 55 F5
Sewards End WICKW SS12 16 D2 8
Seymour Rd SBF/HAD SS7 44 A3
WOS/PRIT SS0 46 B5
Shaftesbury Av SOS SS1 5 J7
Shakespeare Av BCAYE CM11 9 F3 12
RAYL SS6 32 A1
VGE SS16 36 D1
WOS/PRIT SS0 46 C4
Shakespeare Dr WOS/PRIT SS0 46 D4
Shalford Rd BCAYE CM11 9 G3 5
Shanklin Av BCAYW CM12 8 D3
Shanklin Dr WOS/PRIT SS0 45 H4
Shannon Av RAYL SS6 31 F2
Shannon Cl LOS SS9 45 F2
Shannon Wy CVI SS8 69 E1
Sharlands Cl WICKE SS11 11 E5
Sharnbrook SBN/FI SS3 49 G4
Shaw Cl WICKW SS12 16 C3
Sheering Ct RAYL SS6 18 D5 13
Sheldon Cl SLH/COR SS17 51 G4
Sheldon Rd CVI SS8 70 D1
Shellbeach Rd CVI SS8 70 C2
Shelley Pl RAYL SS6 18 D5
Shelley Sq SOSN SS2 47 G4
Shelly Av VGE SS16 36 D1 3
Shelsley Dr VGE SS16 37 F3
Shepard Cl LOS SS9 33 H5
Shepeshall LAIN SS15 25 H5
Shepherds Cl SBF/HAD SS7 43 H2
Shepherds Wk SBF/HAD SS7 43 H2
Sherbourne Cl SOSN SS2 34 D5 1
Sherbourne Dr PIT SS13 27 H2
Sherbourne Gdns SOSN SS2 35 E5
Sheridan Av SBF/HAD SS7 43 E3
Sheridan Cl RAYL SS6 32 A1
Sheringham Cl SLH/COR SS17 64 D1
Sheriton Sq RAYL SS6 19 G4
Sherry Wy SBF/HAD SS7 31 H5
Sherwood Cl VGE SS16 36 D2 4
Sherwood Crs SBF/HAD SS7 43 H2
Sherwood Wy SOSN SS2 48 B4
Shillingstone SBN/FI SS3 49 G5
Shipwrights Cl SBF/HAD SS7 43 E4
Shipwrights Dr SBF/HAD SS7 43 E3
Shire Cl BCAYE CM11 9 G1
Shirley Gdns PIT SS13 28 B3
Shirley Rd LOS SS9 45 F1
Shoebury Av SBN/FI SS3 63 E2
Shoebury Common Rd
SBN/FI SS3 62 B4
Shoebury Rd SOS SS1 48 D5
Shopland Rd RCFD SS4 35 H4
Shorefield SBF/HAD SS7 41 G3
Shorefield Gdns
WOS/PRIT SS0 59 H2 2
Shorefield Rd WOS/PRIT SS0 59 G2
Shortacre BSDN SS14 3 G1
Short Rd CVI SS8 56 A5
SBF/HAD SS7 43 G4
Short St SOSN SS2 4 C1
Shrewsbury Cl VGE SS16 36 C1 13
Shrewsbury Dr SBF/HAD SS7 30 A4 1
Shrubbery Cl LAIN SS15 25 G3 2
Sidmouth Av WOS/PRIT SS0 46 C1
Sidwell Av SBF/HAD SS7 42 B5
Sidwell Cha SBF/HAD SS7 42 B5
Sidwell La SBF/HAD SS7 42 B5
Sidwell Pk SBF/HAD SS7 42 B5
Silva Island Wy WICKW SS12 17 E3 6
Silverdale RAYL SS6 31 H3
SBF/HAD SS7 30 C4
SLH/COR SS17 50 C5
Silverdale Av WOS/PRIT SS0 46 D4
Silverdale East SLH/COR SS17 50 C5
Silvermere VGE SS16 36 D1 4
Silverpoint Marine CVI SS8 71 F1
Silversea Dr WOS/PRIT SS0 45 H4
Silverthorn Cl RCFD SS4 22 C4
Silverthorne CVI SS8 69 G1
Silvertown Av SLH/COR SS17 64 C2
Silvertree Cl HOC/HUL SS5 20 C2 1
Silver Wy WICKE SS11 10 B5
Sinclair Wk WICKW SS12 16 C3
Sirdar Rd RAYL SS6 31 G3
Sir Walter Raleigh Dr RAYL SS6 19 F4
Sixth Av CVI SS8 55 F5
Skylark Cl BCAYE CM11 9 F4
The Slades VGE SS16 39 F4
Smallgains Av CVI SS8 56 C5
Small Gains La ING CM4 7 G2
Smallgains La ING CM4 7 H2
Smartt Av CVI SS8 55 H5 1
Smither's Cha SOSN SS2 47 G1
Smith St SBN/FI SS3 63 E3
Smythe Rd BCAYE CM11 7 G5
Snakes La SOSN SS2 45 H1
Snowdonia Cl PIT SS13 28 B3
Soane St PIT SS13 28 A3
Softwater La SBF/HAD SS7 43 G3
Somerset Av RCFD SS4 22 D5
WOS/PRIT SS0 46 A2
Somerset Crs WOS/PRIT SS0 46 A2
Somerset Gdns PIT SS13 28 A5 3
Somerset Rd LAIN SS15 25 E5
Somerton Av WOS/PRIT SS0 45 H2
Somerville Gdns LOS SS9 58 C1
Somnes Av CVI SS8 55 F3
Sonning Wy SBN/FI SS3 49 G5
The Sorrells SLH/COR SS17 65 E2
The Sorrels SBF/HAD SS7 30 A4
South Av SOSN SS2 4 E1
VGE SS16 50 A2
South Beech Av WICKE SS11 16 C1 1
Southborough Dr WOS/PRIT SS0 46 A4
Southbourne Gdns
WOS/PRIT SS0 46 A2
Southbourne Gv HOC/HUL SS5 21 G2
WOS/PRIT SS0 46 A3
Southchurch Av SBN/FI SS3 63 F2 1
SOS SS1 5 F4
Southchurch Bvd SOS SS1 48 B5
Southchurch Hall Cl SOS SS1 5 H4
Southchurch Rd SOS SS1 4 C3
Southcliff SBF/HAD SS7 41 H2
South Colne VGE SS16 3 K5
Southcote Crs BSDN SS14 27 F3
Southcote Rw BSDN SS14 27 G3
South Crs WOS/PRIT SS0 46 C1
South Crockerford VGE SS16 39 F2
Southend Arterial Rd BSDN SS14 26 C1
LAIN SS15 24 C2
RAYL SS6 30 D3
SBF/HAD SS7 31 F3
Southend Rd BCAYE CM11 13 F1
BCAYW CM12 9 E4
RCFD SS4 35 E3
SBN/FI SS3 49 F3
SLH/COR SS17 51 F2
WICKE SS11 17 F1
Southend Road Main Rd
HOC/HUL SS5 21 E3
Southernhay BSDN SS14 2 D3
LOS SS9 45 E1
Southfalls Rd CVI SS8 71 E1
Southfield Cha BCAYW CM12 24 B2
Southfield Cl SBF/HAD SS7 43 H1
Southfield Dr SBF/HAD SS7 43 H1
South Hanningfield Wy
WICKE SS11 10 C2
Southlands Rd BCAYE CM11 15 E2
South Mayne PIT SS13 27 H5
South Pde CVI SS8 70 D2
South Rdg BCAYE CM11 9 F4
South Riding BSDN SS14 27 F5
South Rd BCAYE CM11 15 E3
Southsea Av LOS SS9 45 E4
South St RCFD SS4 35 E2
South View Cl RAYL SS6 32 A3
Southview Dr WOS/PRIT SS0 46 B4
Southview Rd HOC/HUL SS5 21 G1
South View Rd SBF/HAD SS7 41 H3
Southwalters CVI SS8 55 G5
South Wash Rd LAIN SS15 25 H1
Southway VGE SS16 37 G4
Southwell Rd SBF/HAD SS7 42 B2
Southwick Gdns CVI SS8 69 G1
Southwick Rd CVI SS8 69 G1
Southwold Crs SBF/HAD SS7 41 H1
Southwood Gdns RAYL SS6 32 C3
Sovereign Cl RCFD SS4 34 D1 1
Spa Cl HOC/HUL SS5 21 F2
Spains Hall Pl VGE SS16 3 G4
Spanbeek Rd CVI SS8 56 A4 5
Sparkbridge LAIN SS15 24 D5 10
Spa Rd HOC/HUL SS5 21 E2
Sparrows Herne VGE SS16 2 D7
Spellbrook Cl WICKW SS12 17 E2
Spencer Gdns RCFD SS4 22 C3
Spencer Rd SBF/HAD SS7 30 A5
Spenders Cl BSDN SS14 27 E3
Spindle Beams RCFD SS4 35 E2
The Spinnakers SBF/HAD SS7 41 G1
Spinney Cl WICKE SS11 17 E1
The Spinneys HOC/HUL SS5 21 E3
LOS SS9 33 G4
RAYL SS6 32 B2
The Spinney BCAYW CM12 9 E1
Spire Rd LAIN SS15 25 F4
Sporhams VGE SS16 2 A6
Springfield SBF/HAD SS7 43 G2
Springfield Dr WOS/PRIT SS0 46 C3
Springfield Rd BCAYW CM12 7 E5
CVI SS8 71 E1
WICKE SS11 11 E5
Springfields VGE SS16 39 G3
Spring Gdns RAYL SS6 31 F1
Springhouse La SLH/COR SS17 65 F1
Springhouse Rd SLH/COR SS17 50 D5
Springwater Cl LOS SS9 32 D4
Springwater Gv LOS SS9 32 D4
Springwater Rd LOS SS9 32 C3
Spruce Cl LAIN SS15 25 F2
Sprundel Av CVI SS8 70 C2
Squirrels VGE SS16 37 E3
Stacey Dr VGE SS16 37 F4
Stacey's Mt BCAYE CM11 14 D3
Stadium Rd SOSN SS2 47 F4
Stadium Wy SBF/HAD SS7 31 F4
Staffa Cl WICKW SS12 17 E3
Stafford Cl LOS SS9 33 H5
Stafford Gn VGE SS16 36 C2
Stagden Cross BSDN SS14 39 G1
Stambridge Rd RCFD SS4 35 E1
Staneway VGE SS16 37 G3
Stanfield Rd SOSN SS2 47 F4
Stanford-le-Hope By-pass
SLH/COR SS17 51 F1
Stanford Rd CVI SS8 69 H1
SLH/COR SS17 64 A3
Stanier Cl SOS SS1 5 G3
Stanley Rd CVI SS8 56 B5
RCFD SS4 22 B1
SBF/HAD SS7 42 A1
SOS SS1 5 F5
Stanley Ter BCAYW CM12 8 D4
Stanmore Rd WICKE SS11 17 G2 4
Stannetts LAIN SS15 25 E3 2
Stansfield Rd SBF/HAD SS7 29 G4
Stansted Cl BCAYE CM11 9 G3 6
Stanway Rd SBF/HAD SS7 41 H1
Stapleford End WICKE SS11 17 G3 2
Staplegrove SBN/FI SS3 62 B1
Star La SBN/FI SS3 49 H3
Station Ap CVI SS8 55 G3
HOC/HUL SS5 21 F2 2
LAIN SS15 37 F1
SOS SS1 4 C4
SOSN SS2 47 E4
VGE SS16 40 A2
WICKE SS11 10 C5 2
Station Av RAYL SS6 19 F5
SOSN SS2 47 F3
WICKE SS11 10 B4
Station Crs RAYL SS6 19 G5
Station La PIT SS13 40 B1
Station Rd BCAYW CM12 8 C3
CVI SS8 70 D2
HOC/HUL SS5 21 F2
LOS SS9 45 F3
RAYL SS6 19 F5
SBF/HAD SS7 55 E1
SOS SS1 62 A1
WICKE SS11 10 B3
WOS/PRIT SS0 59 F1
Station Wy VGE SS16 2 D4
Stebbings VGE SS16 37 F2
Steeple Cl RCFD SS4 22 C5
Steeplefield LOS SS9 33 F5
Steeplehall PIT SS13 39 H1
Steeple Hts SBF/HAD SS7 29 G5 2
Steli Av CVI SS8 55 G4
Stella Maris Cl CVI SS8 71 E1
Stephenson Rd LOS SS9 32 D5
Stevens Cl CVI SS8 56 C5
Stevenson Wy WICKW SS12 16 B3
Stewart Pl WICKW SS12 17 E3 7
Steyning Av SOSN SS2 48 B4
Stile La RAYL SS6 31 G1
Stilemans WICKE SS11 10 C5 3
Stirling Av LOS SS9 44 C4
Stirling Cl RAYL SS6 19 E3
Stirling Pl PIT SS13 28 A3
Stock Cl SOSN SS2 47 E2
Stock Rd BCAYE CM11 9 E1
BCAYW CM12 9 E3
SOSN SS2 47
Stockwell Cl BCAYE CM11 13 G
Stockwood SBF/HAD SS7 30
Stokefelde PIT SS13 28
Stonechat Rd BCAYW CM12 9
Stonehill Cl LOS SS9 45
Stonehill Rd LOS SS9 45
Stoneleighs SBF/HAD SS7 30
Stormonts Wy VGE SS16 37
Stornoway Rd SOSN SS2 5
Stour Cl SBN/FI SS3 62 D
Strangman Av SBF/HAD SS7 43
Strasbourg Rd CVI SS8 56
Stratford Gdns SLH/COR SS17 64
Stroma Gdns SBN/FI SS3 62
Stromburg Rd CVI SS8 55
Stromness Pl SOSN SS2 5
Stromness Rd SOSN SS2 5
Struan Av SLH/COR SS17 50
Stuart Cl CVI SS8 56
SOSN SS2 47
Stuart Rd SOSN SS2 47
Stuart St SOSN SS2 47 F
Stuart Wy BCAYE CM11 9 H
Stublands BSDN SS14 27
Sturrocks VGE SS16 39
Sudbrook Cl WICKW SS12 16 C
Sudbury Cl HOC/HUL SS5 21
Sudeley Gdns HOC/HUL SS5 21
Suffolk Av LOS SS9 45
Suffolk Dr LAIN SS15 25
Suffolk Wy CVI SS8 55
Sugden Av WICKW SS12 15
Sullivan Wy VGE SS16 36
Summercourt Rd
WOS/PRIT SS0 59 H
Summerdale BCAYW CM12 8
Summerwood Cl SBF/HAD SS7 43 F
Sumpters Wy SOSN SS2 35
Sunbury Ct SBN/FI SS3 49
Sunnedon VGE SS16 3
Sunningdale CVI SS8 56 B
Sunningdale Av LOS SS9 45
Sunnybank Cl LOS SS9 33
Sunnyfield Gdns HOC/HUL SS5 20
Sunnymede Cl SBF/HAD SS7 30
Sunny Rd HOC/HUL SS5 21
Sunnyside VGE SS16 36 C
Sun St BCAYW CM12 8
Surbiton Av SOS SS1 5
Surbiton Rd SOSN SS2 5
Surig Rd CVI SS8 55
Surrey Av LOS SS9 45
Surrey Wy LAIN SS15 24
Sussex Cl CVI SS8 55
LAIN SS15 25
Sussex Wy BCAYW CM12 7
CVI SS8 55 H
Sutcliffe Cl WICKW SS12 16
Sutherland Bvd LOS SS9 44
Sutherland Pl WICKW SS12 16
Sutton Court Dr RCFD SS4 35
Sutton Rd RCFD SS4 35
SOSN SS2 4
Suttons Rd SBN/FI SS3 63
Swale Rd SBF/HAD SS7 43
Swallowcliffe SBN/FI SS3 49
Swallow Cl RAYL SS6 19 E
Swallow Dl VGE SS16 3
Swallow Dr SBF/HAD SS7 41
Swallow Rd WICKE SS11 10
The Swallows BCAYE CM11 9
Swanage Rd SOSN SS2 4
Swan Cl LAIN SS15 25 H
Swan La WICKE SS11 10
Swan Md VGE SS16 3
Swans Green Cl SBF/HAD SS7 30 D
Swanstead VGE SS16 39
Sweet Briar Av SBF/HAD SS7 42
Sweet Briar Dr LAIN SS15 25 G
Sweyne Av HOC/HUL SS5 21
WOS/PRIT SS0 4
Sweyne Cl RAYL SS6 19
Swinborne Ct PIT SS13 28 A
Swinborne Rd PIT SS13 28
Sycamore Cl CVI SS8 69
RAYL SS6 19 E
Sycamore Gv SOSN SS2 47
Sydervelt Rd CVI SS8 55
Sydney Rd LOS SS9 44
SBF/HAD SS7 41
Sykes Md RAYL SS6 31
Sylvan Cl CVI SS8 70 A
LAIN SS15 25 E
Sylvan Tryst BCAYW CM12 9 E
Sylvan Wy LAIN SS15 24
LOS SS9 44
Symons Av LOS SS9 33

T

abora Av CVI SS8 55 G4
ailors Ct SOSN SS2 47 E1
ailors Wy SOSN SS2 47 E1
aits SLH/COR SS17 65 E2
akely End VGE SS16 2 D5
akely Ride VGE SS16 2 D4
albot Av RAYL SS6 19 F5
allis Cl SLH/COR SS17 64 B1
allis Rd LAIN SS15 25 G3
alza Wy SOSN SS2 47 E1
amarisk SBF/HAD SS7 41 H2
anfield Dr BCAYW CM12 8 D3
angham Wk BSDN SS14 26 C4
angmere Cl WICKE SS11 17 G2 5
ankerville Dr LOS SS9 45 E3
answell Av PIT SS13 28 A4
answell Cl PIT SS13 28 A5
aranto Rd CVI SS8 70 C1
asman Cl SLH/COR SS17 51 E5 5
attenham Rd LAIN SS15 25 E3
attersall Gdns LOS SS9 44 B5
aunton Dr WOS/PRIT SS0 46 A2
aveners Green Cl
WICKW SS12 16 D2 9
avistock Dr BCAYW CM12 6 C5 9
avistock Rd LAIN SS15 25 F3 4
LAIN SS15 25 F4 6
eagles LAIN SS15 25 H5
eigngrace SBN/FI SS3 62 C1
eignmouth Dr RAYL SS6 19 G3
emple Cl LAIN SS15 25 F4 7
SBF/HAD SS7 44 A3
emplewood Ct SBF/HAD SS7 43 G3
emplewood Rd PIT SS13 28 A5
SBF/HAD SS7 43 G3
emptin Av CVI SS8 70 D1
endring Av RAYL SS6 18 D5
ennyson Av SOSN SS2 47 G4
ennyson Cl LOS SS9 44 B4
ennyson Dr PIT SS13 40 A2
ensing Gdns BCAYW CM12 8 C4
enterfields PIT SS13 28 B3
eramo Rd CVI SS8 70 C1 2
erence Webster Rd WICKW SS12 16 C2
erling VGE SS16 3 F4
erminal Cl SBN/FI SS3 63 E2
erminus Dr VGE SS16 40 A2
erms Av CVI SS8 55 H4 7
erni Rd CVI SS8 70 C1
he Terrace SBN/FI SS3 63 E3
ewkes Rd CVI SS8 56 C4
hackerey Rw WICKW SS12 16 C3 3
hames Cl LOS SS9 44 B5
RAYL SS6 31 F2
SLH/COR SS17 65 F1
hames Crs SLH/COR SS17 51 G4
hames Dr LOS SS9 44 B5
hames Haven Rd SLH/COR SS17 65 F1
hameside Crs CVI SS8 69 G1
hames Rd CVI SS8 69 G2
hames Vw VGE SS16 37 F5
hear Cl WOS/PRIT SS0 46 B2
helma Av CVI SS8 55 H5
heobalds Rd LOS SS9 44 D5
hetford Pl LAIN SS15 25 G2
heydon Crs BSDN SS14 27 G2
hielen Rd CVI SS8 55 H4
hird Av CVI SS8 55 F5
SLH/COR SS17 50 D5
WICKE SS11 17 F2
hirlmere Rd SBF/HAD SS7 30 B4
hisselt Rd CVI SS8 55 H4
histle Cl LAIN SS15 26 A2
histledown BSDN SS14 3 H1
histley Cl LOS SS9 45 G2
homas Dr CVI SS8 55 F4
homasin Rd PIT SS13 28 B2
homas Rd PIT SS13 28 D4
hompson Av CVI SS8 71 E1
horington Av SBF/HAD SS7 31 G5
horington Rd RAYL SS6 32 B2 4
hornbush LAIN SS15 25 H5
horndale SBF/HAD SS7 31 E4 3
horndon Park Cl LOS SS9 44 D1
horndon Park Crs LOS SS9 44 C1
horndon Park Dr LOS SS9 44 C1
horney Bay Rd CVI SS8 69 G2
hornford Gdns SOSN SS2 47 E1
hornhill LOS SS9 45 F2
hornton Wy LAIN SS15 36 D1
horolds VGE SS16 39 F3
horpe Bay Gdns SOS SS1 61 H3
horpe Cl HOC/HUL SS5 21 G4
horpedene Gdns SBN/FI SS3 62 C2
Thorpe Esp SOS SS1 61 H3
Thorpe Hall Av SOS SS1 61 H1 2
Thorpe Hall Cl SOS SS1 61 H1
Thorpe Rd HOC/HUL SS5 21 G4
Thorp Leas CVI SS8 70 A2
Thors Oak SLH/COR SS17 64 D2
Threshelford VGE SS16 2 B5
Throwley Cl PIT SS13 40 B1
Thundersley Church Rd
SBF/HAD SS7 42 A1
Thundersley Gv SBF/HAD SS7 42 C1
Thundersley Park Rd
SBF/HAD SS7 42 A3
Thurlow Dr SOS SS1 61 G1
Thurlstone SBF/HAD SS7 43 F1
Thurston Av SOSN SS2 48 B5
Thynne Rd BCAYE CM11 9 F3
Tickfield Av SOSN SS2 47 E4
Tidworth Av WICKE SS11 10 D3
Tilburg Rd CVI SS8 55 H5
Tillingham Gn LAIN SS15 24 D5
Tillingham Wy RAYL SS6 18 D5
Tilney Turn VGE SS16 39 F2
Timberlog Cl BSDN SS14 27 F5
Timberlog La BSDN SS14 27 F5
Timbermans Vw VGE SS16 39 G3
Tinker's La RCFD SS4 35 E2
Tintern Av WOS/PRIT SS0 46 B4
Tippersfield SBF/HAD SS7 42 B2 4
Tiptree Cl LOS SS9 45 G2
Tiptree Gv WICKW SS12 16 C1 2
Tiree Cha WICKW SS12 17 E3
The Tithe WICKW SS12 16 A2
Toledo Cl SOS SS1 4 E4
Toledo Rd SOS SS1 4 E4
Tollesbury Cl WICKW SS12 16 D2 10
Tollgate SBF/HAD SS7 31 F5
Tomkins Cl SLH/COR SS17 64 B2
Tonbridge Rd HOC/HUL SS5 21 G1
Tongres Rd CVI SS8 55 H5
Toppesfield Av WICKW SS12 16 B3
Torney Cl VGE SS16 36 C2
Torquay Cl RAYL SS6 19 G3 3
Torquay Dr LOS SS9 45 F5
Torrington SBN/FI SS3 62 C1
Torsi Rd CVI SS8 70 C1 3
Totman Cl RAYL SS6 31 G3
Totman Crs RAYL SS6 31 F3
Toucan Cl SBN/FI SS3 49 H5 8
Toucan Wy VGE SS16 2 D7
Tower Av LAIN SS15 25 F4
Tower Court Ms WOS/PRIT SS0 59 H2
Towerfield Cl SBN/FI SS3 62 D2
Towerfield Rd SBN/FI SS3 62 D2
Townfield Rd RCFD SS4 35 E2
Townfield Wk SBN/FI SS3 49 H2 1
Towngate BSDN SS14 2 C2
Town Sq BSDN SS14 2 D2
Trafalgar Rd SBN/FI SS3 62 C2
Trafalgar Wy BCAYW CM12 7 E5
Travers Wy PIT SS13 27 H5
Treecot Dr LOS SS9 45 H2
Treelawn Dr LOS SS9 45 G2
Treelawn Gdns LOS SS9 45 G2
Trenders Av RAYL SS6 19 E2
Trenham Av PIT SS13 28 C4
Trent Cl WICKW SS12 16 C2
Tresco Wy WICKW SS12 17 E3
Trevor Cl BCAYW CM12 12 C1
Trimley Cl BSDN SS14 26 D4
Trindehay LAIN SS15 37 H1
Trinder Wy WICKW SS12 15 H2
Trinity Av WOS/PRIT SS0 59 H2
Trinity Cl BCAYE CM11 13 F2
LAIN SS15 25 F5
RAYL SS6 31 H2
Trinity Rd BCAYE CM11 13 F2
RAYL SS6 31 H2
SOSN SS2 5 H1
Tripat Cl SLH/COR SS17 52 A4
Triton Wy SBF/HAD SS7 31 E5
Truman Cl LAIN SS15 24 D5 11
The Trunnions RCFD SS4 35 E2
Truro Crs RAYL SS6 19 F3
Tudor Av SLH/COR SS17 50 D5
Tudor Cl LOS SS9 32 D4
RAYL SS6 32 A1
SBF/HAD SS7 42 C1
Tudor Ct LAIN SS15 26 A1 4
Tudor Gdns LOS SS9 45 E3
SBN/FI SS3 62 C3
Tudor Rd CVI SS8 69 E1
LOS SS9 32 D4
WOS/PRIT SS0 46 D4
Tudor Wy HOC/HUL SS5 21 G4
WICKW SS12 15 H1
Tunbridge Rd SOSN SS2 47 E4
Tunstall Cl PIT SS13 40 B1
Turner Cl SBN/FI SS3 63 E1
Turold Rd SLH/COR SS17 50 D5
The Turpins BSDN SS14 26 D4
Twinstead WICKW SS12 16 D2
Twyzel Rd CVI SS8 56 B4 4
Tye Common Rd BCAYW CM12 12 B3
Tyefields PIT SS13 28 B4
Tyelands BCAYW CM12 8 C5
Tyler Av LAIN SS15 25 F5
Tylers Av BCAYW CM12 7 E5
SOS SS1 4 D4
Tylewood SBF/HAD SS7 43 F4
Tylney Av RCFD SS4 22 D5
Tyms Wy RAYL SS6 19 H4 2
Tyrel Dr SOS SS1 4 E3
Tyrells HOC/HUL SS5 21 E4
Tyrone Cl BCAYE CM11 13 F2
Tyrone Rd BCAYE CM11 13 F2
SOS SS1 61 H3
Tyrrell Rd SBF/HAD SS7 41 G4
Tyrrells Rd BCAYE CM11 13 G2

U

Ullswater Rd SBF/HAD SS7 30 B4
Ulster Av SBN/FI SS3 62 B3
Ulting Wy WICKE SS11 11 F5
Una Rd PIT SS13 29 E5
Underhill Rd SBF/HAD SS7 42 B3
Underwood Sq LOS SS9 44 D4
Union La RCFD SS4 34 D1
Upland Cl BCAYW CM12 8 C1 10
Upland Dr BCAYW CM12 8 C1
Upland Rd BCAYW CM12 8 C1
LOS SS9 58 D1 2
Uplands Cl HOC/HUL SS5 21 G3
SBF/HAD SS7 41 G2
Uplands Park Rd RAYL SS6 19 G4
Uplands Rd HOC/HUL SS5 21 G3
SBF/HAD SS7 41 G3
Upper Av PIT SS13 28 D3
Upper Lambricks RAYL SS6 19 H4
Upper Market Rd WICKW SS12 10 C5 4
WICKW SS12 10 B5 1
Upper Mayne LAIN SS15 26 A4
Upper Park Rd WICKW SS12 16 C4
Upper Rd BCAYE CM11 15 E3
Upton Cl SLH/COR SS17 64 C2
Upway RAYL SS6 19 G5
The Upway BSDN SS14 26 C4
Urmond Rd CVI SS8 55 H5
Uttons Av LOS SS9 58 A1
Uxbridge Cl WICKE SS11 17 E2

V

Vaagen Rd CVI SS8 56 A5
Vadsoe Rd CVI SS8 56 A4 6
Vale Av SOSN SS2 47 F4
Valence Wy VGE SS16 37 F2
The Vale ING CM4 7 G3
VGE SS16 39 E3
Valkyrie Rd WOS/PRIT SS0 59 G1
Vallance Cl SOSN SS2 48 B3
Valley Rd BCAYE CM11 9 E3
Valmar Av SLH/COR SS17 64 A3
Vanderwalt Av CVI SS8 70 C1 4
Van Diemens Pass CVI SS8 71 E1
Vange Corner Dr SLH/COR SS17 38 C5
Vange Hill Dr VGE SS16 3 K5
Vange Park Rd SLH/COR SS17 38 C5
The Vanguards SBN/FI SS3 63 E2
Vanguard Wy SBN/FI SS3 63 E1
Vardon Dr LOS SS9 44 C3
Vaughan Av SOSN SS2 5 K1
Vaughan Cl RCFD SS4 22 D3
Vaughan Williams Rd
LAIN SS15 25 F3 5
Vaulx Rd CVI SS8 56 A5
Venables Cl CVI SS8 70 B1
Venlo Rd CVI SS8 56 A4 7
Vermeer Crs SBN/FI SS3 63 F1
Vermont Cl PIT SS13 28 B3
Vernon Av RAYL SS6 19 E4
Vernon Rd LOS SS9 44 D5
Vestry Cl LAIN SS15 25 F4
Vicarage Cl CVI SS8 69 E1
LAIN SS15 25 F5 5
Vicarage Hl SBF/HAD SS7 42 C4
Vickers Rd SOSN SS2 34 C5
Victor Av PIT SS13 28 C5
Victor Dr LOS SS9 58 C1
Victor Gdns HOC/HUL SS5 21 G3
Victoria Av RAYL SS6 19 E3
SOSN SS2 4 B1
VGE SS16 37 F3 1
WICKW SS12 10 A5
Victoria Cl LAIN SS15 25 E4 3
Victoria Crs LAIN SS15 25 F3 6
WICKW SS12 16 A1
Victoria Dr LOS SS9 45 F5
Victoria Rd LAIN SS15 25 E4 4
LOS SS9 58 B1
RAYL SS6 19 H5
SLH/COR SS17 64 B2
SOS SS1 5 H4
VGE SS16 39 E4
Victor Mew Cl WICKW SS12 16 C3
Vikings Wy CVI SS8 69 E1
Viking Wy WICKE SS11 10 C3
Village Dr CVI SS8 69 F1
Village Hall Cl CVI SS8 69 E1 2
Villa Rd SBF/HAD SS7 41 H2
Villiers Wy SBF/HAD SS7 42 C1
Vincent Cl SBN/FI SS3 62 D2
SLH/COR SS17 65 G1
Vincent Wy BCAYW CM12 6 C5
The Vintners SOSN SS2 47 E1
Virginia Cl SBF/HAD SS7 29 G4
Vista Rd WICKE SS11 17 E1
Voorburg Rd CVI SS8 56 C5 1
Vowler Rd VGE SS16 37 E2
Voysey Gdns PIT SS13 28 A2

W

Waalwyk Dr CVI SS8 56 B5
Waarden Rd CVI SS8 55 H5
Waarem Av CVI SS8 55 H5
Wakefield Av BCAYW CM12 8 D3
Wakering Av SBN/FI SS3 63 E2
Wakering Rd SBN/FI SS3 48 D4
SBN/FI SS3 63 F1
Wakescolne WICKE SS11 17 F2
Waldegrave VGE SS16 2 E5
Waldringfield BSDN SS14 26 C4
Walker Dr LOS SS9 44 B4
Walkers Sq SLH/COR SS17 64 C3
Walkey Wy SBN/FI SS3 63 G1
Wallace Dr WICKW SS12 16 D3
Wallace St SBN/FI SS3 63 E2
Wallis Av SOSN SS2 47 E4 2
Wall Rd CVI SS8 71 E1
Walnut Ct HOC/HUL SS5 21 F1 2
Walsingham Cl LAIN SS15 25 F4 8
Walsingham Rd SOSN SS2 47 G3
Walsingham Wy BCAYW CM12 7 E5
Walters Cl LOS SS9 33 F5
Waltham Crs SOSN SS2 47 G3
Waltham Rd RAYL SS6 19 E5
Walthams PIT SS13 28 A4
Walthams Pl PIT SS13 28 A4
Walton Ct LAIN SS15 25 F3 7
Walton Rd SOS SS1 61 G3
Wambrook SBN/FI SS3 49 G5
Wamburg Rd CVI SS8 56 C5
Wansfell Gdns SOS SS1 48 C5
Warburtons SLH/COR SS17 65 E1
Warner Cl BCAYE CM11 9 G4 2
Warners Bridge Cha RCFD SS4 35 E5
Warners Gdns SOSN SS2 34 D5
Warren Cha SBF/HAD SS7 42 D2
Warren Cl RAYL SS6 31 F3
Warren Dr WICKE SS11 11 F5
Warrene Cl SLH/COR SS17 64 C3
Warren Rd LOS SS9 44 B3
The Warren BCAYW CM12 8 B1
Warrington Sq BCAYW CM12 8 C2 3
Warrior Sq SOS SS1 4 D4
Warrior Sq East SOS SS1 4 D3
Warrior Sq North SOS SS1 4 D3
Warrior Square Rd SBN/FI SS3 63 E4
Warwick Cl CVI SS8 55 H4
RAYL SS6 32 A2
SBF/HAD SS7 30 A4
Warwick Dr RCFD SS4 35 E4
Warwick Gdns RAYL SS6 32 A2
Warwick Gn RAYL SS6 32 B2
Warwick Pl VGE SS16 36 C2
Warwick Rd RAYL SS6 32 A2
SOS SS1 61 G3
Washington Av LAIN SS15 24 D5
Wash Rd LAIN SS15 25 F2
Watchfield La RAYL SS6 31 F2
Waterdene CVI SS8 55 F4
The Waterfalls VGE SS16 37 E3 2
Waterford Rd SBN/FI SS3 62 C3
Waterfront Wk BSDN SS14 26 C2
Waterhale SOS SS1 48 D5
Waterloo Rd SBN/FI SS3 62 C2

Waterville Dr VGE SS16 39 H2
Waterworks La SLH/COR SS17 51 H3
Watkins Cl PIT SS13 28 C2
Watlington Rd SBF/HAD SS7 41 G4
Watson Cl SBN/FI SS3 62 C2
Waverley Crs WICKE SS11 10 B2
Waverley Rd LAIN SS15 25 H2 3
SBF/HAD SS7 41 H1
Wavertree Rd SBF/HAD SS7 41 G2
Wayletts LAIN SS15 24 D4
LOS SS9 32 C5
The Weald CVI SS8 55 F5
Weare Gifford SBN/FI SS3 62 B1
Weaverdale SBN/FI SS3 49 H5 9
Weavers VGE SS16 39 G2
Weavers Cl BCAYE CM11 9 E3 7
Webster Rd SLH/COR SS17 64 D2
Websters Wy RAYL SS6 31 G1
Wedgwood Wy RCFD SS4 22 B2
Weelkes Cl SLH/COR SS17 64 B1
Weel Rd CVI SS8 70 C2
Weir Farm Rd RAYL SS6 31 F3
Weir Gdns RAYL SS6 31 F3
Weir Pond Rd RCFD SS4 35 E1
Weir Wynd BCAYW CM12 8 D4
Welbeck Cl HOC/HUL SS5 21 G4
Welbeck Dr VGE SS16 36 D2
Welbeck Ri VGE SS16 36 D2 5
Welbeck Rd CVI SS8 69 H2
Welch Cl SOSN SS2 48 B3
Wellingbury SBF/HAD SS7 41 H1 2
Wellington Av WOS/PRIT SS0 45 H5
Wellington Ms BCAYW CM12 6 C5
Wellington Rd RAYL SS6 20 A4
Well La ING CM4 7 H1
Well Md BCAYW CM12 13 F1 8
Wells Av SOSN SS2 34 C5
Wellsfield RAYL SS6 19 H4
Wellstead Gdns WOS/PRIT SS0 46 A3
Wellstye Gn BSDN SS14 27 F3
Wendene VGE SS16 39 G2
Wendon Cl RCFD SS4 22 B4 2
Wenham Dr WOS/PRIT SS0 46 D4
Wensley Rd SBF/HAD SS7 43 E2
Wentworth Rd SOSN SS2 47 F3
Wesley Gdns BCAYW CM12 6 C5 10
Wesley Rd SOS SS1 5 F5
Wessem Rd CVI SS8 56 A4 8
West Av VGE SS16 36 B2
West Beech Av WICKE SS11 16 C1
West Beech Cl WICKE SS11 16 D1
Westborough Rd WOS/PRIT SS0 46 A4
Westbourne Cl HOC/HUL SS5 21 H1 1
SBF/HAD SS7 43 G1
Westbourne Gdns BCAYW CM12 7 E5 2
Westbourne Gv WOS/PRIT SS0 46 A2
Westbury RCFD SS4 22 B4
Westbury Rd SOSN SS2 47 H4
Westcliff Av WOS/PRIT SS0 59 H2
Westcliff Dr LOS SS9 45 E5
Westcliff Gdns CVI SS8 70 D1
Westcliff Pde WOS/PRIT SS0 59 H2
Westcliff Park Dr WOS/PRIT SS0 46 C4
West Cloister BCAYE CM11 9 E3 8
West Crs CVI SS8 55 G5
West Cft BCAYE CM11 9 E4 2
The Westerings HOC/HUL SS5 21 F3
Westerland Av CVI SS8 56 C5
Western Approaches LOS SS9 33 H4
Western Esp CVI SS8 70 A2
WOS/PRIT SS0 59 G2
Western Ms BCAYW CM12 8 D3
Western Rd BCAYW CM12 8 D3 3
LOS SS9 44 B5
RAYL SS6 31 E2
SBF/HAD SS7 31 H5
Westfield LAIN SS15 24 D3
Westfield Cl RAYL SS6 19 E3
WICKE SS11 11 E5
Westgate BSDN SS14 2 C2
West Gn SBF/HAD SS7 41 G1
West Hook VGE SS16 36 C3
Westlake Av PIT SS13 28 D5
Westleigh Av LOS SS9 45 E4
Westley Rd VGE SS16 37 F4
Westman Rd CVI SS8 70 D1
West Mayne LAIN SS15 24 D5
Westmede VGE SS16 37 F2 2
Westminster Dr HOC/HUL SS5 20 D2
WOS/PRIT SS0 46 A4
Weston Rd SOS SS1 4 C5
West Park Av BCAYW CM12 8 D2
West Park Crs BCAYW CM12 8 D2
West Park Dr BCAYW CM12 8 D3
West Point Pl CVI SS8 68 D1
West Rdg BCAYW CM12 8 D5
West Rd SBN/FI SS3 62 C2
WOS/PRIT SS0 46 D5
West St LOS SS9 58 B1
RCFD SS4 34 D1
WOS/PRIT SS0 46 D4
West View Dr RAYL SS6 31 E2
Westwater SBF/HAD SS7 41 G2
West Wood Cl SBF/HAD SS7 43 F2 2
Westwood Gdns SBF/HAD SS7 43 G2
Westwood Ldg SBF/HAD SS7 43 F1
Westwood Rd CVI SS8 70 A1
Wetherland VGE SS16 2 B4
Wethersfield Cl RAYL SS6 18 D5 14
Wethersfield Wy WICKE SS11 17 G3
Weybourne Cl SOSN SS2 47 G3
Weybourne Gdns SOSN SS2 47 G3
Weybridge Wk SBN/FI SS3 49 G5
Weydale SLH/COR SS17 51 G4
Weymarks LAIN SS15 25 G4
Wharf Cl SLH/COR SS17 64 C3 3
Wharf Rd SLH/COR SS17 52 A5
SLH/COR SS17 64 D5
Wheatear Pl BCAYE CM11 9 F4 1
Wheatfield Wy VGE SS16 36 D2
Wheatley Cl RCFD SS4 22 C4
Wheatley Rd SLH/COR SS17 51 G4
Wheelers La SLH/COR SS17 52 A4
The Wheelwrights SOSN SS2 47 F1
Whernside Av CVI SS8 56 B4
Whinhams Wy BCAYW CM12 8 C2
Whist Av WICKE SS11 11 E4
Whistler Ri SBN/FI SS3 63 F1
Whitcroft VGE SS16 37 F3
Whitefriars Crs WOS/PRIT SS0 59 F2
Whitegate Rd SOS SS1 4 D4
Whitehall La SLH/COR SS17 51 H2
White Hart La HOC/HUL SS5 21 F3
White House Cha RAYL SS6 31 H3
Whitehouse Mdw LOS SS9 33 H5
White House Rd LOS SS9 33 G5
Whitelands Cl WICKE SS11 10 D4 1
Whiteshott VGE SS16 2 C6
Whitesmith Dr BCAYW CM12 8 B2
Whiteways BCAYE CM11 9 G3
CVI SS8 70 C2
LOS SS9 33 G5
Whitfields SLH/COR SS17 65 E2
Whitmore Ct BSDN SS14 27 F2
Whitmore Wy BSDN SS14 26 C4
Whittingham Av SOSN SS2 48 B4
Whybrews SLH/COR SS17 65 E2 3
Whytewaters VGE SS16 39 G3
Wick Beech Av WICKE SS11 16 D1
Wick Cha SOSN SS2 48 B5
Wick Crs WICKW SS12 16 D3
Wick Dr WICKW SS12 16 C1
Wickford Av PIT SS13 27 H5
Wickford Rd WOS/PRIT SS0 59 H2 3
Wick Gln BCAYW CM12 8 C1
Wickham Pl VGE SS16 3 G4
Wickhay LAIN SS15 2 A3
Wick La WICKE SS11 16 D1
Wicklow Wk SBN/FI SS3 62 B2
Wickmead Cl SOSN SS2 48 B4
Widgeons PIT SS13 28 B5
Wiggin's La BCAYW CM12 12 B1
BCAYW CM12 12 B2
William Rd PIT SS13 28 D5
Williamsons Wy SLH/COR SS17 51 E4
Willingale Av RAYL SS6 18 D5
The Willingales LAIN SS15 24 D5 12
Willingale Wy SOS SS1 48 D5
Willmott Rd SOSN SS2 34 C5
Willow Cl CVI SS8 69 G1
HOC/HUL SS5 21 G2
LOS SS9 33 F5
Willow Dr RAYL SS6 19 F4
Willowfields LAIN SS15 25 F2
Willowhill SLH/COR SS17 50 D4
The Willows BCAYE CM11 13 G1 5
SBF/HAD SS7 41 G2
SOS SS1 48 D5
Willow Wk HOC/HUL SS5 21 G2
SBF/HAD SS7 43 G3
Wills Hl SLH/COR SS17 64 C1
Wilmslowe CVI SS8 56 C4
Wilrich Av CVI SS8 70 C1
Wilsner PIT SS13 28 B4
Wilson Cl SLH/COR SS17 64 B4 2
Wilson Rd WOS/PRIT SS0 4 A6
Wimarc Crs RAYL SS6 19 E4
Wimbish End PIT SS13 28 A5
Wimborne Rd SOSN SS2 4 E2
Wimbourne LAIN SS15 24 D4 1
Wimhurst Cl HOC/HUL SS5 21 F1 3
Winbrook Cl RAYL SS6 31 H3
Winbrook Rd RAYL SS6 31 H3
Winchcombe Cl LOS SS9 45 F3 1
Winchester Cl LOS SS9 33 G4
Winchester Gdns LAIN SS15 25 F2 1
Wincoat Cl SBF/HAD SS7 41 H3
Wincoat Dr SBF/HAD SS7 41 G3
Windermere Rd SBF/HAD SS7 30 B4
SOS SS1 5 G3
Windmill Hts BCAYW CM12 9 E5
Windsor Av SLH/COR SS17 51 F4
Windsor Cl CVI SS8 70 A1
Windsor Gdns HOC/HUL SS5 22 A4
SBF/HAD SS7 43 F2
WICKE SS11 10 C4
Windsor Rd PIT SS13 28 D3
WOS/PRIT SS0 46 D5
Windsor Wy RAYL SS6 31 H2
Winfields PIT SS13 28 B3
Winifred Rd PIT SS13 28 A5
Winsford Gdns WOS/PRIT SS0 45 H2
Winstree PIT SS13 28 A3
Winter Folly LAIN SS15 37 H1 2
Winter Gardens Pth CVI SS8 55 F2
Winterswyk Av CVI SS8 70 D1
Winton Av WOS/PRIT SS0 59 H2
Wiscombe Hl VGE SS16 37 F3
Witchards VGE SS16 2 E4
Withypool SBN/FI SS3 49 G5 1
Wittem Rd CVI SS8 56 A4
The Witterings CVI SS8 55 H4
Woburn Pl BCAYW CM12 6 C5 11
Wollaston Crs PIT SS13 28 C1
Wollaston Wy PIT SS13 28 B2 6
Woodberry Cl CVI SS8 55 H3 6
LOS SS9 44 D1
Woodberry Rd WICKE SS11 17 F2 4
Woodbrooke Wy SLH/COR SS17 51 G4
Woodburn Cl SBF/HAD SS7 43 E2
Woodcote Ap SBF/HAD SS7 29 G4 6
Woodcote Crs PIT SS13 28 B5
Woodcote Rd LOS SS9 45 H4
Woodcotes SBN/FI SS3 49 H5
Woodcote Wy SBF/HAD SS7 29 G4
Woodcroft Cl SBF/HAD SS7 43 F2 3
Woodcutters Av LOS SS9 44 D1
Wood End Av HOC/HUL SS5 21 E3
Woodend Cl SBF/HAD SS7 43 F2 4
Wood Farm Cl LOS SS9 45 E2
Woodfield Gdns LOS SS9 58 C1
Woodfield Park Dr LOS SS9 45 H5
Woodfield Rd LOS SS9 45 H5
SBF/HAD SS7 44 B3 2
Woodgrange Cl SOS SS1 61 F1 1
Woodgrange Dr SOS SS1 5 G5
Wood Gn PIT SS13 28
Woodham Park Dr SBF/HAD SS7 41
Woodham Rd SBF/HAD SS7 41
Woodhurst Rd CVI SS8 69
Woodland Cl SBF/HAD SS7 44
Woodlands Av RAYL SS6 31
Woodlands Cl HOC/HUL SS5 21
RAYL SS6 31
VGE SS16 39
Woodlands Dr SLH/COR SS17 38
Woodlands Pk LOS SS9 44
Woodlands Rd HOC/HUL SS5 21
WICKW SS12 16
The Woodlands SBN/FI SS3 63
Woodleigh Av LOS SS9 45
Woodley Wk SBN/FI SS3 49 H4
Woodlow SBF/HAD SS7 31
Woodmanhurst Rd
SLH/COR SS17 51 E4
Woodpond Av HOC/HUL SS5 21
Woodside LOS SS9 44
Woodside Av SBF/HAD SS7 29
Woodside Cha HOC/HUL SS5 21
Woodside Cl SBF/HAD SS7 32
Woodside Rd HOC/HUL SS5 20
Woodside Vw SBF/HAD SS7 29
The Woods SBF/HAD SS7 44
Woodstock LAIN SS15 24 C5
Woodstock Crs HOC/HUL SS5 21 E2
LAIN SS15 24
Woodview VGE SS16 36 B2
Woodville Cl RCFD SS4 22
Woodville Rd CVI SS8 70
Woolifers Av SLH/COR SS17 51
Woolmergreen LAIN SS15 25
Woolshotts Rd WICKW SS12 15
Worcester Cl SLH/COR SS17 64 C1
VGE SS16 36 C1
Worcester Dr RAYL SS6 32
Wordsworth Cl SOSN SS2 47 G4
Worthing Rd LAIN SS15 24
Wraysbury Dr LAIN SS15 25 G2
Wren Av LOS SS9 32
Wren Cl BCAYE CM11 9 F4
LOS SS9 33
SBF/HAD SS7 29
Wrexham Rd LAIN SS15 37
Wroxham Cl SBF/HAD SS7 32
Wyatts Dr SOS SS1 61
Wyburn Rd SBF/HAD SS7 31
Wyburns Av RAYL SS6 31
Wyburns Av East RAYL SS6 31
Wycombe Av SBF/HAD SS7 29 F5
Wykes Gn BSDN SS14 26
Wynters VGE SS16 2
Wythefield PIT SS13 27

Y

Yamburg Rd CVI SS8 70 C1
Yarnacott SBN/FI SS3 62
Yeovil Cha WOS/PRIT SS0 46
Yew Cl LAIN SS15 25
York Av SLH/COR SS17 51
York Cl RAYL SS6 32
York Ri RAYL SS6 32
York Rd BCAYW CM12 6
RAYL SS6 32
RCFD SS4 22
SOS SS1 4
Young Cl LOS SS9 33

Z

Zandi Rd CVI SS8 70 C2
Zealand Dr CVI SS8 70
Zelham Dr CVI SS8 71
Zider Pass CVI SS8 71

Index - featured places

Aaron House Clinic of Physiotherapy
WOS/PRIT SS0 46 A3
Abbotts Hall Infant School
SLH/COR SS17 64 D1
Adams Business Centre
BSDN SS14 27 G2
Airborne Industrial Estate
LOS SS9 45 F1
Airport Business Park
SOSN SS2 34 D5
Alleyn Court & Eton House School
SBN/FI SS3 48 D3
Alleyn Court Preparatory School
WOS/PRIT SS0 46 B5
Annandale Clinic
WOS/PRIT SS0 46 A3
Appleton School
SBF/HAD SS7 41 H2
The Art Gallery
LOS SS9 58
Arthur Bugler Junior & Infant School
SLH/COR SS17 64
Ashingdon Surgery
RCFD SS4 22

sh Tree Surgery
SLH/COR SS17 ... 51 G5
allards Walk Surgery
LAIN SS15 ... 25 H4
arons Court Infant School
WOS/PRIT SS0 ... 4 A4
arstable School
BSDN SS14 ... 27 G5
asildon College
VGE SS16 ... 2 B6
asildon District Council
BCAYE CM11 ... 13 H4
asildon District Council
BCAYW CM12 ... 8 D4
asildon District Council
BSDN SS14 ... 2 D2
asildon District Council
LAIN SS15 ... 25 F5
asildon District Council
WICKW SS12 ... 16 B1
asildon Hospital
VGE SS16 ... 38 A3
asildon Rugby Football Club
BSDN SS14 ... 27 E2
asildon & Thurrock Community Health Council
BSDN SS14 ... 2 E2
asildon United Football Club
BSDN SS14 ... 26 D2
asildon Zoo
VGE SS16 ... 38 D4
eauchamps High School
WICKE SS11 ... 11 F5
eecroft Art Gallery
WOS/PRIT SS0 ... 59 H2
elfairs Community College
LOS SS9 ... 44 D4
elfairs Swimming Pool
LOS SS9 ... 44 D4
enfleet Business Centre
SBF/HAD SS7 ... 42 A4
he Billericay School
BCAYW CM12 ... 9 E5
illericay Swimming Pool
BCAYW CM12 ... 8 D2
illericay Town Council
BCAYW CM12 ... 8 D3
illericay Town Football Club
BCAYW CM12 ... 8 B4
lenheim County Primary School
LOS SS9 ... 45 G3
luehouse County Infant School
LAIN SS15 ... 25 F5
ournemouth Park Junior & Infants School
SOSN SS2 ... 47 F4
ournes Green Junior School
SOS SS1 ... 62 A1
riarswood Clinic
CVI SS8 ... 55 G4
rightside County Junior & Infant School
BCAYW CM12 ... 6 B5
risco County Junior & Infant School
PIT SS13 ... 28 A3
rocks Business Park
WICKE SS11 ... 17 E2
romfords School
WICKW SS12 ... 16 A2
romfords Sports Centre
WICKW SS12 ... 16 A3
rook Natural Health Centre
CVI SS8 ... 69 F1
rook Road Industrial Estate
RAYL SS6 ... 31 G3
urnham Road Clinic
LOS SS9 ... 44 D5
uttsbury County Infant School
BCAYW CM12 ... 7 E5
uttsbury Junior Gm School
BCAYW CM12 ... 7 E5
anvey County Junior & Infant School
CVI SS8 ... 69 G1
anvey Island Football Club
CVI SS8 ... 71 E2
anvey Village Surgery
CVI SS8 ... 69 F1
apitol Industrial Centre
WICKE SS11 ... 17 F3
arnarvon Medical Centre
SOSN SS2 ... 47 E4
he Carpet Gallery
CVI SS8 ... 56 B5
Castledon School
WICKW SS12 ... 16 A3
Castle Point Borough Council
SBF/HAD SS7 ... 42 D1
Castlepoint Museum
CVI SS8 ... 71 E1
Castle View School
CVI SS8 ... 56 A3
Cater Museum
BCAYW CM12 ... 9 E3
Cecil Jones High School
SOSN SS2 ... 48 A3
Cedar Hall School
SBF/HAD SS7 ... 31 E5
Chalkwell Hall Junior School
LOS SS9 ... 45 H5
Chalvedon School
PIT SS13 ... 28 A5
Charfleet Industrial Estate
CVI SS8 ... 68 D1
Chartwell Gallery
SOSN SS2 ... 4 C3
Chinese Herbal Medical Centre
WOS/PRIT SS0 ... 59 G1
Chinese Medical Centre
WOS/PRIT SS0 ... 4 A3
Church View Surgery
RAYL SS6 ... 31 G1
Civic Halls
CVI SS8 ... 70 A1
Clements Hall Leisure Centre
HOC/HUL SS5 ... 21 H4
The Clinic
SBF/HAD SS7 ... 42 A3
College St Pierre
LOS SS9 ... 45 H5
Co-ordinated Industrial Estate
SBF/HAD SS7 ... 31 G4
Cornelius Vermuyden School
CVI SS8 ... 55 F4
Cornwallis Business Centre
BSDN SS14 ... 26 B3
Corringham County Primary School
SLH/COR SS17 ... 51 H5
Corringham Health Centre
SLH/COR SS17 ... 65 G1
Cranes Industrial Centre
BSDN SS14 ... 27 G1
Craylands Clinic
BSDN SS14 ... 27 F4
Crays Hill County Primary School
BCAYE CM11 ... 15 E2
Cricketers Retail Park
PIT SS13 ... 15 H5
Cricketers Retail Park
WICKW SS12 ... 16 C5
Crown College
WOS/PRIT SS0 ... 46 D5
Crown & County Court
BSDN SS14 ... 2 C1
Crown Court
SOSN SS2 ... 4 C1
Crown Hall
RAYL SS6 ... 31 F1
Crowstone Preparatory School
RCFD SS4 ... 35 G3
Crowstone Preparatory School
WOS/PRIT SS0 ... 59 E1
Darlinghurst School
LOS SS9 ... 45 G4
Deanes Secondary School
SBF/HAD SS7 ... 31 F5
De La Salle RC School
BSDN SS14 ... 26 C3
Dipple Medical Centre
PIT SS13 ... 40 A1
District Council Offices
RAYL SS6 ... 31 G1
Doggetts CP School
RCFD SS4 ... 23 E5
Downhall Primary School
RAYL SS6 ... 19 G3
Earls Hall Infant School
WOS/PRIT SS0 ... 46 C2
Eastgate Business Centre
BSDN SS14 ... 2 E3
East Thurrock Football Club
SLH/COR SS17 ... 65 G1
Eastwood Gm Infant School
LOS SS9 ... 45 G1
Eastwood Gm Junior School
LOS SS9 ... 33 G5
Eastwood High School
LOS SS9 ... 45 G1
Eastwood Industrial Estate
LOS SS9 ... 32 D5
Edward Francis Community Junior School
RAYL SS6 ... 19 H5
Edwards Hall Junior & Infant School
LOS SS9 ... 32 D4
Eldon Way Industrial Estate
HOC/HUL SS5 ... 21 F2
Elms Business Park
WICKW SS12 ... 16 D4
Essex County Council
BSDN SS14 ... 27 F4
Essex County Council
CVI SS8 ... 55 F5
Essex County Council
PIT SS13 ... 28 B1
Essex County Council
RAYL SS6 ... 31 G1
Essex County Council
RCFD SS4 ... 34 D1
Essex County Council
SBF/HAD SS7 ... 42 C2
Essex County Council
SOSN SS2 ... 47 F1
Eversley CP School
PIT SS13 ... 28 B5
The Eye Clinic
LOS SS9 ... 44 B4
The Eye Clinic
SBN/FI SS3 ... 62 C3
Fairhouse Junior & Infant School
BSDN SS14 ... 3 J2
Fairways Primary School
LOS SS9 ... 44 D2
Felmore County Infant School
PIT SS13 ... 28 A3
Fitzwimarc Secondary School
RAYL SS6 ... 19 H5
Franklin Way Practice
WICKE SS11 ... 10 D5
Friars County Junior School
SBN/FI SS3 ... 63 E1
The Fryerns Medical Centre
BSDN SS14 ... 27 F3
Gable Hall Gm School
SLH/COR SS17 ... 51 E4
The Gallery
SBF/HAD SS7 ... 42 A5
Garfield Gallery
RAYL SS6 ... 31 G1
Ghyllgrove County Junior School
BSDN SS14 ... 26 B4
Giffards County Junior & Infant School
SLH/COR SS17 ... 51 E5
Glebe Infant School & U H I
RAYL SS6 ... 19 F5
Glenwood School
WICKW SS12 ... 29 F4
Grange Primary School
WICKW SS12 ... 16 A2
Great Berry CP School
VGE SS16 ... 36 C2
Great Oaks Clinic
BSDN SS14 ... 2 D2
Greensted County Infant School
BSDN SS14 ... 27 F5
Greensward College
HOC/HUL SS5 ... 21 F1
Greensward Surgery
HOC/HUL SS5 ... 21 G1
Grove Junior & Infant School
RAYL SS6 ... 32 B2
Hadleigh Business Centre
SBF/HAD SS7 ... 43 H4
Hadleigh Castle
SBF/HAD SS7 ... 43 H5
Hadleigh Clinic
SBF/HAD SS7 ... 43 F3
Hadleigh Junior School
SBF/HAD SS7 ... 43 H3
Hamstel Primary School
SOSN SS2 ... 48 A4
Hassenbrook School
SLH/COR SS17 ... 64 D2
Hassengate Medical Centre
SLH/COR SS17 ... 64 B1
Hawkesbury Road Doctors Surgery
CVI SS8 ... 69 F1
Herons Gate Trading Estate
BSDN SS14 ... 27 H1
Highlands Surgery
LOS SS9 ... 44 C4
Hilltop Junior & Infant School
WICKE SS11 ... 11 F5
Hinguar Primary School
SBN/FI SS3 ... 63 E2
Hockley Primary School
HOC/HUL SS5 ... 20 D2
Hollywood Bowl
BSDN SS14 ... 26 C2
Holt Farm Infant School
RCFD SS4 ... 22 C5
Holy Family School
SBF/HAD SS7 ... 42 A2
Ilford Trading Estate
BSDN SS14 ... 27 F1
International Business Centre
CVI SS8 ... 69 E1
International Business Park
CVI SS8 ... 68 D1
Island Golf
CVI SS8 ... 55 G3
Island Surgery
CVI SS8 ... 70 B2
Janet Duke County Infant School
LAIN SS15 ... 25 G5
John Cotgrove Gallery
LOS SS9 ... 58 B1
The Jones Family Practice
HOC/HUL SS5 ... 21 E3
Jotmans Hall Primary School
SBF/HAD SS7 ... 41 G2
Kents Hill Junior School
SBF/HAD SS7 ... 42 A2
Kents Hill Road Surgery
SBF/HAD SS7 ... 42 A1
King Edmunds School
RCFD SS4 ... 22 D3
The King John School
SBF/HAD SS7 ... 43 E3
Kingsdown School
LOS SS9 ... 33 H5
Kingston CP School
SBF/HAD SS7 ... 30 B5
Kingswood County Junior & Infant School
VGE SS16 ... 3 F4
Kingswood Medical Centre
VGE SS16 ... 3 F5
Kingswood Surgery
VGE SS16 ... 2 E4
Lady of Lourdes RC School
LOS SS9 ... 45 H4
Laindon Health Centre
LAIN SS15 ... 25 E5
Laindon Park CP School
LAIN SS15 ... 25 H3
Laindon Road Clinic
BCAYW CM12 ... 8 D5
The Laindon School
LAIN SS15 ... 25 E3
Laurence Industrial Estate
SOSN SS2 ... 34 A5
Lee Chapel CP School
VGE SS16 ... 2 A5
Leigh Beck Primary School
CVI SS8 ... 70 D1
Leigh Junior & Infant School
LOS SS9 ... 58 B1
Leigh Parish Council
LOS SS9 ... 45 F5
Lincewood County Junior & Infant School
VGE SS16 ... 37 E3
Lingwood Clinic
SLH/COR SS17 ... 64 B3
Little Margraves Industrial Estate
UPMR RM14 ... 36 C5
London Road Surgery
RAYL SS6 ... 19 E5
London Road Surgery
WICKW SS12 ... 16 B1
Long Gallery
BSDN SS14 ... 3 F3
Long Road Surgery
CVI SS8 ... 69 F1
Lubbins Park Primary School
CVI SS8 ... 70 B2
Lychgate Industrial Estate
SBF/HAD SS7 ... 30 B2
Lynn Tait Gallery
LOS SS9 ... 58 A1
Manor County Junior & Infant School
BSDN SS14 ... 26 D3
Manor Trading Estate
SBF/HAD SS7 ... 30 A4
Markhams Chase Leisure Centre
LAIN SS15 ... 25 G5

Matching Green Surgery BSDN SS14 27 E3
Mayflower Comprehensive School BCAYW CM12 7 F5
Mayflower Retail Park BSDN SS14 27 E1
Merrylands Junior School LAIN SS15 24 D5
Millhouse County Junior & Infant School LAIN SS15 25 F3
Milton Hall Junior School WOS/PRIT SS0 59 H1
Montgomerie Infant School SBF/HAD SS7 29 G4
Mosque WOS/PRIT SS0 59 H1
Nevendon Trading Estate PIT SS13 28 A2
The New Surgery BCAYW CM12 9 E2
Nicholas Comprehensive School LAIN SS15 25 G4
Noak Bridge Medical Centre LAIN SS15 26 A1
Noak Bridge Primary School LAIN SS15 26 A2
North Crescent School WICKW SS12 16 C1
North Shoebury Surgery SBN/FI SS3 49 G5
Northwick Park Junior & Infant School CVI SS8 55 E5
Oaklands Farm Industrial Estate BCAYE CM11 7 H4
Old Westcliffians Rugby Football Club RCFD SS4 34 B3
Olympic Business Centre BSDN SS14 27 G1
Palace Theatre WOS/PRIT SS0 46 C5
Park School RAYL SS6 19 E2
Pembroke Business Centre BSDN SS14 27 F1
Pipps Hill Retail Park LAIN SS15 25 H3
Pitsea County Junior & Infant School PIT SS13 39 H1
Pitsea Health Clinic PIT SS13 39 H1
Pitsea Leisure Centre PIT SS13 40 A1
Pitsea Swimming Pool PIT SS13 40 A1
Porters Grange Junior & Infant School SOS SS1 5 F3
Prince Avenue Primary School WOS/PRIT SS0 46 C1
Priory Park Industrial Estate SOSN SS2 47 F2
Priory School WOS/PRIT SS0 46 D3
Prittlewell C of E School SOSN SS2 47 E4
Prout Industrial Estate CVI SS8 71 E1
Purdeys Industrial Estate RCFD SS4 35 F2
Quest End Industrial Estate RAYL SS6 19 F2
Quilters Junior & Infant School BCAYW CM12 8 D4
Radford Business Centre BCAYW CM12 8 C2
Rawreth Industrial Estate RAYL SS6 19 E3
Rayleigh Lanes Indoor Market RAYL SS6 31 G1
Rayleigh Primary School RAYL SS6 31 F1
Regent Leisure Centre SLH/COR SS17 64 C3
Richmond Avenue Junior School SBN/FI SS3 62 C2
Riverside Industrial Estate RCFD SS4 35 E2
Robert Drake Primary School SBF/HAD SS7 30 A4
The Robert Frew Medical Centre WICKW SS12 17 E3
Rochford Adult Community College RCFD SS4 35 F1
Rochford District Council RCFD SS4 35 E1
Rochford Parish Council RCFD SS4 34 D1
Rochford Primary School RCFD SS4 34 D1
Rochford Swimming Pool Services RCFD SS4 35 F1
Rose Villa Surgery PIT SS13 40 A1
Rosshill Industrial Park SOSN SS2 47 G2
The Royals Shopping Centre SOS SS1 4 D5
Runwell CP School WICKE SS11 10 C3
Runwell Parish Council WICKE SS11 10 D3
Ryedene County Primary School VGE SS16 39 G3
Sacred Heart RC School SOS SS1 5 G3
St Anne Line Junior School LAIN SS15 2 A2
St Bernards High School WOS/PRIT SS0 59 H1
St Christopher School LOS SS9 45 G2
St Cleres School SLH/COR SS17 64 B4
St Georges RC School SBN/FI SS3 62 D1
St Hildas School WOS/PRIT SS0 46 B5
St Johns School BCAYW CM12 9 E2
St Josephs RC Primary School SLH/COR SS17 64 C2
St Josephs RC School CVI SS8 56 A5
St Katherine School CVI SS8 55 H4
St Margarets School PIT SS13 40 D1
St Michaels Preparatory School LOS SS9 44 D5
St Nicholas C of E Primary School WICKE SS11 18 B1
St Nicholas School SOSN SS2 48 B4
St Peters RC Primary School BCAYE CM11 13 H2
St Teresa RC School RCFD SS4 22 C5
St Thomas More High School for Boys WOS/PRIT SS0 45 H3
Scimitar Park Industrial Estate PIT SS13 28 C1
Scott Park Surgery LOS SS9 33 G4
Seedbed Business Centre SBN/FI SS3 63 E2
Shoeburyness High School SBN/FI SS3 62 C2
Skillion Business Centre BSDN SS14 26 B3
Smilers Industrial Estate PIT SS13 29 E3
Sooriakumaran Surgery SOSN SS2 46 D2
Sopwith Crescent WICKE SS11 17 G3
South Benfleet Gm Primary School SBF/HAD SS7 41 H4
Southbourne Grove Surgery WOS/PRIT SS0 46 A2
South East Essex College SOSN SS2 4 B1
South East Essex Sixth Form College SBF/HAD SS7 42 D1
Southend Adult Community College SOS SS1 5 H4
Southend Borough Council SOSN SS2 4 B1
Southend Borough Football Club WOS/PRIT SS0 34 A5
Southend County Court SOS SS1 4 D4
Southend High School for Boys SOSN SS2 46 D3
Southend Hospital N H S Trust WOS/PRIT SS0 46 B3
Southend Rugby Football Club SOSN SS2 35 E5
Southend United Football Club SOSN SS2 46 D4
South Essex Clinical Trials Centre LOS SS9 44 C4
South Essex Health Authority RAYL SS6 31 F2
Southfields Industrial Park LAIN SS15 24 C4
South Green County Infant & Junior School BCAYW CM12 13 E1
South Green Surgery BCAYE CM11 13 F1
Southview Park Surgery VGE SS16 39 E3
South West Essex Magistrates Court BSDN SS14 2 C1
Stadium Trading Estate SBF/HAD SS7 31 F4
Stanford Industrial Estate SLH/COR SS17 64 B3
Stock Industrial Park SOSN SS2 47 F2
Strand Gallery SOSN SS2 5 K2
Sunnymede County Junior School BCAYE CM11 9 G4
Swaines Industrial Estate RCFD SS4 22 D5
Swan Mead Junior School VGE SS16 3 J3
The Sweyne Park School RAYL SS6 19 F
Swimming Pool SLH/COR SS17 51 E
Temple Sutton Primary & Infant School SOSN SS2 47 H
Thameside Community Health Care VGE SS16 3 K
Thameside Community Healthcare N H S Trust BCAYW CM12 9 E
Thorpe Bay School SOS SS1 48 C
Thorpe Bay Surgery SOS SS1 61 H
Thorpedene Gm Junior School SBN/FI SS3 62 B
Thorpe Hall School SBN/FI SS3 48 D
Thundersley Junior & Infant School SBF/HAD SS7 30 D
The Tile Gallery LOS SS9 45 H
UCI Cinema BSDN SS14 26 C
Waterside Farm Sports Centre CVI SS8 55 F
Wellesley Hospital SOSN SS2 47 H
Westborough Primary School WOS/PRIT SS0 46 D
Westcliff High School for Boys WOS/PRIT SS0 45 H
Westcliff High School for Girls LOS SS9 45 H
Westcliff Leisure Centre WOS/PRIT SS0 59 H
Westerings Primary School HOC/HUL SS5 21 E
Western Road Surgery BCAYW CM12 8 D
Westfleet Trading Estate WICKE SS11 17 E
West Leigh Junior & Infant School LOS SS9 45 E
Westmayne Industrial Park LAIN SS15 24 B
West Road Mosque WOS/PRIT SS0 46 D
Westwood Primary School SBF/HAD SS7 43 G
Whitmore County Junior & Infant School BSDN SS14 27 F
Wickford Health Centre WICKW SS12 10 B
Wickford Junior School WICKW SS12 16 E
Wickford Swimming Pool WICKW SS12 10 B
William Read CP School CVI SS8 69 G
Winter Gardens Junior School CVI SS8 55 G
Woodham Ley CP School SBF/HAD SS7 29 G
Woodlands Comprehensive School VGE SS16 2 D
Wyburns City Junior School RAYL SS6 32 A

Page 6

5

Beresford Ct
Colville Ms
Dolphin Gdns
Edward Cl
Granville Cl
Lorrimore Cl
Oakley Dr
Queen's Gate Ms
Tavistock Dr
Wesley Gdns
Woburn Pl

Page 16

1

Bridge House Cl
Charlotte Av
Farnes Av
Laburnum Cl
Lavender Wy

2

Bannister Gn
Beazley End
Erskine Pl
Horkesley Wy
Ingrave Cl
Mackenzie Cl
Pleshey Cl
Sewards End
Taveners Green Cl
Tollesbury Cl

3

Balfour Cl
Buchanan Gdns
Caladonia La
Chatton Cl
Chisholm Ct
Drummond Pl
Grant Cl
Lamont Cl
Maclaren Wy
Munro Ct
Nicholson Gv
Ogilvie Ct
Robertson Dr
Rose Cl

Page 25

3

Arne Ct
Arne Ms
Bramley Gdns
Tavistock Rd
Vaughan Williams Rd
Victoria Crs
Walton Ct

5

The Cloisters
Convent Cl
Friars Cl
Lych Ga
Vicarage Cl

Page 36

1

Alnwick Cl
Amersham Av
Cambridge Cl
Flint Cl
Ipswich Ms
Lancaster Dr
Maple Tree La
Monmouth Ms
Oakham Cl
Osterley Dr
Oxford Cl
Reading Cl
Shrewsbury Cl
Worcester Cl

Page 49

5

Barrington Cl
Blackwater Cl
Dovecote
Midsummer Meadow
Milbanke Cl
Montgomery Ct
Osprey Cl
Toucan Cl
Weaverdale

Notes

Notes

Notes